THE
WAR
AGAINST
CHRISTIANITY

Roger Chappell
205 232 5991

THE
WAR
AGAINST
CHRISTIANITY

HISTORY AND GEOGRAPHY OF
ANCIENT AMERICA
IN THE
BOOK OF MORMON
600–51 BC

TROY J. SMITH

CFI
An Imprint of Cedar Fort, Inc.
Springville, Utah

ISBN 13: 978-1-4621-1771-0

Published by CFI, an imprint of Cedar Fort, Inc.
2373 W. 700 S., Springville, UT 84663
Distributed by Cedar Fort, Inc., www.cedarfort.com

Library of Congress Cataloging-in-Publication Data

Names: Smith, Troy J., author.
Title: War against Christianity / Troy J. Smith.
Description: Springville, Utah : CFI, [2015] | "2015 | Includes
  bibliographical references.
Identifiers: LCCN 2015032942 | ISBN 9781462117710 (perfect bound : alk. paper)
Subjects: LCSH: Book of Mormon--Criticism, interpretation, etc. |
  Christians--Violence against. | Persecution. | War--Religious
  aspects--Mormon Church. | War--Religious aspects--Church of Jesus Christ
  of Latter-day Saints.
Classification: LCC BX8627 .S625 2015 | DDC 289.3/22--dc23
LC record available at http://lccn.loc.gov/2015032942

Cover design by Shawnda T. Craig
Cover design © 2016 Cedar Fort, Inc.
Edited by Deborah Spencer
Typeset by Jessica B. Ellingson

Printed in the United States of America

10 9 8 7 6 5 4 3 2 1

Printed on acid-free paper

CONTENTS

CONTENTS

ACKNOWLEDGMENTS

My gratitude to the following people:

My wife, Debbie—her unwavering faith and love for the Lord and His great work of redemption has provided a light for my path. Her patience and support throughout the period of research and writing has made everything possible.

My oldest daughter, Kimberlly, has continually given love and support for my work since she was thirteen years of age.

My daughter Shauna painstakingly edited books one and two and taught me the art of punctuation and form.

My friend Tim Jimenez read the manuscripts for books one and two. His reaction and observations were extremely important to the process.

My son Carlin read the manuscript and designed and completed all the maps for publication.

My friend Roger Chappell read the manuscript and has helped me in numerous ways to prepare this series for publication and marketing.

All of my children have always shown amazing support through-out the entire period of research and writing.

Thank you,
Troy Smith

INTRODUCTION

THE BOOK OF MORMON is a unique and remarkable resource for spiritual growth and understanding. It is, as the prophet Joseph Smith told the twelve apostles in 1841, "the most correct of any book on earth, and the keystone of our religion, and a man [will] get nearer to God by abiding by its precepts, than by any other book."[1] Its principal authors were prophets of God who wrote according to the promptings of the Spirit.[2] Their righteous insights impart an essence of spirituality that turns our attention toward the heavens.

The Book of Mormon contains many gems of truth regarding the identity of God. It is another witness of Jesus Christ, the Only Begotten Son of God and the Savior of all mankind. It enlarges our understanding of the gospel by expanding our awareness of the Lord's plan for mankind throughout the world. Within its pages are contained the accounts of two unrelated parties from different eras, who broke off from Old World biblical cultures and established new cultures in the Western Hemisphere. It holds a wealth of political, cultural, religious, and geographical information about the nations that resulted.

The primary account, a history of the Nephites covering a period of a thousand years (600 BC through AD 420), was compiled and condensed by the prophet Mormon from records that were first established by the prophet Nephi in obedience to the commandments of God. Two sets of gold plates, the large plate of Nephi and the small plate of Nephi, were handed down from generation to generation throughout Nephite history. Near the end of the Nephite civilization, Ammaron passed them to Mormon, a young boy at the age of eleven when Ammaron first informed him of the plates. Mormon willingly shouldered the four-fold responsibility of protecting all Nephite records during the most vulnerable period, abridging the large plate of Nephi, recording the events of his day, and burying the records in the earth to preserve them for the purposes of the Lord.

At Mormon's death, the responsibility, pertaining to a portion of the records, fell to his son, Moroni—the last and only survivor of the Nephite destruction. Moroni labored alone, destitute of family and friends, to finish Mormon's account of the demise of his people, abridge the account of the Jaredite prophet Ether, write the final book, which bears his name, seal up the fully abridged record, and bury it in the earth, where it would be preserved for the restoration of the gospel in the latter days. In AD 421, he buried this record in the Hill Cumorah, less than 20 miles south of Lake Ontario in present-day Upstate New York, where it lay undisturbed for 1,406 years.[3]

The prophet Ether's account, the "Book of Ether," contains a concise history of the Jaredites, a great culture that preceded the Nephites in the Western Hemisphere until their complete annihilation through internal warfare in *ca.* 250–220 BC. During the last Jaredite civil war, Ether worked under extreme hardship, though sheltered and preserved by the hand of God, to produce a comprehensive summary of approximately 2000 years of Jaredite history. The Nephite king Mosiah II later translated it from the Jaredite to the Nephite language by the power of God, through the gift of the Urim and Thummim.[4] Finally, as noted above, Moroni condensed Ether's account into 15 short chapters that are packed with pertinent facts about the earliest Book of Mormon culture, and that also contain marvelous revelations given to the prophet Mahonri Moriancumer (the brother of Jared) and to the prophet Ether.

The Bible and the Book of Mormon have sharply contrasting origins. The source materials that constitute the Holy Bible were passed down from scribe to scribe and culture to culture, through many generations of copies, handwritten on perishable materials, before they were brought together in one volume of scripture in AD 1611. On the other hand, the prophets Mormon and Moroni compiled the Book of Mormon from original records, which had been maintained and preserved on metal plates within the Nephite culture. The Plates of Mormon and the small plate of Nephi were ultimately passed directly to the latter-day times by the angel Moroni, who returned to the earth in AD 1823 to direct the young prophet Joseph Smith to the spot where he had previously buried them. The Bible was translated into English by scholars, who frequently disagreed on the meaning of words and phrases in the original text, whereas Joseph Smith translated the Book of Mormon in approximately three months by means of the Urim and Thummim, working with one primary scribe, Oliver Cowdery.[5]

The individuals who kept the Nephite records safeguarded them carefully to ensure they did not fall into the hands of wicked men, who would alter or destroy them.[6] The precise history of each record is known and in all probability was unaltered once engraved on metal plates, whereas the histories of the biblical records are concealed within the mists of the Dark Ages. Only through Providence was the Bible preserved with reasonable accuracy, which is corroborated by the other scriptural witness of Jesus Christ—the Book of Mormon.

When compared to the ubiquitous but obscure archaeological record, the rare Pre-Columbian[7] codices,[8] the Spanish colonial documents,[9] and the traditional oral histories of the American Indian cultures, the Book of Mormon shines with crystalline clarity. Furthermore, it provides a true historical foundation to build upon.

Conversely, the Book of Mormon does not provide abundant data concerning artifacts or specific details of Nephite or Jaredite daily life. Such information is incidental within accounts that focus on gospel principles, revelations, prophecies, and historical events, as well as human relationships, successes, failures and tragedy. In general, the physical details of Nephite and Jaredite culture are not included in the Book of Mormon account, which is the very nature of the archaeological record and a principal focus of the cultural records listed above.

If the correct correlation between the Book of Mormon and the archaeological record could be determined, then understanding of each would be greatly enlarged. Ambiguities in the Book of Mormon could be elucidated, incorrect interpretations of the archaeological record could be identified and corrected, and the true history of the Pre-Columbian cultures of the Western Hemisphere would be brought to light.

THE PAGAN WAR AGAINST CHRISTIANITY

The pagan conspiracy to destroy Christianity is a primary focus of this book, as considered in Part 2. Based upon the scanty information provided in the small plate of Nephi,[10] it seems that a significant intrusion of pagan religion into Nephite culture did not occur until around 200 BC, following the merger of the Nephite and Mulekite cultures in Zarahemla. It will be shown that during the entire pre-Christ period in Zarahemla, which lasted approximately 234 years,[11] there was a constant deadly struggle between pagan dissenters and the Christian Nephites.

The prophet Mormon was quite explicit in identifying the true character of this struggle, which afflicted the Nephites not only during the Zarahemla pre-Christ period, but throughout the last 200 years of Nephite history as well. Ultimately, it caused the total destruction of the Christian Nephite culture. As will be shown, the underlying cause of dissent and resulting violence was an organized subversive movement, connected from period to period by way of Satan. These movements were attached to an aggressive and barbaric pagan subculture that warred tirelessly and viciously against the civilized world of Nephite Christianity.

Pagan cults were obsessed with the destruction of the Nephites. Through time, that obsession naturally evolved into a well-orchestrated conspiracy, especially when combined with the secrecy of the Gadianton robbers. The pagan movement first influenced or caused each Nephite episode of dissent, and then gained momentum as a result. Recurring episodes of disobedience and repentance among the Nephites are the earmarks of this intense war between religious philosophies. Rather than identifying the unending cycle of transgression and repentance as the fruits of a people without discipline, this book seeks to identify the elements of the religious struggle that took place during a large portion of the final 600-year period.

In AD 385, the movement would attain a magnitude sufficient to bring about the total extinction of the Nephite culture and the elimination of Christianity from the Pre-Columbian World. The pagan faction became the instrument of destruction but would have had no success were it not for the transgression of the Christian

Nephites against principles of righteousness, and the consequent withdrawal of the Lord's protective hand.

The term "pagan," as used in this book, refers to non-Christian religious cults in the Book of Mormon, which in most if not all cases were violently anti-Christian. Generally, the non-Christian religions were polytheistic in nature, though the term pagan is not dependent upon that criterion. It is a Latin term and is not used in either the Bible or the Book of Mormon.

TWO GEOGRAPHICAL PERSPECTIVES IN THE BOOK OF MORMON

The subject of geography, as presented in the Book of Mormon, is a second primary focus of this book and is examined in Part 3. The geographic history of the Nephites is naturally divided by the Great Storm of AD 34. During the pre-Christ period, the geographic perspective of the writers of the Book of Mormon was limited exclusively to the land southward. The land northward was viewed as a far and distant land.

This is in direct opposition to the Post-Christ Period, with the exception of the visitation of the Savior in AD 34 in the land of Bountiful. For Mormon, who lived in the land northward, the land southward was a far and distant land. This book focuses exclusively upon the pre-Christ period from 589 to 51 BC, while the Nephites resided in the land southward. The Nephite period from 51 BC to AD 34, as well as the Post-Christ Period and its related geography of the land northward, will be addressed in future publications.

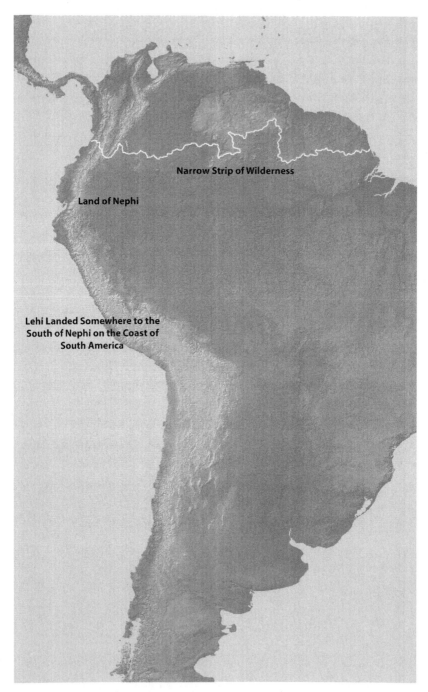

MAP 1.0: Land Southward of the Book of Mormon

PART 1

BOOK OF MORMON CULTURAL FOUNDATIONS

CHAPTER 1.1

BASIC RELATIONSHIPS BETWEEN BOOK OF MORMON CULTURES

ALL OF THE PEOPLES of the Book of Mormon emanated from biblical stock. Each culture originated from a flight to escape wicked and perilous conditions. Around 2000 BC, the earliest Post-Flood New World culture, identified in the Book of Mormon as the Jaredites, fled from the confusion at the Tower of Babel and the tyranny of Nimrod,[12] the enemy of God and oppressor of the righteous.[13]

The people of Lehi fled in 600 BC from the impending destruction of Jerusalem, known to them through revelations from God. Mulek, the youngest son of Zedekiah,[14] in his flight from Jerusalem approximately eleven years after Lehi's departure, avoided certain death at the hands of Nebuchadnezzar. This Babylonian king had overthrown Zedekiah and had slain all of Mulek's brothers.

Mulek is not mentioned in the Old Testament. The Book of Mormon gives the only known information about him—four brief references,[15] which identify him as a son of Zedekiah and allude to his departure from the land of Judah and subsequent voyage to the New World. There is no detailed account of his escape from the Old World, as there is for the people of Lehi and the people of Jared. There is no account of the Mulekite culture, which descended from Mulek and his associates, as there is for the Nephite and Jaredite cultures. Though Mulek's party arrived in the Western Hemisphere shortly after the Nephites, the two cultures were completely unaware of one another for almost 400 years.

In this chapter, Book of Mormon cultures are addressed in the order they appear in the Book of Mormon. The Nephites (descendants of Lehi through the lineage of his son Nephi) kept the history contained in the Book of Mormon. Therefore, the other cultures are introduced as they interacted with, or came into the awareness of the Nephites.

CA. 600 BC
NEPHITE ORIGINS

During the first year of Zedekiah's reign (*ca.* 600 BC),[16] many prophets went into the streets of Jerusalem to sound the warning of forthcoming destruction.[17] When Lehi heard the warnings, he prayed earnestly to the Lord on behalf of his people.[18] The heavens were opened up to him, and he saw for himself the calamities that were imminent, if the people did not repent.[19] This knowledge became a burden to him, and he joined with the other prophets in raising the voice of warning.[20] Soon the Lord told Lehi in a dream to flee the city, because wicked men were angered by his prophesies and sought his life.[21] He immediately uprooted his family, forsaking their home, fortune, and the land of their inheritance.[22]

They fled with Zoram[23] and the family of Ishmael[24] into the wilderness to the south of Jerusalem and then moved generally toward the south/southeast along the eastern shore of the Red Sea.[25] As they traveled through the dry and barren land, a compass called the "ball"[26] (Liahona), provided by the Lord,[27] guided them through the more "fertile parts of the wilderness."[28]

Following the death of Ishmael at a place called Nahom,[29] they turned eastward.[30] At length, after eight years of wandering across 1500 miles of desert wasteland, they arrived at a place they called Bountiful on the coast of "Irreantum, which, being interpreted, is many waters."[31]

While in the wilderness, Lehi had continued to receive revelations from God concerning the coming destruction of Jerusalem.[32] Nephi, Lehi's fourth son, had sought the Lord with all his heart that he might be allowed to see the things his father had been shown.[33] Because of his faith and righteousness, he was blessed with the same revelations.

In Bountiful, the Lord showed Nephi where to find ore, from which he made tools.[34] Nephi then designed and constructed a ship using those tools, according to detailed instructions from the Lord.

After the ship was finished, they put into the waters of Irreantum, again directed by the Liahona.[35] After sailing for many days, they "did arrive in the promised land."[36]

NEPHITE REVELATIONS CONCERNING THE FALL OF JUDAH

Upon settling in the Western Hemisphere, Lehi informed his sons about a revelation he received concerning the destruction of Jerusalem. "For behold, said he, I have seen a vision, in which I know that Jerusalem is destroyed; and had we remained in Jerusalem we should also have perished."[37] Shortly thereafter Lehi died.

In the years following the death of his father, Nephi received additional revelations concerning their former homeland. He prophesied to his children concerning the great destruction that had come to Jerusalem at the hands of the Babylonians following their departure:

"I have made mention unto my children concerning the judgments of God, which hath come to pass among the Jews . . . according to all that which Isaiah hath spoken, and I do not write them.

"Wherefore, it hath been told them [Judah] concerning the destruction which should come upon them, immediately after my father left Jerusalem; nevertheless, they hardened their hearts; and according to my prophecy they have been destroyed, save it be those which are carried away captive into Babylon.

"And now this I speak because of the spirit which is in me."[38]

Nephi's younger brother, Jacob, also a prophet of God, also testified of Jerusalem's destruction, saying, "And now I, Jacob, would speak somewhat concerning these words. For behold, the Lord has shown me that those who were at Jerusalem, from whence we came, have been slain and carried away captive."[39]

NEPHITE REVELATIONS VERIFIED: DISCOVERY OF THE PEOPLE OF ZARAHEMLA

The first Book of Mormon reference to the Mulekites (people of Zarahemla) is found in the Book of Omni, Chapter 1, verses 12–19, which were written by Amaleki, the last contributor to the Book of Omni (and to the small plate of Nephi). Amaleki wrote concerning the discovery of the people of Zarahemla.

Mosiah, "being warned of the Lord,"[40] had fled out of the land of Nephi, the place of their first inheritance, with all who would go with him. They traveled through uninhabited wilderness for many days. Having no idea what lay ahead, they relied exclusively on the invisible arm of God for guidance and protection. The willingness of the people of Mosiah to give up everything and follow their spiritual leader into the unknown was an act of great faith. Their journey carried them to the land of Zarahemla, named for the people they found there. At Zarahemla, the Lord rewarded them with a great discovery.

Amaleki said, "Behold, it came to pass that Mosiah discovered that the people of Zarahemla came out from Jerusalem at the time that Zedekiah, king of Judah, was carried away captive into Babylon."[41] The people of Zarahemla, descendants of Mulek and those who had departed Israel with him, were overjoyed because the Nephites had possession of the Plates of Brass, which contained the history of the Jews.[42]

Amaleki failed to mention that the Nephites also had reason to rejoice. The implications of the discovery surely caused a great stir of excitement among the people of Mosiah. The people of Zarahemla provided absolute vindication for the original flight of the people of Lehi from the Old World. For Mosiah and his people, the people of Zarahemla were living proof that the peril in Jerusalem had been real. The prophecies and revelations concerning the fall of the city were true indeed, for Mulek's departure was made necessary by their fulfillment!

Because of this, the Mulekite presence in Nephite society remained an invaluable keystone of Christian faith until the visitation of the Savior would set a new standard. In about 20 BC, almost 200 years after the discovery of the people of Zarahemla, Nephi, the son of Helaman, said, "And now will you dispute that Jerusalem was destroyed? Will ye say that the sons of Zedekiah were not slain, all except it were Mulek? Yea, and do ye not behold that the seed of Zedekiah are with us, and they were driven out of the land of Jerusalem?"[43]

NEPHITES, LAMANITES, AND MULEKITES

The Nephites observed the Hebrew practice of adding a suffix to a man's name (which in English, appears as the suffix "-ite") to denote descendants or followers of an individual. In fact, the convention is more prevalent in the Book of Mormon than it is in the Old Testament. Terms with an -ite suffix, which can be found in the English text of the Book of Mormon, include "Nephite," "Jacobite," "Josephite," "Zoramite," "Lamanite," "Lemuelite," and "Ishmaelite."[44] The terms refer to direct descendants of the male individuals within the original party that came with Lehi.[45] The terms "Nephite" and "Lamanite" held much greater significance than the others—representing and identifying the two primary cultures that immediately developed following the fracture of Nephi's relationship with his brothers Laman and Lemuel.[46] The Nephite culture consisted of Nephites, Jacobites, Josephites, and Zoramites, and after the arrival of the Nephites in Zarahemla around 200 BC, Mulekites.[47] The Lamanite culture was comprised primarily of Lamanites, Lemuelites, and Ishmaelites, as well as dissenters from the Nephites.

Though the majority of Nephite and Lamanite constituents were predominantly of the tribes listed, there was, from the beginning, an important distinction between the two major groups, which superseded blood relationships. Generally, the Nephites were the followers of Christ, or "the people of God,"[48] whereas the Lamanites rejected Christ. Throughout Nephite history, dissenters defected over to the Lamanites,[49] frequently after leaving the Church established within the Nephite culture.[50] After the Lamanite group known as the people of Anti-Nephi-Lehi were converted to Christ, they could no longer remain in the Lamanite land of Nephi, illustrating the dichotomy that existed at that time,[51] prior to the mass Lamanite conversion of 30 BC.[52] In the years leading to the destruction of the Nephites at Cumorah, many Nephites defected to the Lamanites, denying Christ.[53]

In the days of Nephi and Lehi, the sons of Helaman, however, the dichotomy was reversed for a time, following the sudden conversion of the Lamanites, when the majority of the Lamanites accepted the Savior, repented of their sins, and led righteous lives, while wickedness was rampant among the Nephites.[54] During the

Nephite Golden Age (AD 34–194),[55] following the visitation of the Savior, the dichotomy did not exist. Throughout that entire 160-year period, "there were no robbers, nor murderers, neither were there Lamanites, nor any manner of –ites; but they were in one, the children of Christ, and heirs to the kingdom of God."[56]

Minor instances of the –ite suffix are terms such as "Amalekite," "Amulonite," and "Zoramite," which identified descendants or followers of certain Nephite dissenters (apostates), living among the Lamanites, who were more hardened and resistant to the gospel than other Lamanites.[57] Without the fuel of the dissenters' hatred and twisted information, the Lamanites would not have been a major thorn, as they were, in the side of the Nephites.[58]

THE JAREDITES—THE EARLIEST BOOK OF MORMON CULTURE

The Book of Ether contains the account of the Jaredites, a people who came from the Tower of Babel to the New World sometime before 2000 BC. The Book of Ether contains an abbreviated narrative[59] of their history from the time of their departure from Babel until their extinction through civil war around 250–220 BC.[60] Written by a prophet named Ether, it also contains prophecies and revelations, though many were sealed when Joseph Smith translated the book and will be revealed at a later time.

The Nephites never encountered the Jaredites, though the two cultures simultaneously inhabited the New World for approximately 370 years (ca. 589 BC until ca. 220 BC). During that initial period in the land of Nephi, the Nephites were confined exclusively to the land southward and likely were not even aware of the existence of the land northward[61] until they joined with the people of Zarahemla,[62] who had recently migrated from the land northward.[63]

While the Nephites lived in the land of Nephi, they were separated from the land northward by an immense wilderness that stretched across the northern portion of the land southward[64] and posed a massive and formidable barrier between Nephi and the narrow neck of land that led into the land northward.[65] The Jaredites literally covered the face of the land northward,[66] but intentionally reserved the land southward for hunting expeditions.[67] The distance they penetrated into the interior of the south wilderness[68] is unknown, but there is no record of their having traveled as far as the land of Nephi during the period of Nephite habitation.

These things considered, it is concluded that only after the terminal Jaredite civil war had ended and the former culture lay moldering in the dust, amid the ruins of the land northward, did the Nephites learn of them. The first awareness of the Jaredites came to them by way of the people of Zarahemla in about 200 BC.[69]

Before their migration to the land southward,[70] the people of Zarahemla had discovered Coriantumr, the last Jaredite king and the only survivor of the final Jaredite battle, likely after he wandered from the Hill Ramah[71] back to his former homeland[72] in search of other possible survivors.[73] Coriantumr lived with the Mulekites for nine moons (months) before he died.[74]

The Mulekites also acquired a large stone at that time with inscriptions that gave an account of Coriantumr and the final Jaredite war.[75] The inscriptions were apparently engraved by Coriantumr after the battle at Ramah, perhaps while he lived with the Mulekites, for they "spake" of the aftermath of the war, referring specifically to the scattered bones of Coriantumr's people across the land northward. Furthermore, they seem to indicate that Coriantumr had thought deeply and honestly about the final outcome of the war by describing his personal acceptance of the Lord's "judgments" as being "just."

The first direct Nephite encounter with the physical remains of the Jaredites came about 80 years later (121 BC), when King Limhi sent a party of 43 men from the land of Nephi in search of Zarahemla.[76] The party became lost and wandered up through the narrow neck of land into the land northward, through the Mulekite land of Desolation, and into the land of the Jaredites, where they found ruins that covered the face of the land. They found the bones of the former combatants and their "beasts," described as having been "as numerous as the hosts of Israel."[77] The bones lay unburied where they had fallen, bleaching in the sun, disintegrating in the tropical environment.[78] They also found weapons and armor,[79] for the entire land was a battlefield.

Most importantly, they found the twenty-four gold Plates of Ether,[80] which provide a history of the Jaredite civilization. King

Mosiah II translated the Plates of Ether from the Jaredite language to the Nephite language in 92 BC.[81] Moroni abridged the record around AD 400. Joseph Smith translated it from the Nephite language into English in 1829. Without the Book of Ether, nothing would be known today concerning the Jaredites, other than the information that they came from the Tower of Babel, lived in the land northward, and were destroyed "according to [the Lord's] judgments."[82]

CHAPTER 1.2

NEPHITE HISTORY IN THE LAND OF NEPHI
1 NEPHI 18:23–OMNI 1:11

CA. 589 BC

WHEN LEHI, HIS FAMILY, and associates arrived on the shores of the "promised land,"[83] undoubtedly,[84] they all bowed their heads in a prayer of thanksgiving to the Lord. The extreme burden of a long, grueling voyage on an endless sea had suddenly been lifted. The day of their landing was the real beginning of the culture that would flourish and eventually spread throughout the land.

However, the peace and serenity of that day did not last for long. Lehi soon went "the way of all the earth,"[85] and upon his death, Laman and Lemuel immediately amplified their antagonism toward their younger brother, Nephi. Very soon, they were plotting his murder. The story continues with Nephi following the promptings of the Lord to flee with his family and friends into the wilderness.

Their journey carried them many days of travel from the place of their first landing to a highland region[86] where they laid the foundations for the city of Nephi. They lived in that region during the period from *ca.* 588 BC to *ca.* 200 BC. Between 18 and 28 years after the establishment of Nephi,[87] the Lamanites sought out the Nephites, and wars commenced that would characterize the relationship between the Nephites and Lamanites for much of their history.

From that time forth, the Lamanites were a scourge that meted out punishment whenever the Nephites transgressed against God's laws of righteousness.[88] If the Nephites had followed the teachings of their prophets and obeyed God's commandments, they could

17

have remained in the land of Nephi perpetually. Lehi's son Jacob offered a warning to his people concerning the dangers of violating the laws of God, of which they were guilty even in his day: "And the time speedily cometh that except ye repent [the Lamanites] shall possess the land of your inheritance, and the Lord God will lead away the righteous out from among you."[89]

In about 400 BC, and more than a hundred years after Jacob's warning, the people had repented, for which Jacob's grandson Jarom observed, "The word of the Lord was verified, which he spake unto our fathers, saying that: Inasmuch as ye will keep my commandments ye shall prosper in the land."[90] The Lord's promises to his people of blessings for righteousness are as certain as his warnings of destruction for wickedness. Jarom was therefore able to record that the Lamanites were driven out of the land of Nephi in his day.[91]

CYCLES OF TRANSGRESSION AND REPENTANCE

The scriptural accounts of every Biblical and Book of Mormon culture reveal that people of the earth in every age naturally move away from righteousness until the Lord sends adversity to humble them and cause them to repent from their sins. Only then do they find sorrow in iniquity and seek the Lord's favor. According to that principle, it was inevitable that sooner or later the people would once again fall into transgression, and the peace established during the days of Jarom[92] would come to an end.

During the period from 361 BC to 317 BC, while Jarom's son Omni was the keeper of the small Plates of Nephi, there were initially "many seasons of peace." But then the Nephites transgressed, the wars returned, and there followed "many seasons of serious war and bloodshed"[93] between the Nephites and the Lamanites.

The wars intensified during the life of Omni's son, Amaron, and by 279 BC, "the more wicked part of the Nephites" had been destroyed.[94] At that time, Amaron provided the inverse of his grandfather Jarom's statement concerning the Lord's previous warning. He said, "Inasmuch as ye will not keep my commandments ye shall not prosper in the land."[95] The wars continued without abatement over the next two generations. During the last years in the land of Nephi, the Lamanite attacks occurred in ever-increasing frequency and intensity.[96]

CA. 200 BC

Amaleki, the last contributor to the small Plates of Nephi, recorded a brief account concerning one King Mosiah, which other than Nephi, is the only Nephite king mentioned by name in the small Plates of Nephi. During Mosiah's reign, Jacob's warning prophecy[97] was fulfilled. After many generations in the land of Nephi, many cycles of transgression and repentance, and countless battles with the Lamanites, the voice of the Lord came to Mosiah to once again[98] lead the righteous Nephites away from Lamanite aggression. He gathered all who "would hearken to the voice of the Lord,"[99] and collecting their possessions, they departed out of the land of Nephi into the wilderness.

CHAPTER 1.3

THE DISCOVERY OF ZARAHEMLA

CA. 200 BC

HAVING DEFENDED THEIR HOMELAND continually during the preceding years, the people of Mosiah were thoroughly seasoned in the art of war. Yet, notwithstanding their capacity to defend themselves, they saw in their flight from the land of Nephi the opportunity to avoid conflict. They dared to hope that they might live in peace without fear of Lamanite intrusions.

They traveled, likely by means of the Liahona,[100] through a deep and trackless wilderness.[101] The wilderness was so deep and formidable that although it bordered upon the land and city of Nephi, it had remained off limits for habitation through almost 400 years. Subsequent accounts of travel across its considerable expanse attest to the difficulty it presented to even the most able explorer.[102] Finally, after many days, the people of Mosiah "came down into the land which is called the land of Zarahemla."[103] There, they discovered the people of Zarahemla, who were descendants of Mulek and his associates.[104]

During their journey, due to the nature of their flight and the possibility of Lamanite pursuit, they were well equipped for battle and were likely superior in that respect to the people of Zarahemla. Yet as they came into the valley of the Sidon River and began to encounter the Mulekite inhabitants, the people of Mosiah surely exuded an aura of good will through the righteous leadership of Mosiah. The last thing they wanted was to create a new scenario of conflict by subjugating the people of Zarahemla through force of arms. The first unexpected encounter may have had moments of tension heightened by the difficulty of communication,[105] but it was quickly apparent that the two peoples were peaceable, and their common Jewish heritage soon had a powerful impact in drawing them together.

THE MERGER OF THE NEPHITE AND MULEKITE CULTURES

The Book of Omni contains brief statements from each of the last five generations of Nephites that kept the small Plates of Nephi. Amaleki, the last keeper of the plates, provided a few lines concerning the flight of King Mosiah and his people out of the land of Nephi, and the discovery of Zarahemla. His account, which is lengthy by the standard of his four predecessors, describes a completely peaceful union between the two cultures. The people of Zarahemla "were taught in the language of Mosiah."[106] After they were able to communicate, there is little doubt that the Nephites taught them the gospel of Jesus Christ. In the process of time, "the people of Zarahemla, and of Mosiah, did unite together; and Mosiah was appointed to be their king."[107]

The people of Mosiah and the people of Zarahemla were on opposite ends of the spiritual and cultural spectrum. Whereas the people of Mosiah were devout followers of Christ, the people of Zarahemla denied the existence of Christ.[108] The people of Mosiah were literate, while the people of Zarahemla were illiterate. The Nephites had brought the brass plates[109] from Jerusalem and had also kept extensive records of their history in the New World, beginning with their exodus from Jerusalem,[110] but the people of Zarahemla had no written records.

The brass plates obtained by Nephi in 600 BC "contain[ed] the five books of Moses, which gave an account of the creation of the world, and also of Adam and Eve, who were our first parents; And also a record of the Jews from the beginning, even down to the commencement of the reign of Zedekiah, king of Judah."[111] Also included was the genealogy of Lehi's fathers.[112] Therefore, the people of Mosiah, having retained the Jewish and Nephite records, had a precise knowledge of their religious and historical past all the way back to Adam. Moreover, they had retained the spiritual and moral values first taught by Father Adam, the Ancient of Days, and most recently by Lehi, Nephi, and Jacob. The people of Zarahemla, on the other hand, had limited knowledge of their historical and genealogical roots in Israel and no understanding of the religious and moral principles that had set Israel apart from surrounding nations.

In that sense, the people of Mosiah fled from the Lamanites, only to encounter a people similarly engulfed in spiritual darkness. The people of Zarahemla, however, did not have a tradition of hatred for the Nephites that had always been a barrier to the Lamanites' acceptance of truth.[113] Many were therefore receptive of the gospel when taught by the people of Mosiah.

EFFECT OF NEPHITE CULTURE ON THE PEOPLE OF ZARAHEMLA

The people of Zarahemla found in the Nephites all of the characteristics of a highly developed civilization, even in the absence of a homeland and thriving cities. The people of Mosiah were a migrant people without a home, but they possessed all of the elements necessary to establish a civilized nation, including literacy, government, law, and technology. When the people of Zarahemla thus came under Nephite influence, a great transformation took place. Basking in the light of Nephite culture, they quickly ascended in literary knowledge and spiritual understanding. Former religious beliefs and cultural traditions were restored through the influence of the Nephites, and are discussed below.

Christianity: When Mosiah I discovered the people of Zarahemla, Christianity was not found among them, for they "denied the being of their Creator."[114] Many Nephites, like their first fathers Lehi, Nephi, and Jacob, were devoted to the cause of Christ, as illustrated in the stories of Mosiah I, Benjamin, Mosiah II, Abinadi, Alma the Elder, Alma the Younger, and the four sons of Mosiah II.[115] Under the direction of Mosiah I, the gospel was taught to the people of Zarahemla. Many were converted and became a great strength to the Nephites, both spiritually and physically (numerically). Two generations later, Ammon, a descendant of Zarahemla, having a firm testimony of Jesus Christ[116] and of the divine inspiration and priesthood power possessed by Mosiah II,[117] exemplified the change that had come to many of the Mulekites.

Literacy: The Nephites had preserved their written language and instructed each successive generation in the skills of reading and writing.[118] This was one of the first things the people of Zarahemla were taught under Mosiah's direction.[119]

Cultural History: The Nephites taught the people of Zarahemla the history of the world and the history of Israel, as contained in the brass plates. This brought joy and fulfillment to them[120] because it represented their own ancestral history, which had been lost for many generations.

Cultural Significance: The people of Zarahemla had suffered from the inaccuracy and error that is fundamentally inherent in an exclusively oral tradition. In the absence of their religious heritage, they had lost the consciousness of and appreciation for their cultural and tribal significance, as given to them through the power and authority of Jacob's (or Israel's[121]) blessing.[122]

God-fearing Nephites had never denigrated or diminished the importance of their Jewish heritage. They believed the blessings given by Jacob to Manasseh through Joseph[123] to be eternally significant and valid to all who remained true to the commandments of God.

Descendants of Mulek, being of the tribe of Judah, were also given great importance in the brass plates. Theirs was the bloodline of the kings of Judah from whence the Nephites had come, and descendants of Judah were the legitimate nobility of Israel. The Savior of the world would come through their tribal lineage. In the hazy world of war, illiteracy, and pagan religion, the significance of their heritage had paled and ultimately disappeared, but now in the atmosphere of its restored authenticity within Nephite society, it was free to rise out of the mists.

THE PEOPLE OF ZARAHEMLA—A NEWLY ORGANIZED SOCIETY

When discovered by Mosiah, the people of Zarahemla were a recently organized society. They were called the people (or followers) of Zarahemla, their current leader.[124] Therefore, their history as the people of Zarahemla did not precede the man Zarahemla.

The land northward was the location of the original Mulekite landing in the New World. [125] However, the Nephites discovered the people of Zarahemla in the land southward.[126] The Book of Mormon gives no direct indication of why they departed from the land northward. If they were an offshoot of the original Mulekite culture,[127] what happened to the Mulekite heartland in the land northward? Such a culture is never identified in the Book of Mormon, neither in *ca.* 200 BC at the time of the merger, nor when the Nephite northward migrations began approximately 145 years later (55 BC).[128] A logical conclusion is that the entire Mulekite culture departed with Zarahemla into the land southward, leaving no one behind.[129]

The people of Zarahemla had apparently been humbled by adversity. Like the Nephites, their history was plagued by wars and serious contentions, which had reduced their population "from time to time."[130] In spite of their violent past, however, they were "exceedingly numerous,"[131] when discovered by the people of Mosiah. According to Mosiah 25:2, they actually outnumbered the people of Mosiah, which the Nephites felt would be of great benefit for defensive purposes, should the Lamanites again seek them out.[132]

THE PERIOD OF THE KINGS IN ZARAHEMLA— MOSIAH I, BENJAMIN, AND MOSIAH II

D<small>UE TO THE ABSENCE</small> of the first 116 pages of Mormon's abridgment,[133] very little is known of Nephite history in the land of Nephi between *ca.* 589 and *ca.* 200 BC. The cultural and historical information that is provided in the small Plates of Nephi[134] consists of facts without true orientation in a chronological or geographical sense. For instance, the Book of Enos provides information about the Lamanites, but it is general information that might be classified as a number of floating facts concerning the depraved spiritual condition of the Lamanites. Such facts are not anchored to any chronological or geographical framework, that is, to a specific time or location, nor is there any specificity of facts concerning Lamanite leaders and cities, or descriptions of their attacks against the Nephites. Rather, they provide historical and cultural information of a general nature, which pertains to the common origin of the Nephites and the Lamanites and the volatile relationship that existed between the two cultures during the life of Enos.

The same is true of Nephite history, chronology, and geography during the same period. Little specific information is given pertaining to the secular history of the Nephites, such as the settlement, growth, and development of the land of Nephi. No information is provided concerning the kings, not even the king who succeeded Nephi—likely his own son, based on succession by rights of lineage among both kings and judges during the Zarahemla period. There is no specific information pertaining to wars, famines, geography, cities, construction of the temple, the story of "Aminadi and the writings upon the wall of the temple,"[135] the "transgression,"[136]

Amaleki's dissent, and so forth. The account provides little information concerning the degree of peril that required an exodus from the land of Nephi, and no information surrounding specific incidents that occurred prior to, and which contributed to the departure of Mosiah and his followers.[137]

Likewise, information for the first 75 or 80 years in the land of Zarahemla (*ca.* 200–124 BC) is almost nonexistent. It is possible that within the lost pages will one day be discovered[138] books bearing the names of all of the Nephite kings from Nephi through Benjamin, such as the Book of First Mosiah and the Book of Benjamin. The Book of Mosiah, which is presently contained in the Book of Mormon, might then become Second Mosiah. Another possibility is that some books might contain the accounts of more than one king, similar to the way the Book of Alma contains the accounts of Alma and his son Helaman and the Book of Helaman contains the accounts of Helaman (the son of Helaman) and his son Nephi.

CA. 200 BC

KING MOSIAH I

The only information in the Book of Mormon that specifically concerns the reign of King Mosiah, the father of Benjamin, is found in the Book of Omni, the last book of the small Plates of Nephi. Twelve verses in Omni deal with Mosiah[139] and supply brief information about important historical events that occurred during his reign. King Benjamin provided a last reference to the teachings of Mosiah I, which was included in his farewell address to the Nephites.[140] No information pertaining to Mosiah's reign is contained in Benjamin's reference.

In the Omni account, it is revealed that Mosiah was a righteous prophet king who led the Nephites out of the land of Nephi, through the wilderness, and into the land of Zarahemla, where they encountered the Mulekites (the people of Zarahemla). Mosiah "caused that [the people of Zarahemla] should be taught in [the Nephite] language."[141] The people of Mosiah and the people of Zarahemla united together, and Mosiah ruled as king over both peoples. Mosiah's eminent spiritual stature as prophet and seer is highlighted in Omni, verses 12, 13, and 20. The information did not come by way of describing Mosiah, but rather by describing the events surrounding the discovery of Zarahemla and a stone tablet that was brought to King Mosiah by the people of Zarahemla, whereupon he interpreted the engravings on it through the power of God by means of the Urim and Thummim.[142] The account generates more questions than answers, especially surrounding 1) the stone tablet and 2) Mosiah's possession of the Urim and Thummim, which is not referenced previously in the Book of Mormon.

DEPARTURE OF THE PEOPLE OF ZENIFF

Also included in the Book of Omni is a brief passage "concerning a certain number who went up into the wilderness to return to the land of Nephi" during Mosiah's reign.[143] The passage was written by Amaleki and constitutes the last verses of the small plate of Nephi. Amaleki was concerned about his brother, who had accompanied the party out of Zarahemla. Later, in the Book of Mosiah, it is revealed that the eventual leader of the party was a man named Zeniff. The story of the people of Zeniff is closely associated with the establishment of the Church of Christ in the land of Zarahemla. The account of their history in the land of Nephi is included in the following chapter.

KING BENJAMIN

More information is provided about King Benjamin from his sermon to the Nephites than from anywhere else in the Book of Mormon, not as pertaining to his reign, but to his humility and righteousness—even holiness before the Lord. Benjamin was "chosen by [his] people and consecrated by [his father Mosiah], and was suffered by the hand of the Lord that [he] should be a ruler and a king over [them]."[144] Like his father, he was a great spiritual leader as well as a king.

Other than information supplied in Benjamin's final address to his people (such as the above statement), which was delivered at the consecration of his son Mosiah as his successor,[145] the only information provided in the Book of Mormon concerning King Benjamin's reign is found in Words of Mormon 1:12–18 and Omni 1:23-25. Words of Mormon is the transitional book written by Mormon, which bridges the gap between the small plate of Nephi and the second portion of Mormon's abridgment of Nephite history,[146] which he took from the large plate of Nephi.[147]

The passage in the Words of Mormon is interpreted herein as a single, multi-faceted event in which dissenters rose up against King Benjamin and obtained military assistance from Lamanites in the land of Nephi. A Lamanite army came down into the land of Zarahemla, but with Benjamin at the head of the Nephite armies, the Lamanites were defeated and driven out of the land. He then rounded up all the dissenters (rebels) that did not escape to the land of Nephi and punished them for their crimes. He received assistance from "many holy men" to preach the gospel to the people, "and they did speak the word of God with power and with authority; and they did use much sharpness because of the stiffneckedness of the people."[148] Through the efforts of King Benjamin and these prophets, peace was restored to the land of Zarahemla.

124 BC

KING BENJAMIN WAS A PROPHET OF GOD

Through the words of Benjamin, it becomes evident that he was a man of God, and truly choice among the children of God, for he was a prophet sent to declare the word of the Lord. As recorded in Mosiah 3, he told the people that an angel of God had appeared unto him and awakened him from sleep[149] to declare unto him a great and marvelous prophecy of the coming of Christ into the world to walk among men. The angel said that "with power, the Lord Omnipotent who reigneth, who was, and is from all eternity to all eternity, shall come down from heaven among the children of men and shall dwell in a tabernacle of clay."[150]

The Lord would go forth, doing great miracles, and would "suffer temptations, and pain of body, hunger, thirst, and fatigue, even more than man can suffer, except it be unto death; for behold, blood cometh from every pore, so great shall be his anguish for the wickedness and the abominations of his people."[151] Benjamin was told that His name would "be called Jesus Christ, the Son of God, the Father of heaven and earth, the Creator of all things from the beginning; and his mother shall be called Mary."[152]

THE NECESSITY OF THE ATONEMENT OF CHRIST

Through Benjamin's declaration of the coming of the Son of God, we learn the true import of the gospel principle he had already presented: "if ye should serve him who has created you from the beginning, and is preserving you from day to day . . . with all your whole souls yet ye would be unprofitable servants."[153] Benjamin was referring to the Atonement of Christ, without which all would be lost, though we should serve the Lord with all our "heart, might, mind, and strength,"[154] "for all have sinned, and come short of the glory of God,"[155] and "the Lord cannot look upon sin with the least degree of allowance."[156]

Concerning the Atonement, Benjamin said,

> And moreover, I say unto you, that there shall be no other name given nor any other way nor means whereby salvation can come unto the children of men, only in and through the name of Christ, the Lord Omnipotent.
>
> For behold he judgeth, and his judgment is just; and the infant perisheth not that dieth in his infancy; but men drink damnation to their own souls except they humble themselves and become as little children, and believe that salvation was, and is, and is to come, in and through the atoning blood of Christ, the Lord Omnipotent.
>
> For the natural man is an enemy to God, and has been from the fall of Adam, and will be, forever and ever, unless he yields to the enticings of the Holy Spirit, and putteth off the natural man and becometh a saint through the atonement of Christ the Lord, and becometh as a child, submissive, meek, humble, patient, full of love, willing to submit to all things which the Lord seeth fit to inflict upon him, even as a child doth submit to his father.
>
> And moreover, I say unto you, that the time shall come when the knowledge of a Savior shall spread throughout every nation, kindred, tongue, and people.
>
> And behold, when that time cometh, none shall be found blameless before God, except it be little children, only through repentance and faith on the name of the Lord God Omnipotent.[157]

THE PEOPLE ENTER INTO A COVENANT WITH THE LORD

King Benjamin exhorted the people to "consider on the blessed and happy state of those that keep the commandments of God" and "hold out faithful to the end . . . that thereby they may dwell with God in a state of never-ending happiness."[158] Having the influence of the Holy Ghost, he spoke to them with great power and authority. His words had a marvelous effect upon all the people, who were brought to their knees in repentance:

> And they all cried with one voice, saying: Yea, we believe all the words which thou hast spoken unto us; and also, we know of their surety and truth, because of the Spirit of the Lord Omnipotent, which has wrought a mighty change in us, or in our hearts, that we have no more disposition to do evil, but to do good continually.
>
> And we, ourselves, also, through the infinite goodness of God, and the manifestations of his Spirit, have great views of that which is to come; and were it expedient, we could prophesy of all things.
>
> And it is the faith which we have had on the things which our king has spoken unto us that has brought us to this great knowledge, whereby we do rejoice with such exceedingly great joy.
>
> And we are willing to enter into a covenant with our God to do his will, and to be obedient to his commandments in all things that he shall command us, all the remainder of our days, that we may not bring upon ourselves a never-ending torment, as has been spoken by the angel, that we may not drink out of the cup of the wrath of God.
>
> And now, these are the words which king Benjamin desired of them; and therefore he said unto them: Ye have spoken the words that I desired; and the covenant which ye have made is a righteous covenant.
>
> And now, because of the covenant which ye have made ye shall be called the children of Christ, his sons, and his daughters; for behold, this day he hath spiritually begotten you; for ye say that your hearts are changed through faith on his name; therefore, ye are born of him and have become his sons and his daughters.[159]

KING BENJAMIN GIVES THE PEOPLE A NAME

When Benjamin had first directed his son Mosiah to send a proclamation for the gathering of his people to the temple, his stated purpose was twofold:

- To proclaim Mosiah as his successor to the throne.
- To "give this people a name, that thereby they may be distinguished above all the people which the Lord God hath brought

out of the land of Jerusalem; and this I do because they have been a diligent people in keeping the commandments of the Lord."[160]

Receiving the new name was contingent upon their first making a formal covenant before God, "to do his will, and to be obedient to his commandments in all things that he shall command [them], all the remainder of [their] days."[161] Therefore, it was not until after they had, of their own accord, entered into the covenant that Benjamin gave them the name, which was "the children of Christ."[162] It was a name by which they would be known from that time forward.[163] Through this covenant, the people were fully prepared for baptism into the Church of Christ, which would soon be restored to the Nephites through the prophet Alma the Elder.[164]

KING MOSIAH II

The Book of Mosiah, as constituted in the Book of Mormon, represents the first book in the portion of the Plates of Mormon that remained after the first 116 pages were lost. It concerns the period of Nephite history during the life and reign of Mosiah II, exclusively.

The Book of Mosiah was written entirely in the perspective of Mosiah's reign. The initial remarks provide information surrounding his and his brothers' early life, during which they were taught by their father "in all the language of his fathers . . . that they might know concerning the prophecies which had been spoken by the mouths of their fathers, which were delivered them by the hand of the Lord."[165] Their "fathers," unmentioned by name, were the leaders of the Nephites, extending back to Nephi and Jacob, and their father Lehi.

As referenced above, King Benjamin selected Mosiah (his eldest son) as his successor to the throne. He commanded Mosiah to send forth a proclamation to all the people, which consisted of the people of Mosiah and the people of Zarahemla,[166] calling upon them to gather around the temple for the formal public announcement. King Benjamin's final address to the people is included in the Book of Mosiah because it was given during the ceremony to appoint Mosiah as king. Thus, it became a part of Mosiah's record. Benjamin retired and lived out his three remaining years in peace.[167]

Mosiah II is the only Nephite king (for which information is provided) whose reign was not marred by warfare.[168] It was a time of peace and prosperity. That is not to imply that there was no contention, especially near the end of his reign, but that contention never erupted into violence that can be classified as warfare.[169]

121 BC

MOSIAH SENDS AN EXPEDITION TO THE LAND OF NEPHI

Mosiah's reign began in 124 BC. Only three years later, he responded to a desire voiced continually by his people. Many had become overly anxious to know what had happened to the people of Zeniff, who had departed out of Zarahemla to return to the land of Nephi during the reign of Mosiah's grandfather many years before,[170] and "they wearied him with their teasings."[171] Therefore, in 121 BC, Mosiah commissioned "sixteen of their strong men," led by a man named Ammon, to mount an expedition to the land of Nephi in search of the people of Zeniff.[172]

Having no well-known or well-defined route between Zarahemla and Nephi, Ammon's party wandered in the wilderness for 40 days before they came to a hill bordering the city of Shilom on the north side of the city.[173] Looking out from the top of the hill (perhaps from a tower previously constructed there by King Noah[174]), no doubt they could see the city and its surrounding farmland. Shilom was one of two cities[175] in the land of Nephi occupied by the people of Limhi, the grandson of Zeniff. Through Ammon's discovery of the people of King Limhi, the Nephites in Zarahemla would finally learn the rest of the story of Zeniff, which will be recounted from its beginning in the following chapter.

THE RECORD OF THE PEOPLE OF ZENIFF

CA. 200 BC

IT IS APPARENT THAT some of the people who accompanied Mosiah out of Nephi into the wilderness were not impressed with the land of Zarahemla. Missing were the highlands of Nephi and their relatively cool, crisp mountain air. Zarahemla is characterized as a land of fevers, abundant flora, and sweltering heat.[176]

Shortly after Mosiah's arrival in Zarahemla, discontent began to grow among a segment of the people. A movement developed from the discontent in which a considerable number made plans to return to the land of Nephi and contend with the Lamanites for the land of their birthright. They were willing to die for the opportunity to return to their homeland.

There were two return expeditions to the land of Nephi, the first of which was a miserable failure. The leader of the first expedition was "an austere and bloodthirsty man"[177] with great animosity toward the Lamanites. He wanted to annihilate them wherever they were found, which surely would have brought about their own destruction, for the Lamanites greatly outnumbered them. Zeniff wanted to make peace with the Lamanites. He did not want to murder innocent women and children, for he saw much of worth among them.[178]

The leader refused to consider Zeniff's arguments and sought to put Zeniff to death. Fighting broke out between two factions—those who defended Zeniff and those who supported the leader. All but 50 were slain,[179] and the survivors returned to Zarahemla to report the sad news to their wives and children.

KING ZENIFF

Though the first venture into the land of Nephi had ended in failure and disappointment, Zeniff refused to be deterred from his dream of returning to the land of his nativity. He began gathering other Nephites with like feelings, and at length mounted a second expedition. This time he was the leader, and they came peaceably with their families into the land of Nephi. He petitioned Laman, the Lamanite king, to allow them to take possession of the land. King Laman allowed them to take possession of the cities of Lehi-Nephi (Nephi)[180] and Shilom, which were deserted and in disrepair.

The king granted unto him according to his petition, and commanded the Lamanites, which had moved into the area following the departure of the people of Mosiah, to evacuate the land and allow the people of Zeniff to move in. The people of Zeniff began to inhabit the two cities, utilizing the surrounding land for farming. The account of Zeniff is included in the Book of Mosiah[181] and describes their subsequent history through the reign of three kings (the same as the number of kings in Zarahemla during the same period).

KING NOAH

King Zeniff passed the throne to his son, Noah, who became a very wicked and idolatrous king . He replaced all his father's priests with priests who would support him in his wickedness. He became a wine-bibber. He and his priests had many wives and concubines. He burdened the people with heavy taxation to enable him to maintain a luxuriant lifestyle. He "built many elegant and spacious buildings" in the city of Nephi, and "he ornamented them with fine work of wood, and of all manner of precious things." He ordered the renovation of the temple previously built by the prophet Nephi.[182] He had his workmen work all manner of fine work within the walls of the temple of fine wood, and of copper, and of brass. The seats constructed for his priests were elevated above all the rest and were ornamented with pure gold. There, he and his priests could sit to administer to and judge the people.[183]

Their wickedness was displeasing to God, and soon a prophet was sent among the people to warn of the judgments Noah was bringing down upon them. The story of King Noah is reminiscent of the kings of Israel and of Judah, who through their positions of absolute power and influence over the children of Israel frequently led them into idolatry and moral depravity.[184]

CA. 148 BC

ABINADI

God's displeasure with Noah and his people was revealed suddenly, when a prophet named Abinadi, one of Noah's subjects, was commanded by the Lord to go among the people and testify of coming judgment if they did not repent of "their abominations, and their wickedness, and their whoredoms."[185] When word came to King Noah that Abinadi was condemning the people and prophesying their destruction, he was angry and commanded that he be brought to him, that he might slay him. All the people began looking for Abinadi, but he was nowhere to be found.

Two years later, Abinadi again ventured forth among the people, but this time he was in disguise. Again, he prophesied of imminent destruction if they did not repent. Again, the people were angry at his condemnation of their actions. They seized him and carried him before the king. They related to Noah the things he had said concerning them. Noah had him cast into prison while he consulted with his priests concerning what actions they should take.

At length, Abinadi was brought before Noah and his priests to answer the many charges that had been brought against him. They questioned him with the intent of finding reasons to condemn him to death. For Abinadi, it was the opportunity he had sought to deliver the Lord's message to the king, and he was filled with the power of the Holy Ghost. Again, he condemned them for their wickedness. He preached concerning the many commandments of God they were disobeying and warned them of imminent judgment from the Lord.

ALMA BELIEVES THE WORDS OF ABINADI

When Abinadi had finished his sermon,[186] King Noah was angry and commanded his soldiers to cast him into prison to await execution for his crime. "But there was one among them whose name was

Alma, he also being a descendant of Nephi. And he was a young man, and he believed the words which Abinadi had spoken, for he knew concerning the iniquity which Abinadi had testified against them; therefore he began to plead with the king that he would not be angry with Abinadi, but suffer that he might depart in peace."[187]

The king, however, was even more angry and had Alma cast out. He then sent his servants to follow Alma and slay him. Alma, apparently expecting their pursuit, fled while he had the chance, and hid from the assassins. In their anger, King Noah and his priests put Abinadi to death, burning him with fire.

CA. 145 BC

A REBELLION AMONG THE PEOPLE OF NOAH

About three years after Abinadi's death, a portion of Noah's people rebelled against him. The enemies of the king comprised the "lesser part" of the people,[188] but they were led by a powerful and influential man by the name of Gideon.[189] As a result of the political struggle that followed, (including a Lamanite invasion, a retreat led by Noah, and further rebellion among the people) King Noah was slain. As soon as it was confirmed that he was dead, the kingdom was conferred upon his son Limhi, a righteous man, who then took his place as the king.

Limhi had accepted a treaty with the Lamanite king, which he immediately formalized with an oath.[190] It required the people of Zeniff to pay a tribute of half of their possessions and yearly increase to the Lamanites. This would prove to have serious consequences for the people of Limhi, but it was their only choice since they looked death in the face from the Lamanites.

CA. 145–121 BC

THE PEOPLE OF LIMHI SUFFER IN BONDAGE TO THE LAMANITES

Years passed, and the people of Limhi suffered under the burden of Lamanite oppression. Not only were they required to give half of all their increase to the Lamanites,[191] but increasingly, the Lamanites treated them with contempt and physically abused them. To add insult to injury, they "began to put heavy burdens upon their backs, and drive them as they would a dumb ass."[192]

At length, the people of Limhi struck out against their tormentors. They gathered their army together and gave battle to the Lamanites, but they were soundly defeated. Many were killed, and they returned to their land. Twice more, they went against the Lamanites, and twice more, they were smitten and driven back to their own land.[193]

They were humbled before the Lord because they knew the judgments foretold by Abinadi had arrived and were just punishments for their iniquities. Through the loss of so many of their men during these battles, there were many widows in the land, which greatly increased their burden. Limhi called upon each man to give support to the widows and their children. Every man struggled to fulfill these responsibilities, but the Lord blessed them with bounteous crops.[194] The Lord also blessed them by softening the hearts of the Lamanites, and they "began to ease their burdens."[195]

In 121 BC, as King Limhi and his people continued to struggle under the yoke of Lamanite persecution,[196] King Mosiah sent the party of sixteen headed by Ammon in search of the people of Zeniff.[197] Upon their arrival at the hill located on the north side of the city of Shilom, Ammon took three of his men and ventured down into the valley below.[198] They were discovered by King Limhi, who was accompanied by his guards outside the walls of the city.[199] When Limhi learned of their identity, he and they immediately began to plan an escape into the wilderness.

THE FLIGHT OF THE PEOPLE OF LIMHI

Soon, an escape plan was introduced by Gideon to intoxicate the Lamanites who guarded them, which would enable them to slip into the wilderness. The plan was soon put into play. The people of Limhi gathered all their possessions together and made ready to depart on Limhi's command.

Gideon went to the Lamanite guards and gave them the normal tribute of wine. Limhi "also sent more wine, as a present unto them."[200] As expected, the guards drank themselves into a stupor, whereupon the people of Limhi departed out of the city of Nephi into the wilderness. They circled around the city of Shilom in the wilderness, possibly to avoid other Lamanite guards posted there, and only then "bent their course towards the land of Zarahemla, being led by Ammon and his brethren."[201]

After many days, they arrived in the land of Zarahemla and united with the people of Mosiah and became Mosiah's subjects. Limhi presented the record of Zeniff and the record of the Jaredite prophet Ether to King Mosiah.[202]

CHAPTER 1.6

THE CHURCH OF CHRIST IS RESTORED[203]
THROUGH ALMA THE ELDER

CA. 148 BC

A FTER BEING EXPELLED FROM King Noah's court, Alma hid for "many days"[204] from the persistent "searches of the king."[205] He repented of all his iniquities,[206] and then commenced to diligently study the gospel principles, which had been taught by Abinadi.

Alma found refuge in the "borders of Nephi"[207] at "a place which was called Mormon."[208] "Now, there was in Mormon a fountain of pure water, and Alma resorted thither."[209] The "waters of Mormon,"[210] which emanated from a natural spring[211], formed a large pool of water[212] that was clear and pure.

A forest grew in the moist environment created by the Waters of Mormon. The "forest of Mormon"[213] may have represented the outer reaches of the wilderness separating Nephi from Zarahemla, for the wilderness extended continuously all the way from the land of Zarahemla to the borders of Nephi.[214]

All of Alma's needs were met at the Waters and Forest of Mormon. There was pure water to drink, game to eat, and a remote and ideal location to hide, where the people could come in relative safety to hear the word of the Lord. Soon, however, the Waters of Mormon would fill yet another important need.

After an undisclosed period of study, prayer, and revelation,[215] Alma began moving "privately" among the people, teaching them about the Atonement of Christ and the salvation of mankind, which comes only through the Atonement.[216] In time, he began to conduct baptisms in the Waters of Mormon, through which Nephites joined together to solemnize their belief in Christ. They called themselves the Church of Christ, which would thereafter remain among the Nephites until the Nephites would be destroyed at the Hill Cumorah in AD 385.

ALMA'S AUTHORITY TO BAPTIZE

Mormon did not clearly describe the manner in which Alma received his authority to baptize, though he did write that Alma baptized "having authority from the Almighty God."[217] This authority can come in more than one way. Today, new members entering the Church are baptized by the priesthood authority that was given when John the Baptist laid his hands upon Joseph Smith and Oliver Cowdery on May 15, 1829, and which thereafter has been passed down through the Church to the present day. It was by that authority only that Joseph baptized Oliver, for he had not been baptized when he baptized Oliver.

It can be concluded from the series of events in 1829 that the authority to baptize is not contingent upon a person already having been baptized. The basic requirement is simply that they must first be ordained to the priesthood—the Aaronic Priesthood. Unlike Joseph and Oliver, however, in the Church today, a person is baptized prior to receiving the priesthood.

Still, it was necessary only that Joseph receive authority by the laying on of hands by one having the authority to ordain him to the priesthood of God. He therefore had the power to baptize before he was baptized. It was still necessary that he be baptized as well, to enter into the baptismal covenant and to formally take upon himself the name of Christ.

For that reason, Oliver subsequently baptized him. It could have been done in reverse order, since both Joseph and Oliver were ordained to the priesthood by John the Baptist. However, John instructed Joseph to perform the first baptism and afterward Oliver should baptize him.[218]

Considering the source by which Joseph Smith and Oliver Cowdery received their authority to baptize, it follows that Alma's priesthood authority may also have come directly from the heavens. It was later revealed to Joseph Smith that John the Baptist received his authority from an angel of the Lord.[219] Still, the Book of Mormon does not reveal the specific source of Alma's authority.

Given the fact that no baptisms were performed in Zarahemla until Alma's arrival, it is unlikely that Alma received his authority through Nephite priesthood channels that extended back to an earlier time in Nephite history. Otherwise, King Benjamin, a great man of God, would have held the same priesthood authority in the land of Zarahemla to baptize the people who took upon themselves the name of Christ.[220]

THE PEOPLE OF THE CHURCH MEET TOGETHER EACH SABBATH DAY

Following the great day of baptism and church organization, the Church of Christ, under Alma's direction, met together "one day in every week . . . to teach the people, and to worship the Lord their God, and also, as often as it was in their power, to assemble themselves together."[221] Alma called upon his followers to bear one another's burdens and to serve each other in all things.

The Waters of Mormon, like the Sacred Grove in modern times, were held sacred to the Nephites throughout the remainder of their history. As Mormon stated at the very end of the Nephite era (summarizing those events), "And now it came to pass that all this was done in Mormon, yea, by the waters of Mormon, in the forest that was near the waters of Mormon; yea, the place of Mormon, the waters of Mormon, the forest of Mormon, how beautiful are they to the eyes of them who there came to the knowledge of their Redeemer; yea, and how blessed are they, for they shall sing to his praise forever."[222]

CA. 145 BC

KING NOAH LEARNS OF A MOVEMENT AMONG THE PEOPLE

Each week on the Sabbath day, members of the Church would discreetly join together at the border of the land to hear the word of the Lord.[223] Notwithstanding all their caution, it was through these weekly meetings, as well as the proselytizing of the Church among the people of Noah that Noah learned of a "movement among the people."[224] He sent his servants to observe the people and follow them as they went to the place of meeting.

The servants returned to the king and informed him of what they had discovered at the Waters of Mormon. In his wickedness, King Noah saw the people of Alma as nothing more than a rebellion to overthrow his kingdom: "And now the king said that Alma was stirring up the people to rebellion against him; therefore he sent his army to destroy them."[225]

Perhaps Noah's army was gathered without haste, in preference for the element of surprise and careful strategic planning to ensure that no one escaped. After all, Alma's movement had been going on for months, or possibly years. As far as Noah knew, the people of Alma did not even know they had been discovered. When they reached the Waters of Mormon, however, Alma and his people, having been warned of the Lord,[226] were nowhere to be found.

CA. 145–121 BC

THE LAND OF HELAM

Alma and his people fled into the wilderness with their families, tents, flocks, and grain. They had no idea how long it would be before Noah's army would begin their pursuit. No doubt they pushed themselves and their flocks to the very limit of their endurance. They fled for eight days, likely beginning each day at the break of dawn, and continuing until it was night. They went forth in the strength of the Lord, and therefore were able to maintain the extreme tempo of a forced march through approximately 12 hours of daylight.[227]

At the end of eight days, "they came to a land, yea, even a very beautiful and pleasant land, a land of pure water."[228] This appears to be another reference to fountains, or natural springs, the most likely source of pure water. The fountain or fountains may also have formed the headwaters of a river, a possibility which will be considered in Part 3, Chapter 3.3, as pertaining to the most direct and recognizable passageway between the Waters of Mormon and the headwaters of the Sidon River.

The new land was apparently the most beautiful and alluring location they had found since departing from the Waters of Mormon.

It drew them in and forbade them to depart. They stopped, "pitched their tents," and began to till the land and construct buildings.[229] As at the Waters of Mormon, all of their needs were met in the land of Helam, which was likely named after the first member to enter the Church through the waters of baptism.

The people loved Alma and desired that he should be their king. Having recently been victims of Noah's persecution, this speaks volumes for their veneration of Alma and complete trust in his righteousness and equity to all. However, Alma looked past the present into the future, when his reign would come to an end. He could foresee the possibility of a successor like Zeniff's son, Noah, and he refused to be their king. He reminded them of Noah's wickedness and informed them of the Lord's will in the matter. He said, "for thus saith the Lord: Ye shall not esteem one flesh above another, or one man shall not think himself above another; therefore I say unto you it is not expedient that ye should have a king."[230] The people accepted Alma's wisdom.

Years possibly passed, and the people of Alma prospered in the land of Helam. In time, they built the city of Helam. Their lives revolved around the gospel and Alma's teachings, and all was well in Zion. They had no idea that the time would come in the not-too-distant future when their perfect world would be abruptly disrupted.

CA. 121 BC

THE PEOPLE OF ALMA ARE DISCOVERED BY THE LAMANITES

One day, as the people of Alma worked in their fields, a Lamanite army marched into the land of Helam. The people were frightened and ran from their fields. They gathered in the city of Helam. "But Alma went forth and stood among them, and exhorted them that they should not be frightened, but that they should remember the Lord their God and he would deliver them."[231]

The people were encouraged and "began to cry unto the Lord that he would soften the hearts of the Lamanites, that they would spare them, and their wives, and their children."[232] When the Lamanites came to the city, "the Lord did soften [their] hearts," and they did not destroy the people of Alma. "And Alma and his brethren went forth and delivered themselves up into their hands; and the Lamanites took possession of the land of Helam."[233]

THE PRIESTS OF AMULON ACCOMPANY THE LAMANITES

The Lamanite army that appeared in Helam had pursued the people of Limhi into the wilderness. After two days, they could no longer detect the trail and realized they were lost. Completely disoriented, they wandered around for an undisclosed period of time. One day, they chanced upon the priests of Noah, who a number of years earlier had abducted twenty-four of the Lamanite daughters.[234]

Following the abduction, the priests had fled deep into the wilderness to evade the Lamanites who would certainly come looking with vengeance for their daughters. In the wilderness, they made the Lamanite daughters their wives. In the sanctuary of the wilderness, they began to till the land, and in the intervening years, they built a city that they called Amulon, after the name of their leader.

When they were discovered by the Lamanites, Amulon pleaded with them to spare his people. He sent their wives, who also stood before the Lamanites and begged them to spare the lives of their husbands. The Lamanites had compassion on the priests of Noah because of their wives.[235] They did not destroy them, but neither did they leave them in peace. Rather, they took them along in their search for the land of Nephi. Thus, when the Lamanite army wandered into the borders of Helam, the wicked priests of Noah were in their midst.[236]

ALMA GIVES THE LAMANITES DIRECTIONS TO NEPHI

When the Lamanites and Amulonites arrived in Helam, they had been wandering for many days in the wilderness. They petitioned the people of Alma to show them the way back to Nephi, promising in return to leave them in peace.[237] When Alma showed them the way, however, it is apparent that their attitude immediately changed. They "would not keep their promise; but they set guards round about the land of Helam, over Alma and his brethren"[238] before departing in the direction of Nephi.

THE AMULONITES EDUCATE THE LAMANITES

Amulon and his associates were learned men, who likely had been chosen by Noah for their charisma, intellect, and learning, as well as their willing indulgence in physical pleasure. "And it came to pass that Amulon did gain favor in the eyes of the king of the Lamanites; therefore, the king of the Lamanites granted unto him and his brethren that they should be appointed teachers over his people, yea, even over the people who were in the land of Shemlon, and in the land of Shilom, and in the land of Amulon. For the Lamanites had taken possession of all these lands; therefore the king of the Lamanites had appointed kings over all these lands."[239]

Laman, the king of the Lamanites, from whom Amulon gained approval may have been the same Lamanite ruler who only a few years earlier had been found wounded among the dead near the city of Nephi in a battle with the people of Limhi.[240] If so, then he was a man of honor, for he had kept his word to Limhi at that time, even after persuading the people of Limhi to disarm prior to the Lamanite army arriving. His failure to keep the agreement with Alma was likely a result of Amulon's influence.

At this time, the Amulonites were given teaching assignments in various cities, including Shemlon, Shilom, Amulon,[241] and likely Nephi and other cities and lands[242] not identified in the Book of Mosiah. They were wise as to the things of the world. They taught the Lamanites to read and write "the language of Nephi,"[243] and they taught them to keep records like the Nephites, and to communicate in writing with "their own brethren."[244] Though they did not teach them about God, Jesus Christ, the Law of Moses, or the words of Abinadi,[245] they did elevate them culturally by teaching them the wisdom of the world.[246]

Through the influence of the Amulonites, the Lamanites "began to increase in riches, and began to trade one with another and wax great, and began to be a cunning and a wise people, as to the wisdom of the world."[247] Previously, for the most part, they had lived a nomadic-type existence, dwelling in tents and likely depending more on hunting and gathering than agriculture for subsistence.[248] Afterward, they lived to a much greater extent in cities. As a result, the Amulonites became highly respected among the Lamanites, a status that would continue for about 40 years, or until *ca.* 80 BC, when the curse pronounced by Abinadi[249] would come to fruition.[250]

AMULON PERSECUTES ALMA AND HIS PEOPLE

When the Lamanite king assigned the priests of Amulon to various cities to teach and administer to the Lamanites, Amulon reserved the land of Helam for himself. He petitioned the king to give him authority over Helam. His arguments may have revolved around the idea that since Helam was not occupied by Lamanites, the king should make an exception and allow him to have authority over Alma and his people. And, because of his knowledge and understanding of the Nephite culture, he could rule them in wisdom. The king "granted unto Amulon that he should be a king and a ruler over his people, who were in the land of Helam; nevertheless he should have no power to do anything contrary to the will of the king of the Lamanites."[251] Amulon's manipulation of the Lamanite king was typical of the aggressive behavior of Nephite dissenters, which in 73 BC would be elevated to a new standard by Amalickiah.[252]

Amulon's sovereign control of Helam would temporarily have serious consequences for Alma and his people. The political control he had assumed through manipulation of the Lamanite king gave him the power to persecute them. Amulon knew Alma well, and it would not be surprising if he blamed Alma's "insurrection" for causing the rebellion led by Gideon. The internal strife had factored into the fall of King Noah's kingdom to the Lamanites. Thus, in his opinion, it was possibly Alma who had shattered his world of power and influence in King Noah's court.

However, the true reason he was an enemy to Alma was that he was an enemy to God. Revenge against Alma thus became his obsession. It was his very purpose in petitioning the king to give him complete authority in ruling over the people of Alma. Once in power, he immediately exerted unrighteous dominion over them, to punish them for their "crimes" against King Noah, and against him. He began to persecute "Alma and his brethren . . . and cause that his children should persecute their children."[253] It is likely that Alma the Younger was numbered among the children that were persecuted by Amulon's children.

Amulon appointed taskmasters over the people of Alma and subjected them to hard labor. "And it came to pass that so great were their afflictions that they began to cry mightily to God. And Amulon commanded them that they should stop their cries; and he put guards over them to watch them, that whosoever should be found calling upon God should be put to death. And Alma and his people did not raise their voices to the Lord their God, but did pour out their hearts to him; and he did know the thoughts of their hearts."[254]

CA. 120 BC

ALMA AND HIS PEOPLE ARE DELIVERED FROM BONDAGE

The voice of the Lord came to Alma and his people, acknowledging the covenant which they had made with Him upon entering the Church and promising to ease their burdens until they should be delivered from their bondage.[255] "And now it came to pass that the burdens which were laid upon Alma and his brethren were made light; yea, the Lord did strengthen them that they could bear up their burdens with ease, and they did submit cheerfully and with patience to all the will of the Lord."[256]

Because of their faith, the voice of the Lord came to them once more, promising them deliverance on the morrow. The Lord said to Alma, "Thou shalt go before this people, and I will go with thee and deliver this people out of bondage."[257]

They gathered their flocks and their grain throughout the night and prepared for departure in the morning. As promised, "in the morning the Lord caused a deep sleep to come upon the Lamanites, yea, and all their task-masters were in a profound sleep."[258] Unmolested, the people of Alma departed out of Helam into the wilderness. They traveled throughout the day before coming to a halt in the Valley of Alma, which they called thus because Alma had led them out of bondage.

In the Valley of Alma, the people gave thanks to God for their deliverance, for they knew that "none could deliver them except it were the Lord their God."[259] Soon, the voice of the Lord came to Alma, informing him that the Lamanites had awakened from their sleep and were at that moment pursuing them. He said, "Haste thee and get thou and this people out of this land . . . and I will stop the Lamanites in this valley that they come no further in pursuit of this people."[260] It is not recorded, and perhaps they never knew how He accomplished this miracle.

Immediately, the people of Alma continued on their journey. Counting their first day from Helam to the Valley of Alma, they traveled through the wilderness for twelve days before they arrived in the land of Zarahemla, "and king Mosiah did also[261] receive them with great joy."[262]

TABLE 1.0

NEPHITE HISTORY IN THE LAND OF NEPHI FROM 200 TO 120 BC

Year (BC)	People	Event
~200	Mosiah	Mosiah leads his people from the land of Nephi through the wilderness to the land of Zarahemla.
~200	Zeniff	Zeniff convinces some to return with him through the wilderness to Nephi.
~160	Noah	Zeniff confers the kingdom upon his son Noah.
~150	Abinadi	Condemns the people of King Noah for their sins and is delivered by the Lord out of their hands.
~148	Abinadi	Returns and again condemns the people of Noah and becomes a martyr for the gospel.
~148	Alma	Comes to the support of Abinadi, is forced to flee from King Noah and his priests.
~145	People of Alma	Flee eight days from King Noah and establish the city of Helam in the heart of the wilderness.
~145 to ~121	People of Alma	Thrive in the land of Helam for approximately 24 years.

Year (BC)	People	Event
~145	Amulonites	Flee first from Lamanites and then from the people of Noah into the wilderness; Noah is slain by his own people.
~145	Limhi	Becomes the king after Noah's death, surrenders to the Lamanites, and is required to pay tribute of 50 percent.
~143	Amulonites	Abduct Lamanite daughters, flee into wilderness, and inhabit and till the land of Amulon.
~143 to ~121	People of Limhi	As a result of the Lamanite abductions, Lamanite hostility took place, which continued in varying ways until their departure from the land of Nephi approximately 22 years later.
121	Mosiah II	Sends the party of Ammon in search of the people of Zeniff.
121	People of Limhi	Flee from the land of Nephi with Ammon's party and journey through the wilderness to Zarahemla.
121	Lamanites	Pursue the people of Limhi, become lost, and unexpectedly discover the land of Amulon.
121	Amulonites	Are discovered by the Lamanites and are forced to travel with them in search of the land of Nephi.
121	People of Alma	Are discovered by the Lamanites and Amulonites and are persecuted by Amulonites.
120	People of Alma	Flee out of Helam and migrate to Zarahemla.

PART 2

NEPHITE HISTORY—A PAGAN CONSPIRACY

INTRODUCTION

A PREVALENT IDEA WITH RESPECT to the Nephite culture as described in the Book of Mormon is that the Nephites were a predominantly Christian culture throughout their history in the Western Hemisphere. Readers of the Book of Mormon might very well see the Nephite culture as fundamentally, if not exclusively, Christian, largely because it was written by Christian prophets, which cast every subject in a gospel perspective.[263] The same view could even be held by serious students of the Book of Mormon who concentrate on its abundant spiritual and doctrinal content. For many, the idea has never been a subject of consideration and might be considered as unimportant and irrelevant.

A number of non-Mormon archaeologists—critics of Latter-day Saint claims that the Book of Mormon is a true history of Pre-Columbian cultures—have pointed to inconsistencies between the New World archaeological record and the Christian society described in the Book of Mormon. Without looking closely, the critics assume the Book of Mormon paints a homogeneous picture of Christian-based culture. If correct, then the Book of Mormon account would indeed contrast sharply with the abundant pagan iconography found in the ruins of Mesoamerican cities from the Preclassic through the Postclassic eras, as well as other ancient sites outside of Mesoamerica, which were inhabited across the North and South American continents during the same periods of time.

The undeniable fact is this: Pre-Columbian civilization, as preserved in the archaeological record, was generally dominated by polytheistic idol worship. If the ancient cultures of the New World were Book of Mormon cultures, as represented therein, then pagan religion, and specifically idolatry, must have been a significant, if not prevalent, element within the Jaredite and Nephite cultures. It should be evident within the text of the Book of Mormon, as well as in the archaeological record.

In the following chapters, the Pre-Christ Book of Mormon period is systematically considered from the above perspective. Forces that caused dissension and warfare are investigated in detail. As will be observed, pagan religion was deeply entrenched within both Nephite and Lamanite cultures. It was a constant source of discontent and violence through approximately three-fourths of the last 600 years of Nephite history, which began with the *ca.* 200 BC arrival of the Nephites in the land of Zarahemla. Of the 200 years which then preceded the birth of the Savior and the 400 years between His birth and the last comments made by the prophet Moroni, only 160 years (AD 34–194) were blessed by the total absence of pagan religion.

The successful preservation of the Nephite culture over a period of a thousand years was made possible only by the dominance of the Christian faith over the destructive pagan religions. During the pre-Zarahemla period in the land of Nephi, though the record is incomplete, it appears that the Nephites were largely unaffected by Lamanite idolatry. A pagan subculture within the Nephite culture is not identified in the record until the arrival of the Nephites in Zarahemla. It was not until the final Nephite wars, however, that the pagan cults for the first time became the dominant force. The result was the complete eradication of Christianity from the Western Hemisphere in AD 384.

As considered above, the first Nephite period in the land of Nephi (589 BC to *ca.* 200 BC) is covered only briefly in the Book of Mormon. The absence of the first 116 pages[264] of Mormon's abridgment of the large plate of Nephi prevents a clear view of secular Nephite history during that period. Only a glimpse is given in the small plate of Nephi[265] of pagan elements within the Nephite culture during that period, primarily in a short reference to Sherem, an antichrist.[266] Enos made reference to a tradition of Lamanite idolatry during his day, which he contrasted with Nephite tradition, the implication being that the Nephites did not practice idolatry, but instead "did seek diligently to restore the Lamanites unto the true faith in God."[267]

During the pre-Christ period in Zarahemla (*ca.* 200 BC– AD 34), however, Nephite dissenters were always pagan and idol worshipers, according to instances where evidence is provided concerning the form of their religion.[268] Following the establishment of the Church of Christ by Alma the Elder, these dissenters became enemies of the Church, and of the Christian government which protected it. There were likely Nephite dissenters to the Lamanites during the first period in the land of Nephi, but none are referenced in the small plate of Nephi. In the Book of Alma, reference is made to Amalekite dissenters in 91 BC, living among the Lamanites in the land of Nephi.[269] The account of their dissent is not included in the Book of Mormon.

On the surface, it is conceivable that the Amalekites dissented over to the Lamanites during the 400-year period in the land of Nephi. However, in the balance of all related information,[270] it becomes apparent that their dissension occurred in Zarahemla during the days of King Benjamin. The 116 lost pages likely incorporated the story of the Amalekites, probably including an account of the dissenter Amaleki and his dissension from the Nephites.

CHAPTER 2.1

THE PAGAN MENACE IN ZARAHEMLA

IN EVERY AGE OF the world, the work of the Lord, and the people who seek to obey the commandments first given to Adam and Eve have come under attack. Cain was a son of Adam who was completely given over to the influences of Satan. He rose up and destroyed his brother Abel because of jealousy over Abel's offering to the Lord. In his fallen state, he was angry that the Lord had found favor in Abel's offering and had rejected his offering of fruits and vegetables, which bore no resemblance to the sacrifice of Jesus Christ.

Throughout the remainder of the Pre-Flood era, Cain's descendants and followers filled the earth with violence. In the seventh patriarchal generation from Adam, they sought to destroy the City of Zion, but the city was protected by the power of God. As the Lord protected the righteous in Enoch's Zion,[271] He has protected the righteous throughout the history of mankind. He will protect His righteous and obedient people until His Second Coming, when He returns in power and great glory.

In the Nephite culture, the same animosity that was at work in previous times, fueled by Satan, was a continual source of contention. Though the Lamanites hated the Nephites because of the alleged disrespect of Nephi for his elder brothers, the original cause of the hatred was the rebellion of Laman and Lemuel against the commandments of God. As a result of their unbelief and moral depravity, the Lamanites who descended from them were unknowing instruments of the devil. For more than 350 years, the Nephites found it necessary to defend the land of Nephi against violent attacks by the Lamanites.

In approximately 200 BC, Mosiah I listened to the Spirit of God and led his people out of the land of Nephi. In so doing, he removed his people from the immediate threat of Lamanite animosity.

Upon their arrival at the Sidon River, the Nephites encountered the people of Zarahemla, who also had previously rebelled against God, considering their religious roots in Israel. As a result, "they denied the being of their Creator [Jehovah]."[272] Though the two peoples united politically under the rule of King Mosiah, the Mulekites brought with them a primitive form of a pagan religion that in time would gain power and influence among the Nephites. It would become a formidable enemy of righteousness, and a predator against the people of God.

THE VOICE OF DISSENT

Dissenters from the Nephites generally espoused pagan beliefs. They were not merely non-believers of the Christian faith. Many dissenters were apostates from the Church of God who had fallen away or perhaps returned to the pagan religion. However, for the most part, they were more against the teachings of Christ than they were loyal and devout followers of another religious philosophy. In fact, the very things about the Church that angered them were the strict rules of conduct, which required that they obey the commandments of God to remain in good standing in the Church. The pagan gods had no such requirements, but rather allowed them to indulge in all of the pleasures of life without condemnation.

The word "pagan," as used in this book, is a general and rather nondescript term, referring to individuals or organizations having religious traditions that are polytheistic or indigenous.[273] It is for that reason that it is the term of choice in this book, for it sits in juxtaposition to the only true religion, and as such requires no more definitive treatment, except as it is distinguished from Christianity in the Book of Mormon, and as it frequently became a predator to the people of God.

Dissenters "were of a more wicked and murderous disposition" toward the Nephites than even the Lamanites[274] and frequently gave themselves over completely to "the traditions of the Lamanites; giving way to indolence, and all manner of lasciviousness; yea, entirely forgetting the Lord their God."[275] Dissenters, such as

Amalekites and Amulonites, as well as Zoramites (after 74 BC) were known for being more embittered and "hardened" against the Church than the Lamanites.[276] However, they generally found the Lamanites to be highly susceptible to claims of Nephite injustice; therefore, it was not difficult to incite them to violence.[277]

From 92 BC until 30 BC, dissenters repeatedly came to battle against the Nephites, using the Lamanites as pawns. The ultimate purpose was always the same—to destroy Christianity, and it is frequently identified as such in the Book of Mormon.[278] It might thus be concluded that the frequent attacks of dissenters during the reign of the judges (91 BC–AD 34) were part of the general pagan strategy to first take control of Nephite government and then eliminate Christianity from the land of Zarahemla.

The books of Alma, Helaman, and 3 Nephi describe an ever intensifying struggle between the Christian and pagan factions within the Nephite population in Zarahemla. The antagonism was markedly one-sided, and on the part of the Christians was generally a defensive response to pagan aggression. The struggle was terminated suddenly by the Great Storm of AD 34.[279] Each development in this religious, political, and military struggle during the pre-Christ period will be identified in Part 3.

Following the 160-year Nephite Golden Age (AD 34–194), the pagan campaign began again with renewed fury and continued until the Christian Nephites were silenced by genocide at Cumorah in AD 385. The events of the Post-Christ Period will not be addressed in this book.

THE CHURCH OF CHRIST—THE PRIME TARGET OF PAGAN ANIMOSITY

The Church of Christ was established in the land of Zarahemla by Alma the Elder in 121 BC.[280] As the Church began to preach the gospel, anti-church sentiment quickly developed. The purpose of missionary activities was expressly to focus attention upon the Church and to invite all men to come unto Christ. As in the Church of Jesus Christ of Latter-day Saints today, the response was not always positive.

Over the following 30-year period (121–91 BC), the Church spread throughout the land of Zarahemla.[281] As it grew in stature and made inroads into the pagan community, persecution against the Church, as the identity and authority of Christian faith, began to increase.[282] Sometime between 100 and 92 BC, it became so intense that Mosiah issued a proclamation forbidding persecution of the Church by unbelievers.[283]

Following Mosiah's proclamation, pagan hostility toward the Church became secretive.[284] After 91 BC, during the period of the judges, which brought a greater sense of political freedom to Zarahemla, it would again become openly displayed, as demonstrated in Alma Chapters 1, 2, and 14.

The growing animosity against the Church also signaled the growth and development of an organized pagan cult within Zarahemla, which began to flourish at about the same time. The surfacing of organized pagan religion may have been a calculated response to the Church of Christ, with non-Christians seeking to equalize the playing field and raise their level of competition, taking organizational ideas from the Church. Whereas the Church had previously made great strides,[285] the pagan backlash was exceedingly strong when the pagans began to formally organize the existing religious order, or establish new orders.

THE EARLY STAGES OF THE PAGAN CONSPIRACY AGAINST THE CHURCH

A disturbing chain of events is recorded in Mosiah Chapters 26 and 27, which concerned the first appearance and development of pagan influences within the Church established by Alma the Elder. The pagan element was the initial and primary cause of the first serious trouble within the Church.[286] The problem surfaced when church members were led into sin[287] through the influence of unbelievers.[288] The transgressors were "delivered up unto the priests by the teachers; and the priests brought them before Alma, who was the high priest" over the Church.[289] "There were many witnesses against them" that "stood and testified of their iniquity in abundance."[290]

This was a troubling experience for Alma.[291] He asked King Mosiah to "judge [the Church members] according to their crimes."[292] Mosiah apparently saw the infractions as immoral but not criminal offenses. More importantly, he acknowledged the autonomy of the Church and Alma's sole and unmitigated authority to deal with matters relating to the Church. However, when he told Alma that he must judge them, Alma was again distressed.[293] Therefore, he went to the Lord in prayer and received important revelation concerning moral and spiritual requirements for church members.

After Alma established a code of appropriate Christian conduct, many unrepentant members were excommunicated, and their names were removed from the rolls of the Church.[294] Persecution against the Church became intense as non-Christians (unbelievers) began to attack and persecute church members.[295] No doubt many in the ranks of these unbelievers were excommunicated apostates from the Church of Christ, who became bitter enemies of the Church, obsessed with its destruction.[296] As will be considered below, hostility against the Christian Nephites would continue to escalate throughout the remainder of the pre-Christ period.

In summary, the Book of Mormon outlines a substantial period in which pagan factions persecuted the Church of God in Zarahemla. The persecution increased throughout the reign of Mosiah II to such intensity that Mosiah issued his proclamation.[297] His own sons, and Alma the Younger, joined the pagan movement and became secret activists against the Church.[298] After their miraculous conversion to the gospel,[299] they became victims of persecution at the hands of their former colleagues.[300]

A CHESS MATCH BETWEEN THE CHRISTIAN KINGS AND THE PAGANS

The contentions recorded in Mosiah chapters 26 and 27 are not the first references to Nephite dissenters during the reign of the kings. The first such reference is found in Words of Mormon chapter 1, in which the Nephites under the rule of King Benjamin endured "much contention and many dissensions away unto the Lamanites."[301] They also withstood an associated Lamanite attack. King Benjamin drove the Lamanites out of the land and put down the dissenter uprising.[302]

The rebellion was costly to the dissenters. King Benjamin quelled the attempted coup with force of arms and preaching. He shut the mouths of "false Christs," "false prophets," and "false preachers and teachers," and punished them for their crimes.[303] Many of the dissenters fled to the land of Nephi to avoid Benjamin's justice.[304] The subsequent period of peace rested firmly on the foundation of Benjamin's display of power and his administration of justice without compromise, which he augmented by working with prophets to preach the gospel "with power and with authority" throughout the land.[305]

As a result, in 124 BC, Benjamin's son Mosiah inherited a land of peace and prosperity. By virtue of that peace, during the course of his reign, it appears that Mosiah softened the disciplinary atmosphere, which had been imposed by Benjamin following the rebellion.

It was in Mosiah's new atmosphere of impartiality and generosity that proponents of the aggressive pagan religion began to reassert themselves near the end of his reign, as they had done leading up to the rebellion against King Benjamin. As their numbers began to expand rapidly,[306] they once again became arrogant and aggressive. By about 100 BC, Mosiah found that the "unbelievers" had pushed their new found freedom past the limits of reason and had begun to assault the Church of God, which had been established in Zarahemla in about 120 BC, four years after Mosiah had ascended to the throne.

One thing became clear as the pagan movement grew and gained momentum: only the law could restrain the unbelievers. Mosiah therefore found it necessary to impose new laws against persecution of the Church to hold them in check.[307] As mentioned in the previous section, the unbelievers responded not by ceasing their attack against the Church, but by committing their crimes in secret.[308]

A PAGAN CONSPIRACY?

Was the pagan assault an actual conspiracy that extended over many generations in Nephite culture? This question will be considered throughout Part 3. It is revealed in the Book of Mormon that the Lamanites taught their children to hate the Nephites first during the period from 589 to 30 BC[309] and again to hate the children of God during the period from AD 194 to 385.[310] The same could be said for pagans during certain times within the land of Zarahemla, as well as in the land of Nephi. Therefore, the pagan obsession to destroy the Christian Nephites was part of the package of hatred passed from generation to generation. Furthermore, in the sense that knowledge of secret combinations was passed down from generation to generation and from culture to culture, conspiratorial ideas were also passed down.

However, there is one condition, which is taught and demonstrated again and again throughout all the scriptures. In a very real sense there was and is a conspiracy—one that has plagued mankind throughout the history of the earth. It is masterminded by Satan, who, with his cohorts, represents a common thread of discord throughout all generations of the earth, and who works according to a great plan for human failure and destruction.

"For we wrestle not against flesh and blood, but against principalities, against powers, against the rulers of the darkness of this world, against spiritual wickedness in high places."[311] This conspiracy, which is administered under Satan's direction, stirred the wicked in the Nephite culture in the same manner the wicked are influenced today. If there is not a direct physical link to the evil of the past, then Satan himself will provide the link to the wicked in the current era. In time, the ultimate objectives of Satan's conspiracy were brought to fruition in the Nephite culture through the curse of secret combinations in league with idolatry. In the post-Christ era, it would bring to pass the total elimination of the Christian Nephite culture from the Western Hemisphere.

CHAPTER 2.2

THE EVOLVING STATE OF NEPHITE GOVERNMENT

92 BC

GOVERNMENT BY KINGS DEFINED the political structure of the Nephites from the time of Nephi (the son of Lehi)[312] through the reign of Mosiah II. In 92 BC, near the end of his life, Mosiah engineered a change from monarchy to a system of judges. The period of the kings had lasted for approximately 497 years.[313]

91 BC

THE REIGN OF THE JUDGES

In 91 BC, the Nephites obeyed King Mosiah's final command[314] to do away with the tradition of kings. Subsequently, Alma the Younger was appointed as the first chief judge by the voice of the people.[315] No other candidate is mentioned, and, though not stated, it is likely that the people merely ratified Alma the Younger as Mosiah's chosen appointee.

As chief judge, Alma became the most powerful political figure in the Nephite government. The language used in describing the appointment, tenure, or removal of a chief judge was quite similar to the ascendancy, reign, or overthrow of a king.[316] However, the power of the chief judge was diminished from the power of a king because it could be overruled by the voice of the people.[317]

At that time, Alma's father (Alma the Elder) also "conferred" upon him the position of high priest over the Church of Christ.[318] When he voluntarily stepped down from the office of chief judge eight years later to devote his full time to his leadership of the Church,[319] he chose his own successor, a man named Nephihah, likely a descendant of Nephi (judging by his name) and a faithful member of the Church.[320] As with Alma, Nephihah's selection was confirmed by public vote.[321] It can thus be concluded that in the period of the judges, protection of the Church was transferred from the king to the people.

By eliminating monarchical government and instituting a form of democracy, Mosiah made it impossible for an individual, or a minority faction, to destroy the religious freedom of the land without the support of the people. Given the prosperity and growth of the Church of Christ throughout the land at that time,[322] it seemed like an excellent safeguard that would ensure a higher level of stability within Nephite government. The potential for a mass movement of the people to wickedness was, in Mosiah's opinion, very small.[323] However, in the very first year of the judges (91 BC), the appearance of a man named Nehor in the city of Zarahemla[324] provides a disturbing omen of impending calamity, though perhaps for the majority of the Nephites it was little noticed at the time.

For the reader of the Book of Mormon, it is the first significant indication that in an environment of literacy, the primitive pagan religion had acquired sophistication. Nehor had formally organized the pagan religion into a church, which would immediately enter a period of phenomenal growth.[325] If the pagans gained the majority in Zarahemla, it would spell doom for the Christians. Monarchy would have provided much more security for the Christian faith, if only Mosiah could have been certain that righteous kings would have followed him in unending succession.

To be sure, Mosiah was fully aware of the religious trend that was occurring among his people, which could be measured in the recent falling away of the youth from the Church during his reign.[326] If his statement in Mosiah 29:26 is considered, it might be concluded that he did not expect the trend to continue. In verse 27, however, he acknowledged the distinct possibility that iniquity could indeed bring down the judgments of God to the complete destruction of the Nephites, in like manner to the complete destruction of the Jaredite culture, who rested in the dust of the land northward.

Did Mosiah foresee that the order of Nehor would quickly rise to prominence and in only four years (87 BC) attain a near majority and threaten the freedom of the land?[327] Did he anticipate that in the 67th year of the judges (25 BC) idolatry would be practiced by the majority ("more part") of the people?[328] Being a prophet of God, it is quite possible that by revelation Mosiah thoroughly understood the seriousness of the pagan threat.

His understanding of its future development may actually have been a primary reason he favored democracy. A democratic government would place the responsibility in the hands of the people,[329] should they succumb to iniquity,[330] rather than allowing them to be victimized by the actions of an individual.[331]

In parallel modern-day revelation pertaining to the Constitution of the United States of America, the Lord revealed to the Prophet Joseph Smith that men must be free to satisfy the principle of moral agency, "that every man may be accountable for his own sins in the day of judgment."[332] Thus, under any circumstances, whether wickedness or righteousness prevails, democracy allows mankind the freedom to exercise agency.

POLITICAL FREEDOM—NEW OPPORTUNITIES FOR PAGAN LEADERS

In 91 BC, a new era of political freedom began. In the environment of democracy that characterized the period of the judges, an inherent vulnerability was given birth that had not existed during the period of the kings. A public forum was naturally created in which the pagan faction or anyone else in Zarahemla could legitimately contend for political power. A democratic form of government would not prevent the election of pagan leaders, if they could garner a majority vote.

Seizing upon their newfound freedom and political opportunity, the pagans mounted a series of political offensives against Christian Nephite authority. As a second aspect of the assault, pagan dissenters frequently resorted to armed conflict with Lamanite support. [333] Their specific purpose and goal was to destroy the Christian Nephite government, by either political or military means.

With the new political freedom came a greater sense of aggressive religious freedom, in spite of the fact that persecution was still against the law.[334] Pagan ideology came quickly to the forefront. It would be up to the Church of God to spiritually strengthen the people and to exert greater influence than the pagan faction. The stage was thus set for a war of philosophy that frequently would be punctuated by violence. As poignantly illustrated by the final result at Cumorah, it was literally a matter of life and death for the Christian Nephite culture.

CHAPTER 2.3

THE ORDER OF THE NEHORS

IN THE FIRST YEAR of the judges (91 BC), the account is given of a religious leader named Nehor, who established "a church after the manner of his preaching."[335] There were two notable characteristics of Nehor's religion, as he presented it to the Nephites in the streets of Zarahemla. First, he advocated the practice of priestcraft, in which the people should honor and provide for the priests.[336] Through 500 years of history in the New World, priestcraft had never been known among the Nephites.[337] Second, he taught "that all mankind should be saved at the last day, and that they need not fear nor tremble, but that they might lift up their heads and rejoice; for the Lord had . . . redeemed all men; and in the end, all men should have eternal life."[338]

A CONFRONTATION IN THE CITY OF ZARAHEMLA

Nehor had great success in Zarahemla and developed a large following.[339] As he was proselytizing one day in the city of Zarahemla, he encountered a man named Gideon,[340] one of the teachers of the Church of Christ. Gideon had played an important role in the escape of the people of Limhi from the land of Nephi. Other members of the Church accompanied Gideon when Nehor began to "contend with him sharply" over principles of religion. Gideon responded with the admonitions of God. Apparently, Nehor was either confounded, or felt he was losing the debate. He rose up in anger and slew the elderly Gideon with his sword.[341] Immediately, he was seized by the members of the Church who had witnessed his atrocity and taken before the chief judge Alma, where he was sentenced to die for the murder of Gideon. His execution "did not put an end to the spreading of priestcraft through the land."[342] Among the pagans, no doubt he was venerated for sacrificing his life for the cause. The order of Nehor continued to grow rapidly across the land of Zarahemla.

AMLICI SEEKS TO BE KING

Four years later, in 87 BC, a man named Amlici, who belonged to the order of Nehor, acquired such a strong political following that he was able to impose a public vote designed to overturn the judges and restore monarchy, with himself as the first king of a new era. He sought to destroy the very freedom that provided him the political opportunity to do so.

When the vote was held, the majority favored the retention of judges. However, Amlici would not concede defeat. His followers rallied around him and consecrated him as king. He then ordered his new subjects to take up arms and wage war against the Nephites.

The Amlicite war began at the hill Amnihu, which was located eastward of the city of Zarahemla. The Nephite army, led by the chief judge Alma, prevailed and before the day ended, the Amlicites were in full retreat. The Nephites pursued them until darkness fell and then camped for the night. The religious nature of the struggle was emphasized when they named the valley of their encampment after Gideon, who had become a martyr at the hands of Nehor in defense of the gospel.[343] It was as if "Remember Gideon!" was their battle cry.

Alma sent spies to follow the Amlicites as they fled through the darkness toward the southern borders of the land of Zarahemla. The spies returned the following day in great fear and astonishment to report that the Amlicites had united with an army of the Lamanites. The two armies were at that very moment moving down the Sidon River Valley toward the city of Zarahemla.

The Nephites rushed westward, arriving at their city as the enemy combatants arrived from the south. Though greatly outnumbered, the Nephites prevailed through the strength of the Lord, and drove them out of the land.

There is no further mention of the Amlicites in the Book of Mormon. Alma's discourse in Alma 3 concerning the mark of dissenters who "mingleth [their] seed with [the Lamanites]"[344] seems to imply that the Amlicites, who with the Lamanites were driven out of the land, remained in the land of Nephi thereafter. This idea is further implied by the attack of another Lamanite army, likely consisting of Amlicites and Lamanites, a few days later.[345] The second attack may have been an act of retaliation, in response to their first defeat.

ALMA STEPS DOWN FROM HIS POSITION AT THE HEAD OF GOVERNMENT

In 83 BC, four years after the Amlicite war and eight years after entering office as chief judge, Alma, seeing that serious spiritual degeneration had developed within the Church, resigned his position to devote all his attention to restoring order. In the year following the defeat of Amlici (86 BC), Alma had baptized many in the River Sidon, and in 85 BC, 3,500 were baptized.[346]

Notwithstanding the growth, the Church had become lifted up in pride and was in grave circumstances. They had ceased to provide a righteous example for unbelievers.[347] Alma realized it was crucial that he reestablish order.

ALMA'S ECCLESIASTICAL WORK

Alma dedicated himself to preaching "the word of God unto the people [of the Church].[348] He traveled throughout the land of Zarahemla, preaching the gospel of repentance. Beginning his work in the city of Zarahemla, he then traveled eastward to Gideon. In both of these cities, the Church was set in order and purged of those who refused to "repent of their wickedness and humble themselves before God."[349]

In his sermon to the people of Gideon, Alma revealed that he had encountered idolatry within the Church in Zarahemla. His words were plain and cannot be misunderstood, for he said, "I trust that ye are not in a state of so much unbelief as were your brethren . . . I trust that you do not worship idols, but that ye do worship the true and living God."[350]

This was the condition Alma had observed in Zarahemla, not among the ranks of unbelievers, but within the Church of Christ among those who professed to be believers. No doubt idolaters within the Church were heavily influenced by the idolatry practiced by the unbelievers. Many members (or their ancestors) were former pagans who had been converted to the Church of Christ. Alma's statement is a subtle reference to the idolatrous pagan religion that competed with the Church of Christ in Zarahemla for the souls of the Nephites.

It follows that the sudden and dramatic fluctuations in spirituality[351] that had initially stimulated Alma to resign from his political office likely resulted from the powerful influence of the pagan religion. It was not a new phenomenon in Zarahemla. Rather, it was the continuation of the pagan influence on Church members, which had first taken place more than 20 years previously, as referenced in Mosiah 26:1–6. Briefly, it had ensnared Alma himself, and the sons of Mosiah.[352]

ALMA JOURNEYS TO THE CITY OF AMMONIHAH

Alma returned from Gideon to the city of Zarahemla, pausing for a few days of rest before journeying west to the city of Melek. He had great success in Melek, baptizing converts throughout the land.[353] He then traveled northward for three days[354] to the city of Ammonihah.

Like all cities peripheral to the city of Zarahemla, Ammonihah was a city of recent origin, not established before 100 BC, when the people first began moving outward from Zarahemla, following Mosiah's proclamation prohibiting the persecution of the Church of Christ by unbelievers.[355]

Like the Amlicites, the city was under the control of the pagan cult of Nehor.[356] It had been placed at the borders of the land, where—unlike the Amlicites in the center of the land—they could easily take advantage of Lamanite military assistance. Alma would soon find that the Church of God was not to be found in the city of Ammonihah, and that he was not welcome come there.

When he entered the city, he was immediately recognized as the former chief judge and current head of the Church of God.[357] Though he had prayed fervently to the Lord, "that he would pour out his Spirit upon the people who were in the city,"[358] they refused to listen to him. They "reviled him, and spit upon him . . . and cast [him] out of their city."[359]

As Alma traveled away from Ammonihah in deep sorrow because of their wickedness and open hostility to the word of God, an angel appeared to him. He was the same angel who had appeared to him at the time of his conversion and had chastened and instructed him concerning the commandments of God.[360] He commanded Alma to return to Ammonihah to warn them of coming destruction if they did not repent of their sins. For, said the angel, "they do study at this time that they may destroy the liberty of thy people."[361]

Alma returned "speedily" to Ammonihah, entering at the south entrance[362] that lead into a different quarter of the city from that of his first arrival. Shortly before his second arrival, an angel appeared to a man named Amulek and informed him that a holy prophet would soon enter the city. He was commanded to receive Alma. Shortly thereafter, Alma arrived and Amulek took him in, providing him food and shelter. For many days,[363] Amulek sat at Alma's feet and became fully converted to the gospel Jesus Christ. Alma then received revelation that the time had come for the work to commence, and they went forth into the streets to proclaim repentance to the people.[364]

THE WARNINGS OF A PROPHET

Alma was the first to speak, and he began to warn the people of Ammonihah of impending destruction if they did not repent. [365] He told them that they had greater guilt than the Lamanites who sinned in ignorance because of the traditions of their fathers.[366] He added that the sins of the people in Ammonihah were committed in spite of their knowledge of the truth through the witnesses of angels, the gift of the Holy Ghost, and other manifestations from God.[367]

He made reference to their plans to destroy the people of God. Finally, he called them "a hard-hearted and a stiff-necked people," and "a lost and a fallen people."[368] His last statements raised their ire, and they sought to cast him into prison, but according to the will of God, they did not at that time.[369] Amulek then bore a second witness of the things Alma had said.[370]

IMPRISONMENT AND DELIVERANCE

At length, after preaching to the people and contending with the lawyers of the city, the two men were arrested and taken before the chief judge to answer for their crimes. Many of the people who had been converted to the gospel were cast out of the city. Others were rounded up with their wives and children and cast alive with their "holy scriptures" into a fire. Alma and Amulek were escorted to the "place of martyrdom," and were forced to observe the suffering and deaths of those cast into the fire.[371]

The two men were held in prison for many days following the martyrdom of the people, suffering many deprivations and various forms of torture.[372] One day, the priests and judges came in for their daily session of mockery and intimidation. Each tormentor took his turn slapping their faces and taunting them, telling them to call upon God for deliverance.

After the last man had finished, the power of God came suddenly upon Alma and Amulek. Alma rose to his feet and cried out, "How long shall we suffer these great afflictions, O Lord? O Lord, give us strength according to our faith which is in Christ, even unto deliverance." He and Amulek immediately received strength and "broke the cords with which they were bound."[373] Their captors began to flee but were so frightened they fell to the ground before reaching the door.[374]

Suddenly, an earthquake stuck with great intensity. The walls of the prison collapsed, killing everyone inside except Alma and Amulek, who came forth from the ruins unharmed. The people of the city fled in fear, "even as a goat fleeth with her young from two lions."[375]

Alma and Amulek departed the city of Ammonihah and traveled over to the neighboring land of Sidom. There they found the new converts who had been driven from Ammonihah after accepting the gospel. They related to them the account of their miraculous deliverance from the prison.

They also found Zeezrom, one of the lawyers who had tormented the two missionaries in the streets of Ammonihah. He was afflicted with a burning fever, due in part to an overwhelming sense of guilt, believing the people in Ammonihah had killed the two men and that he was responsible. Upon his request, the two men went to his bedside and healed him with a priesthood blessing.[376] Zeezrom was baptized and became a great emissary of the gospel from that day forward.[377]

In Ammonihah the people remained unrepentant, "ascribing all the power of Alma and Amulek to the devil."[378] Amulek's entire family disowned him, including his father.[379] The people of the city continued in their wickedness and abominations. Nevertheless, a prophet of God had pronounced the judgments of God upon them. Very soon those judgments would be at their door.

THE ORDER OF NEHOR IN THE LAND OF NEPHI

Prior to Nehor's confrontation with Gideon in 91 BC,[380] he had experienced great success as he preached among the Nephites. The people had begun "to support him and give him money. And he began to be lifted up in the pride of his heart, and to wear very costly apparel, yea, and even began to establish a church after the manner of his preaching."[381]

The above statement in the first chapter of Alma gives the impression that the order of Nehor was established by Nehor at that time. It therefore comes as a bit of a surprise when it is disclosed in Alma chapter 21 that the Amalekites and Amulonites in the land of Nephi also belonged to the Order of the Nehors and "had built synagogues after the order of the Nehors."[382] The surprise stems from the fact that Nehor had only recently organized his church in Zarahemla. It becomes apparent that the synagogues, which were standing in Nephi in about 92 BC,[383] had been built at an earlier time. Likely, they were standing well before Nehor began establishing his church and priestcraft in the land of Zarahemla.

The feat of establishing a church in both lands seems especially difficult, considering the complete lack of communication between Zarahemla and Nephi at that time—the product of two conditions. First, Nephi was separated from Zarahemla by the great wilderness, which alone prevented direct communication between the two lands. Second, the two cultures were separated by Lamanite hostility. As a result of the hostility, there could be no free and peaceful exchange of ideas, Cwith or without the geographic barrier.

Some have suggested the possibility that Nehor was a native of Nephi, and that he first established his church in Nephi before migrating to the land of Zarahemla to establish it there. However, when the sons of Mosiah journeyed from Zarahemla to Nephi to preach the gospel, they could not hide their identity from the

TROY SMITH

Lamanites.[384] By the same token, if Nehor had come from the land of Nephi, it would have been quite apparent to the Nephites, and his country of origin would have been reported in the account. It is therefore highly doubtful that Nehor was a Lamanite, Amalekite, or Amulonite by birth. No doubt there was a simple explanation among the Nephites as to how the Order of the Nehors had been established in both lands.

In conclusion, it is only at first impression that the Order of the Nehors—whether in Zarahemla or in Nephi—might be construed to have been an offshoot of Nehor's preaching. Such a conclusion, however, is based purely on name recognition. If all of the information provided in the Book of Mormon is considered, however, a more plausible source of the religious order becomes evident, one which incorporates and blends together certain elements in the Mulekite past and cultural experience. This information is examined as follows:

THE JAREDITE CITY OF NEHOR

Nehor was the name of a capital city of the Jaredites throughout a large portion of Jaredite history. The city's rise to prominence coincided with the illegitimate reign of Kib's eldest son, Corihor, who rebelled against his father when he was 32 years of age. Corihor "went over and dwelt in the land of Nehor; and he begat sons and daughters, and they became exceedingly fair; wherefore Corihor drew away many people after him.[385]

> And when he had gathered together an army he came up unto the land of Moron where the king dwelt, and took him captive, which brought to pass the saying of the brother of Jared that they would be brought into captivity.
>
> Now the land of Moron, where the king dwelt, was near the land which is called Desolation by the Nephites.
>
> And it came to pass that Kib dwelt in captivity, and his people under Corihor his son until he became exceedingly old; nevertheless Kib begat Shule in his old age, while he was yet in captivity.
>
> And it came to pass that Shule was angry with his brother; and Shule waxed strong, and became mighty as to the strength of a man; and he was also mighty in judgment.

Wherefore, he came to the hill Ephraim, and he did molten out of the hill, and made swords out of steel for those whom he had drawn away with him; and after he had armed them with swords he returned to the city Nehor, and gave battle unto his brother Corihor, by which means he obtained the kingdom and restored it unto his father Kib. (Ether 7: 5–9)

In the above verses, it is apparent that the capital city, or "the place where the king dwelt"[386] was transferred from Moron to Nehor when Kib was brought into captivity. Shule was born in the land of Nehor, and there he grew to adulthood. After he attacked the city of Nehor and wrested the kingdom from Corihor[387], his father Kib gave the kingdom to him. Shule continued to rule from Nehor.[388]

THE JAREDITE CITY OF NEHOR AND THE RISE OF JAREDITE IDOLATRY—THE FIRST OF TWO HYPOTHESES

Turning to the curse of idolatry, the first reference appears during Shule's reign in Nehor, as described in Ether 7:23–26. It seems apparent that the curse was in place before Shule came to power but was not acknowledged until the influence of Shule's righteousness and spiritual discernment was reflected in the Jaredite record. It follows that the ancient capital of Nehor was the official birthplace of Jaredite idolatry, which played a primary role in Corihor's violent overthrow of his father's kingdom. The following chain of events, which includes a link to the Nephites, is projected from the scenario set forth in Ether Chapter 7:

- Corihor rebelled against his father Kib and went over and dwelled in the land of Nehor.

- In the land of Nehor, Corihor became involved in idolatry, and under its diabolical influence, his rebellion against Kib evolved into a calculated plan to obtain his father's kingdom. Idolatry was therefore closely associated with insurrection in the city of Nehor.

- The sedition that resulted in the establishment of Nehor as the new capital of the Jaredites was the first aberration in the Jaredite tradition of righteousness, as established by Jared and his brother (Mahonri Moriancumer). Though it had been prophesied by the brother of Jared that monarchy would lead to captivity,[389] the rapidity, or promptness by which it took place must have been appalling. Until Corihor's rebellion, the principles of righteousness taught continually by Jared and his brother throughout their long lives had been passed down from generation to generation. Orihah and Kib had each in turn lived their lives according to those principles. It is also apparent that Shule's rise to power immediately restored the tradition of righteousness. It required Shule's righteous rule to awaken the people—and to awaken Corihor as well—to an awareness and understanding of the evil that had settled over them during Corihor's reign.

- Under Shule's righteous influence, Corihor repented of the evil he had done, and Shule responded by giving him power in his kingdom. Shule also gave power and authority to the prophets of God to teach the gospel throughout the entire land. By this means, the curse of idolatry was lifted, and the Jaredites prospered once more.[390]

- Having first provided the foundation for Corihor's rebellion in the third generation of the kings, and throughout the remainder of Jaredite history, idolatry in league with secret combinations posed a dangerous menace to peace and prosperity, first resurfacing with Omer's eldest son Jared only two generations later (the fifth generation of the kings),[391] and again with Heth, another three generations later (the eighth generation).[392]

- More than a thousand years later in *ca.* 250–220 BC, Jaredite civilization ended abruptly, when a new partnership between Jaredite idolatry and secret combinations ultimately caused the entire civilization to self-destruct in violence.

- Fortunately for the Mulekites, they were not forced into the Jaredite terminal war, which was a war between the two elite Jaredite lineages for the right to the throne. The Mulekites lived within the boundaries of the land of Desolation, which neighbored the southern border of the Jaredite world. In fact, Desolation was "the place of their first landing."[393]

- The land of Desolation can be described as the adjacent land to the south of the Jaredites, which extended northward from the "line Bountiful and the land Desolation"[394] to the borders of

Moron the first and last Jaredite capitol.[395] The Mulekites were far enough away from the terminal Jaredite war, both geographically and culturally, to survive its devastation, but near enough to discover Coriantumr, the last survivor directly involved in the Jaredite conflict. The Mulekites remained in Desolation until it became desolate and uninhabitable as a result of the curse caused by the Jaredites.

- The Mulekites embraced the Jaredite pagan religion as a result of their interaction with the Jaredites during, approximately, the last 375 years of Jaredite civilization. This can be determined from the fact that "they denied the being of their Creator" (Jehovah), when discovered by the Nephites,[396] in combination with the information that they had come from the land northward[397] and many bore Jaredite names.[398]

In spite of having witnessed the Jaredite holocaust, they preserved and nurtured the seed of the idolatry, which (in league with the secret combinations) had personally engineered the Jaredite extinction. When discovered by the people of Mosiah, they were largely under its influence. Considering the second (Mulekite) scenario, as projected above (items 7 and 8), in which the Mulekites interacted with and were influenced by the Jaredite culture,[399] it was not out of character for the Mulekite pagan religion to be known as the Order of the Nehors, or in other words, the order of the people of the Jaredite land of Nehor—the land of its origination.

TIMING IS OF ESSENCE

Building on the above foundation, the operation of the Order of the Nehors in the land of Nephi prior to the establishment of a church in Zarahemla by Nehor[400] becomes a significant factor. According to Alma 21:4, near the end of 92 BC, Aaron (Mosiah's son), on the first day of his mission, while preaching to the Lamanites in a city called Jerusalem observed that the inhabitants of the city "had built synagogues after the order of the Nehors; for many of the Amalekites and the Amulonites were after the order of the Nehors." Three pieces of information in the Book of Mormon place Aaron's observation of the pagan synagogues at this time, shortly before Mosiah's appointment of Alma to the judgment seat in Zarahemla:

- Following the departure of Aaron and his brethren[401] from Zarahemla, Mosiah spent a considerable amount of time translating the twenty-four gold Plates of Ether from the Jaredite language into the Nephite language.[402] He then ordered them to be written and distributed among his people. Subsequently, time was allowed to observe their reaction.[403]

- After these things transpired, while the end of 92 BC approached, Mosiah made his formal petition to the Nephites to change the form of their government from kings to judges. There had to be the time for Mosiah's preparation, time for his petition to be distributed among the people, and time for the people to respond and vote to ratify Alma as the first chief judge. It was not a day of electronic ballets.

- In contrast to Mosiah's extensive two-pronged project, his sons may have reached the land of Nephi in no more than 40 days, and likely less.[404] Upon their arrival, they immediately parted company,[405] whereupon Aaron went directly to the Lamanite city of Jerusalem and entered a synagogue of the Nehors.[406] The exact time at which the missionaries reached the land of ? (Removed)Nephi depends upon how late in the year (92 BC) they left Zarahemla.[407] However, based on Alma 16:21 and 17:4, they began their mission in Nephi at or near the end of 92 BC, because they returned at the end of the fourteenth year of the reign of the judges[408] after "teaching the word of God for the space of fourteen years among the Lamanites."[409]

It is thus concluded that at or near the end of 92 BC, Aaron encountered Amalekites[410] and Amulonites[411] practicing the religion of Nehor in synagogues built according to the Nehor manner of construction,[412] while Alma was appointed to the judgment seat at the beginning of 91 BC. The precise time and order of the two series of events is of little consequence, since both occurred at approximately the same time. However, the fact that the synagogues were already standing points to an earlier date when the pagan cult was first established in the land of Nephi.

TRACING THE INITIAL SPREAD OF THE RELIGION OF NEHOR FROM ZARAHEMLA TO NEPHI—THE SECOND HYPOTHESIS

Mormon's transitional book (The Words of Mormon) contains the only reference to "dissensions away unto the Lamanites" during the period of the kings in Zarahemla.[413] Conversely, the Amalekites are the only dissenters in the land of Nephi identified by name whose origin is unknown and who were already living there in 92 BC as the period of the kings came to a close. The fact that the Amalekites were affiliated with the order of Nehor, which had Jaredite and therefore Mulekite roots,[414] supports the hypothesis that the Amalekites were dissenters from the land of Zarahemla, possibly the same who had fled from King Benjamin's justice.[415] According to this hypothetical scenario, which is a logical derivative of the known facts, the Amalekites introduced the Mulekite pagan religion among the Lamanites. Its establishment in the land of Nephi thus occurred before Nehor was born.

In Zarahemla, Nehor later organized the religion into a church, at which time it became variously known as the "order and faith of Nehor,"[416] the "profession of Nehor,"[417] and the "order of the Nehors."[418] By 83 BC the "profession of Nehor" was established in the Nephite city of Ammonihah.[419] Considering Aaron's abovementioned experience with the synagogue of the Nehors, it becomes obvious that the man Nehor did not design the synagogues. Rather, the manner of their construction, like the religion, was passed down from the Jaredites to the Mulekites.

The religion was thus being practiced by the Mulekites in Zarahemla when the Nephites arrived. It had been practiced in Zarahemla for about 110 years when Nehor organized it into a church around 92 BC. It follows that if the Amalekites introduced it to Lamanites in the land of Nephi during the days of King Benjamin, then it had been practiced in the land of Nephi for somewhere between 65 and 80 years before Nehor established his church in Zarahemla.

NEHOR'S DESTRUCTIVE INFLUENCE AMONG THE LAMANITES

Though thousands of Lamanites were brought to a knowledge of Christ through the efforts of Aaron and his brethren, the work was greatly hindered by the religious sect commonly referred to in the Book of Mormon as the order of Nehor. As discussed previously in this chapter, this pagan religion was likely established by the Amalekites in the land of Nephi long before Nehor established a church by the same name in the land of Zarahemla.

Because of the unconcealed hatred of the order of Nehor toward the gospel,[420] Aaron received a cold reception in Jerusalem.[421] An Amalekite's angry response to Aaron's teachings reflected the general pagan hostility against Christianity. He said, "How knowest thou that we have cause to repent? How knowest thou that we are not a righteous people? Behold, we have built sanctuaries, and we do assemble ourselves together to worship God. We do believe that God will save all men."[422]

His response was similar to the response the patriarch Noah received from the children of men as he preached the gospel of repentance: "And, also, after that they had heard [Noah], they came up before him, saying: Behold, we are the sons of God; have we not taken unto ourselves the daughters of men? And are we not eating and drinking, and marrying and giving in marriage? And our wives bear children, and the same are mighty men, which are like unto men of old, men of great renown. And they hearkened not unto the words of Noah."[423]

Soon Aaron realized it was futile to try to preach to the inhabitants of Jerusalem, and he departed from the city. He then journeyed to a small village called Ani-Anti, where he found Muloki, Ammah, and others of his brethren. He joined them in teaching the people of Ani-Anti, but again they found it was impossible to penetrate the wall of resistance and animosity. They departed Ani-Anti and went to the city of Middoni, where they were apprehended and imprisoned in bonds, suffering many afflictions before King Lamoni and Ammon intervened.[424] Aaron's experience was only the beginning of an account of horrors at the hands of the Nehors in the land of Nephi.

LAMANITE CONVERSIONS

The conversion of King Lamoni,[425] his father (the king over all the land),[426] his brother Anti-Nephi-Lehi, and thousands of their people through the missionary efforts of the sons of Mosiah[427] is one of the most beautiful and remarkable accounts in the Book of Mormon. It illustrates that there were choice spirits among the Lamanites, though raised in an environment of utter spiritual darkness. When through the miraculous intervention of the Lord[428] they were brought to a knowledge of God, they embraced the gospel with all their might, mind, heart, and strength. None of them ever fell away.[429]

Lamoni's father sent out a proclamation to his people, in which he commanded them to give the missionaries free passage throughout the land to teach the gospel in their homes, temples, and synagogues. At that time, circa 91 BC, the Lamanites had not yet moved eastward across the land of Nephi into the east wilderness.[430] That would not occur until the period between 81–77 BC, when on two separate occasions they were driven there by the Nephite armies.[431] Therefore, the mission was likely limited to the greater highland region surrounding the cities of Nephi and Shilom, and the region bordering along the shores of the west sea.

Throughout the 14 year period from 91 to 77 BC, the sons of Mosiah, and the other missionaries who accompanied them, taught the Lamanites with remarkable success.[432] They "[established] churches and [consecrated] priests and teachers throughout the land. . . . Thousands were brought to the knowledge of the Lord."[433]

During that period, entire cities of Lamanites were converted to Christianity, whereas only one Amalekite and no Amulonites were converted, and in cities where they lived, the Lamanites under their influence also resisted the gospel.[434] Hostility escalated continually through time until, in the beginning of the 11th year of the judges (81 BC),[435] the Lamanites who had not been converted "were stirred up by the Amalekites and by the Amulonites to anger against their brethren." They began to make preparations to overthrow the king.[436] The king passed away at that time, after conferring the kingdom upon his son, Anti-Nephi-Lehi.[437]

Seeing the preparations for war, the sons of Mosiah and their companions went to the land of Ishmael to counsel with Anti-Nephi-Lehi and Lamoni concerning how to defend themselves.[438] Instead of preparing a defense, however, the people of Anti-Nephi-Lehi,[439] ashamed of their previously murderous lives, buried their weapons of war,[440] refusing to take the life of a fellow human being, even in defense, for fear of offending God.

When the Lamanite army came into their land, the people of Anti-Nephi-Lehi prostrated themselves upon the ground, showing no resistance whatsoever. The unbelieving Lamanites were cut to the heart, because "their brethren would not flee from the sword, neither would they turn aside to the right hand or to the left, but ... they would lie down and perish, and praised God even in the very act of perishing under the sword."[441]

A thousand and five believers were slain that day. An even greater number of the aggressors, their consciences seared, threw down their arms and joined their brethren on the ground. The majority, however, were even more furious and blamed the Nephites for teaching the people the gospel. In a rage, they departed from the land of Nephi and headed straight for the land of Zarahemla to inflict their vengeance upon the Nephites.[442]

81 BC

"THE WICKED SHALL SLAY THE WICKED"[443]

Three months and eleven days had passed since Alma and Amulek were delivered from the prison in Ammonihah. Nothing had changed. The people of that city carried on their business, just as they were doing when Alma first warned them of coming destruction. The markets were likely bustling with activity. Perhaps court was in session and the judges were hearing complaints brought before them by "concerned" lawyers.

Imagine the irony of that day. Without doubt, the priests of Nehor had continued with their plans to overthrow the Nephite government in Zarahemla. Conceivably, the plan to destroy the "liberty of [the] people"[444] was in its final stages. All that likely remained was to send an envoy to the land of Nephi to stir up the Lamanites to assist them in their quest for justice against the Nephites.

What shock they must have felt when suddenly the alarm was sounded that the city was under siege by a Lamanite army. That was impossible! The Lamanites were on their side! On that day,[445] however, an army of the Lamanites entered the land of Zarahemla from the wilderness on the western perimeter[446] and began to attack Ammonihah.

The Lamanites had come straight from the bloodletting in the land of Nephi.[447] Now, with their hatred and rage fueled by Nephite dissenters belonging to the order of Nehor,[448] they wanted to spill Nephite blood. They had no idea that the inhabitants of Ammonihah, which lay in their path, were also of the "order and faith of Nehor"[449] and were likewise bent on the destruction of the Nephites and Christianity.[450] Had they known the intentions of the Ammonihahites, they would have gladly united with them to make war against the Nephites.

Instead, they attacked the city of Ammonihah with all the venom of their anger. As Alma had prophesied,[451] the "great city was destroyed, which they [had] said God could not destroy, because of its greatness."[452] No one survived the attack.

THE NEPHITES RESCUE THE HOSTAGES—THE LAMANITES ARE DRIVEN INTO THE EAST WILDERNESS

Afterward, the Lamanite army fled into the south wilderness with captives taken from the bordering city of Noah. Chief Captain Zoram and his two sons Aha and Lehi led the Nephite army that soon pursued them. Knowing that Alma had the spirit of prophecy, they appealed to him "to know whither the Lord would that they should go into the wilderness in search of their brethren, who had been taken captive by the Lamanites."[453] Alma went and "inquired of the Lord concerning the matter," and then returned to inform Zoram and his sons that "the Lamanites [would] cross the river Sidon in the south wilderness, away up beyond the borders of the land of Manti," and to promise them that the Lord would "deliver unto [them their] brethren."[454] Following Alma's instructions, they intercepted and surprised the Lamanites in the south wilderness, rescuing all the captives and sending the Lamanites fleeing for their lives.[455] Their flight carried them into the east wilderness. (See Appendix A, Map A-4.)

Using the east wilderness as a base of operations, this Lamanite army apparently returned several times during that same year (81 BC) before finally being convinced they could not succeed against the Nephite armies. Through a series of battles with the Nephites, the judgments of God were visited upon them, and they were slain and driven back "into the east wilderness."[456]

In Zarahemla, the Nephites then enjoyed three years of peace.[457] During the same three-year period (80–78 BC),[458] the Lamanites suffered greatly in the east wilderness. In the above series of events, which began with the destruction of Ammonihah, a branch of the order of Nehor from the land of Nephi became the means by which the judgments of God were carried out against a second branch of the same pagan cult in the city of Ammonihah. Afterward, the Nephites, in defending the land of Zarahemla, became instruments of the Lord to carry out judgment against the wicked branch from Nephi. Both branches of Nehor were guilty of persecuting the servants of God, and of murdering innocent men, women, and children for their belief in Christ.

THE PEOPLE OF ANTI-NEPHI-LEHI SUFFER MORE PERSECUTION

In about 78 BC, the Lamanites, consisting of Lamanites and Amalekites (minus the Amulonites) returned to the land of Nephi.[459] They had been punished by Zoram's army and had subsequently suffered from internal contention, which apparently raged for the better part of three years.[460] The fire of their hatred and wrath, far from being extinguished, continued to burn out of control.

The Amalekites were especially vengeful, for they and the Amulonites had provoked the original murderous reaction to the Lamanite conversions.[461] Their goals for Nephite destruction—so carefully conceived and meticulously planned—had been completely frustrated. Upon their arrival in Nephi, the Amalekites again stirred the Lamanites to violence against the people of Anti-Nephi-Lehi. Once again, plans were made to attack them. As in the initial assault four years previous,[462] the people of Anti-Nephi-Lehi refused to defend themselves.[463]

The sons of Mosiah were "moved with compassion"[464] for their Lamanite brethren. They entreated King Anti-Nephi-Lehi to go with them to the land of Zarahemla where they would be protected by the Nephite armies. At first, Anti-Nephi-Lehi resisted, saying "the Nephites will destroy us because of the many murders and sins we have committed against them."[465] Ammon therefore posed a question to him. He said, "I will go and inquire of the Lord, and if he say unto us, go down unto our brethren, will ye go?"[466]

> And the king said unto him, Yea, if the Lord saith unto us go, we will go down unto our brethren, and we will be their slaves until we repair unto them the many murders and sins which we have committed against them.
>
> But Ammon said unto him; It is against the law of our brethren, which was established by my father, that there should be any slaves among them; therefore let us go down and rely upon the mercies of our brethren.
>
> But the king said unto him: Inquire of the Lord, and if he saith unto us go, we will go; otherwise we will perish in the land. (Alma 27:8–10)

Ammon went to the Lord in prayer. He received revelation that he and his brethren must lead the people of Anti-Nephi-Lehi out of Nephi, "for," as the Lord said, "Satan has great hold on the hearts of the Amalekites, who do stir up the Lamanites to anger against their brethren to slay them."[467] In obedience to God, the king gathered all the people, and their flocks and herds, and they departed with the sons of Mosiah out of the land. They entered the wilderness that separated Nephi from Zarahemla[468] and traveled eastward until they came near the land of Manti, which was situated near the headwaters of the Sidon River.[469]

77 BC

REFUGE AT LAST

Arriving at a location near Manti in the beginning of the year,[470] the people of Anti-Nephi-Lehi pitched their tents in the wilderness[471] and waited while the sons of Mosiah traveled north to the city of Zarahemla to petition the people to allow them to dwell in their land.[472] The Nephites graciously received them and allowed them to inhabit the land of Jershon, which was located along the eastern seaboard, far from the Lamanite city of Nephi. Jershon extended northward along the coastline from the border of Nephi on the south[473] to the border of Bountiful on the north.[474] The people of Ammon, as they were called from that time forth, settled near the southern border of Jershon.[475] Their descendants would become a great blessing to the Nephites, both spiritually and militarily.

SUMMARIZING THE HISTORY OF THE NEHORS IN ZARAHEMLA AND NEPHI

As discussed previously in this chapter, the account of Aaron's observation of the of the Nehors in the land of Nephi is crucial to a complete understanding of the pagan cult known after 92 BC as the Order of the Nehors. Based solely upon that singular event, the entire history of the Order of the Nehors can be projected with a reasonable level of confidence. Two hypotheses were set forth previously, which propose a Jaredite origin for the Order of the Nehors and provide the means by which it was transferred from the Jaredite to the Nephite culture. The salient points of the two hypotheses are combined in the following projected scenario:

- A primitive religion, based on the pagan religion passed down among the Jaredites from the city of Nehor, was practiced by the Mulekites at the time of their discovery by the people of Mosiah. It was primitive in the sense that the Mulekites were illiterate and uneducated at that time.

- After approximately 110 years under the progressive influence of the Nephites, the original Mulekite religion was formally organized into a church by a man named Nehor, which was called by his name. The order of Nehor was Nehor's personalized version of the Mulekite pagan religion, with its most noticeable and unique characteristic being that it represented the first establishment of a professional clergy (the practice of priestcraft) in the entire history of the Nephites.[476]

- The organization of Nehor's church may have been patterned after the Church of Christ, which was established by Alma the Elder in Zarahemla approximately 30 years previously.

- Nehor's name has clouded the issue of the source of the order of Nehor, for it seems that the name did not originate with him. Instead he was likely named after the Jaredite city where Jaredite pagan religion was first established, similar to a possible scenario in which Mormon's father was named after the Waters of Mormon,[477] where the Church of Christ was established through Alma the Elder.[478]

- Notwithstanding the presence of the Order of the Nehors among the Lamanites, Nehor did not establish his church in the land of Nephi. This can be concluded from the complete lack of communication of the order of Nehor in the land of Zarahemla with the Order of the Nehors in the land of Nephi, which was directly illustrated in the destruction of the city of Ammonihah in 81 BC, as outlined above in the section entitled "The Wicked Shall Slay the Wicked."

- The Amalekites came to the Lamanite land of Nephi from the land of Zarahemla. They did not dissent away while the Nephites were in the land of Nephi.

- The Mulekite pagan religion was introduced into the land of Nephi by the Amalekites.

- It was later embraced by the Amulonites. One of their beliefs, (even while they remained in Noah's court) was similar to that of the Amalekites with respect to believing in a universal salvation for "all the ends of the earth," without consideration for righteousness or wickedness.[479]

THE DISAPPEARANCE OF THE ORDER OF NEHORS FROM THE BOOK OF MORMON

In 77 BC, the sons of Mosiah led away the people of Anti-Nephi-Lehi from certain destruction at the hands of the order of Nehor.[480] After their departure from the land of Nephi, the Amalekites continued to incite the Lamanites against them. Notwithstanding all of their defeats at the hands of the Nephite armies, they were able to gather a large army and pursue the people of Anti-Nephi-Lehi to the land of Zarahemla.

This party of Amalekites and Lamanites had only recently returned from the east wilderness,[481] and therefore they knew very well the route of travel taken by the fleeing party along and through the narrow strip of wilderness. The narrow strip of wilderness is first identified in Alma 22:27, according to which it "ran from the sea east even to the sea west and round about on the borders of the seashore." It ran "through the borders of Manti, by the head of the river Sidon, running from the east toward the west." By the narrow strip of wilderness, "were the Lamanites and the Nephites divided."[482] The Lamanites may have utilized this narrow strip of wilderness to move their armies and supplies.[483]

The Amalekites and Lamanites did not follow immediately, because there was time for the Anti-Nephi-Lehies to settle in the land of Jershon, and time for the Nephites to move their armies into position in the region. However, probably with their spies and their scouts, the Lamanite army was able to learn of the whereabouts of the people of Ammon, as the people of Anti-Nephi-Lehi were called after their arrival in the land of Zarahemla.

The Lamanites had recently returned to Nephi upon realizing they could not satisfy their lust for vengeance against the Nephites.[484] They knew it was suicidal to return to the land of Zarahemla, but they were in an uncontrollable rage through the influence of the Amalekites and refused to stop until either they, or the Nephites were destroyed. They went against the Nephite armies in Jershon, and in a "tremendous" battle, the likes of which at that time had never been witnessed in the entire history of the Nephites, "tens of thousands of the Lamanites were slain and scattered abroad."[485] The year 77 BC came to a close as the people of Zarahemla mourned the loss of so many of their valiant men,[486] lost by the end of the first 15 years of the "reign of the judges."[487]

It appears that almost everyone associated with the order of Nehor was destroyed in the wars between 87 and 77 BC. Many of the Amlicites were either slain or were compelled to flee to the land of Nephi, for there is no further mention of them by name.[488] The people of Ammonihah were destroyed in 81 BC. The Amulonites were largely destroyed by the Lamanites or driven deep into the east wilderness during the period from 80 to 78 BC. The Amalekites were not completely destroyed in the final battle of 77 BC, but their numbers were substantially reduced. It is apparent that the order of Nehor was effectively eliminated from both the land of Zarahemla and the land of Nephi, for it is never again mentioned in the Book of Mormon. Soon, however, another pagan sect would ascend to dominance within the land of Nephi.

CHAPTER 2.4

THE ZORAMITES

ALMOST IMMEDIATELY FOLLOWING THE final battle of the Nehor War,[489] the Zoramites took up the torch of pagan animosity. Near the end of 75 BC, Alma received word that a man named Korihor had been murdered by the Zoramites in a land called Antionum.[490] He also learned that the Zoramites, who had only recently settled Antionum,[491] "were perverting the ways of the Lord, and that Zoram, their leader, was leading the hearts of the people to bow down to dumb idols."[492]

KORIHOR

Earlier in the latter half of the same year,[493] Korihor had come into the land of Zarahemla preaching a doctrine that was contrary to the word of God and mocking the Christian belief in the coming of Christ and the doctrine of the remission of sins. He said that such foolish traditions were the "effect of a frenzied mind."[494]

In time, Korihor had gained a large following of men and women, for he taught, in sharp contrast to the principles of the gospel, the typical pagan concept that there is no punishment for our sins. His particular variation, however, was that there was no Christ[495] and no hereafter.[496] A person could therefore "eat, drink, and be merry,"[497] for there would be no consequences at the end of this life (the end of a person's existence).

Korihor's first recorded stop was in the land of Jershon, where he began to disseminate his ideas among the people of Ammon. His preaching had no effect on the people of Ammon, who had sacrificed much for the privilege of embracing Christianity. They had experienced the miraculous power of God, which had transformed them from a murderous people immersed in spiritual darkness into a people filled with love and kindness. Korihor's arguments held the same air of contempt and tone of indifference as those of the Amalekites and Amulonites, members of the cult of Nehor, whose ideas they had rejected. Korihor was taken before Ammon, the high priest of the Church in Jershon, who ordered him cast out of the land.

Undaunted, Korihor journeyed from Jershon to the land of Gideon, where he continued his denunciation of the Christian faith and traditions. The people of Gideon seized him and carried him before their chief judge and their high priest. Korihor told the high priest, Giddonah, that their foolish gospel ordinances and priestly performances had been "laid down by ancient priests, to usurp power and authority over [the people], to keep them in ignorance, that they may not lift up their heads, but be brought down according to [the words of the priests]."[498] He said the priests enslaved the people by teaching them "that they should, if they did not do according to their words, offend some unknown being, who they say is God—a being who never has been seen or known, who never was nor ever will be."[499] Seeing the "hardness of his heart," the high priest and the chief judge ordered him bound and delivered to the city of Zarahemla to be judged by Alma, the high priest over the Church, and Nephihah, the chief judge over all the land.[500]

When he stood before Alma and Nephihah, Korihor again denounced and belittled the Christian traditions of the Nephites. He declared his alleged belief that there was no God, and further stated that he would not believe unless Alma showed him a sign. This grieved Alma, who told him he had received signs enough.[501] Korihor again insisted,[502] whereupon Alma relented and showed him a sign. It was a sign Korihor did not want to see. By the power of God he was cursed that he would no longer be able to speak.

In that moment, Korihor suddenly became speechless. In the moment of his surprise, he acknowledged that the power of God had stricken him, for he wrote, "I know that nothing save it were the power of God could bring this upon me."[503] He told Alma and Nephihah that "the devil... [had] appeared unto [him] in the form of an angel of light and said unto [him]: Go and reclaim this people, for they have all gone astray after an unknown God." [504] The devil had taught Korihor the words to speak to the Nephites.

Korihor pleaded with Alma to remove the curse. Alma replied that if he removed the curse, Korihor would simply continue in the same path of leading away many people to destruction. "Therefore," he said, "it shall be unto thee even as the Lord will."[505] The Lord did not remove the curse. Korihor was cast out and found it necessary to go from house to house begging for food.

Defeated and humiliated, Korihor soon departed the city of Zarahemla and journeyed to the land of Antionum, which was located "east of the land of Zarahemla, which lay nearly bordering upon the seashore" at the southern border of the land of Jershon.[506] It is likely that Antionum was the home of Korihor's kinsmen and friends and the place from which he had launched his crusade against the Church of Christ for three reasons:

- He taught some of the same ideas that were taught by the Zoramites, including the labeling of Christian Nephite doctrines as foolish or silly, and the denial of Jesus Christ as the Son of God.

- His first recorded stop was among the people of Ammon, whose city was the nearest Nephite city to the Zoramite city of Antionum.

- While suffering from his involuntary humility after being smitten by the hand of God, he journeyed from Zarahemla to Antionum. This required that he again pass by the people of Ammon to arrive at the southeastern border of the land.

This last point tells that in spite of witnessing and acknowledging the power of God, he remained true to his religious bias and was more at home with idolaters than with Christians. In Zarahemla, he had been cast out, but he was treated much worse by the Zoramites in Antionum. Ultimately, they ran upon him and trampled him under their feet "until he was dead."[507]

Korihor had accused Alma and other leaders of the Church of Christ of "leading away the people after the silly traditions of their fathers, for the sake of glutting on the labors of the people."[508]

In reality, the Zoramites, with whom he sought refuge after being stricken speechless, openly practiced priestcraft,[509] whereas the Christians did not. But then, Korihor admitted to Alma that all his words were given to him by the father of lies,[510] who appeared to him and told him what to say.[511]

CA. 77 BC

THE ZORAMITES

In a maneuver very similar to that of the people of Ammonihah a few years earlier (at the western perimeter of the land of Zarahemla), the Zoramites settled the land of Antionum, which was located to the south of Jershon against the border of the "wilderness south."[512] In that location, they could quickly tap into a reservoir of Lamanite warriors, because the east wilderness, both north and south of the Zarahemla/Nephi boundary, was full of Lamanites,[513] driven there first during the wars of 81 BC[514] and again in 77 BC.[515] This was a source of great concern to the Nephites,[516] because any correspondence of dissenters with the Lamanites would quickly rekindle flames of Lamanite hatred and animosity.

ALMA'S MISSION TO THE ZORAMITES

Alma was saddened by the news of the Zoramites, and he knew the only way to rescue them was to bring about a change in their hearts. He immediately called a powerful missionary team comprised of Aaron, Ammon, Omner, Amulek, Zeezrom, and two of his sons, Shiblon and Corianton, to join him on a mission to Antionum.[517] Arriving in Antionum in late 75 BC, they were shocked by what they found there.

The Zoramites, who took their name from their leader, a man named Zoram,[518] worshipped once a week, but they did not so much as acknowledge God during the rest of the week. On their day of worship, they observed a set prayer and ritual, which each person would perform individually. The prayer was a pompous display of pride and arrogance. Inside their synagogue, they had built a tower called a Rameumptom (interpreted in the Nephite language as "holy stand"[519]), which would accommodate only one person at a time. Each individual in turn would climb the steps to the top of the tower, raise his hands "towards heaven,"[520] and recite the following prayer:

> Holy, holy God; we believe that thou art God, and we believe that thou art holy, and that thou wast a spirit, and that thou art a spirit, and that thou wilt be a spirit forever.
>
> Holy God, we believe that thou hast separated us from our brethren; and we do not believe in the tradition of our brethren, which was handed down to them by the childishness of their fathers; but we believe that thou hast elected us to be thy holy children; and also thou hast made it known unto us that there shall be no Christ.
>
> But thou art the same yesterday, today, and forever; and thou hast elected us that we shall be saved, whilst all around us are elected to be cast by thy wrath down to hell; for the which holiness, O God, we thank thee; and we also thank thee that thou hast elected us, that we may not be led away after the foolish traditions of our brethren, which doth bind them down to a belief of Christ, which doth lead their hearts to wander far from thee, our God.
>
> And again we thank thee, O God, that we are a chosen and a holy people. Amen. (Alma 31:15–18)

THE MISSIONARIES GO FORTH IN THE STRENGTH OF THE LORD

Witnessing the wicked state of the Zoramites, Alma was appalled especially by the wickedness of many which were "brethren" in the Church of Christ. He led the missionaries in a prayer that the Lord would give them the strength and wisdom to teach the word and "bring these, our brethren, again unto thee."[521] He then "clapped his hands upon all them that were with him," and as he did so, "they were filled with the Holy Spirit."[522] They then separated and went among the people, taking no thought for their own physical needs.

"And the Lord provided for them that they should hunger not, neither should they thirst; yea, and he also gave them strength, that they should suffer no manner of afflictions, save it were swallowed up in the joy of Christ. Now this was according to the prayer of Alma; and this because he prayed in faith."[523]

They taught the people in their synagogues, in their houses, and in their streets.[524] They had success only among the poor, who were not allowed to worship in the synagogues because of their poverty and the coarseness of their clothing. The leaders considered the poor in their ragged condition to be filthy and unworthy to go into a house of worship. In their humble and dejected circumstance, they were receptive of the gospel, and many were brought to repentance.[525]

A "great multitude" of the poor came to Alma as he taught the people on the hill Onidah.[526] They asked him how they could worship God when they had been cast out of the synagogues.[527] Alma responded that a person does not need a synagogue to communicate with God.[528] They need only open their heart and pray, wherever they may be.[529]

Seeing that the poor were drawn to the gospel, Alma turned away from the crowd of hardened and resistant Zoramites to whom he had been speaking and devoted his attention to the poor. As he spoke, he compared the word of God to a seed, that once planted in the heart must be nourished, to enable it to grow and take root and finally to produce fruit.[530] The plant that begins to grow must be nurtured, or it will wither and die, not because it is a bad seed, but because it was planted in barren ground and deprived of essential spiritual nutrients.[531] He concluded by saying, "And now, my brethren, I desire that ye shall plant this word in your hearts, and as it beginneth to swell even so nourish it by your faith. And behold, it will become a tree, springing up in you unto everlasting life."[532]

INDICATIONS OF IDOLATRY IN THE ZORAMITE CULT

The Zoramites, like the order of Nehor,[533] did not believe in Christ.[534] The fact that they bowed down to dumb idols,[535] while at the same time offering up weekly prayers to God, reveals that they were polytheistic. A prevailing belief in more than one God is also alluded to in Alma 33:1 when the poor Zoramites, in response to Alma's above comparison of the word of God to a seed,[536] asked him "whether they should believe in one God, that they might obtain this fruit of which he had spoken, or how they should plant the seed, or the word of which he had spoken."[537] Alma's response was that indeed there was only one God, and they could begin to exercise their faith by praying to Him wherever they might be.[538] It was not necessary to go into a synagogue before praying to the Lord.

THE ATONEMENT OF JESUS CHRIST

Alma then focused his attention on the Son of God, the only way a person may come to the Father. He said that if they believed the scriptures, then they must believe in Christ.[539] He referred them to the ancient prophets of Israel—specifically to Zenos, Zenock, and Moses, who had all spoken of Christ, the Savior and Redeemer of mankind.[540]

After Alma had completed his discourse, "he sat down upon the ground."[541] Amulek then stood and spoke further to them about the Atonement of Christ.[542] He said that Alma "hath exhorted you unto faith and to patience."[543]

> Yea, even that ye would have so much faith as even to plant the word in your hearts, that ye may try the experiment of its goodness.
>
> And we have beheld that the great question which is in your minds is whether the word be in the Son of God, or whether there shall be no Christ. (Alma 34:4–5).

Amulek then taught them about the Atonement, whereby "Christ shall come among the children of men, to take upon him the transgressions of his people, and that he shall atone for the sins of the world; for the Lord God hath spoken it."[544] He exhorted them to have faith in Christ,[545] repent of their sins,[546] receive the Holy Ghost[547] and worship the Lord with humility[548] and patience[549]—a timeless message for all generations of the children of God.

A MIXTURE OF PAGAN AND CHRISTIAN IDEAS

Due to the perpetual existence of pagan religions in the Nephite culture, the Nephites lived in a strange world in which the people frequently believed the scriptures while freely entertaining ideas and practices from the pagan religion. For example, in 83 BC, Alma had observed idolatry among the members of the Church in Zarahemla.[550]

Proponents of idolatry took license to blend the two religious traditions together whenever it suited their purposes, creating a temporary hybrid of the two. A previously noted example of this was the unbeliever Nehor, who spoke of the Lord, but described Him as one who would welcome everyone into the fold of God without the necessity of repentance and regardless of the life lived. Nehor apparently considered the Lord to be one of many gods, as did the Zoramites. The people could be easily confused by such rhetoric, as illustrated by the poor people in the city of Antionum.

PREPARATIONS FOR WAR

Upon concluding their sermons to the poor in Antionum, Alma and Amulek traveled over to the land of Jershon.[551] Likely as previously agreed upon, all of the missionaries, with the possible exception of Corianton,[552] promptly departed Antionum upon completion of their work and rejoined Alma and Amulek in Jershon.[553]

In the land of Antionum, the political and religious leaders of the Zoramites met together to assess the effect of the Christian missionaries on the people. The reports from the various sectors were dismal, for the people no longer had respect for the priests, and their "craft" (ability to make a living) had been destroyed.[554] They gathered the people throughout the land of Antionum to covertly learn the mind of all the people individually—whether they did or did not believe in the words of the missionaries. Then they expelled those who were "in favor of the words which had been spoken by Alma and his brethren."[555]

The outcasts went over to neighboring land of Jershon, where the people of Ammon received them with open arms. In this way, the converted Zoramites were separated from the wicked and unbelieving Zoramites. The leader of the Zoramites sent word to the people of Jershon (the people of Ammon), demanding that they not give refuge to the outcasts.[556] He threatened them with war if they did not also cast them out."[557]

The people of Jershon ignored the ultimatum. They fed and clothed the refugees and gave them land in Jershon. As 75 BC came to an end,[558] the Zoramites "began to mix with the Lamanites and to stir them up also to anger against them."[559] Soon they began gathering "for war against the people of Ammon and also against the Nephites."[560]

In preparation for the impending war, the Nephites sent the people of Ammon out of that region past the city of Zarahemla to the land of Melek near the western border of the land.[561] In the commencement of 74 BC,[562] they moved their armies into position within the land of Jershon to defend against the Zoramite and Lamanite armies.

74 BC

MORONI TAKES COMMAND OF THE NEPHITE ARMIES

During the Nehor Wars (87–77 BC), the leadership of the Nephite armies was in the able hands of Chief Captain Zoram and his two sons, Aha and Lehi. In the interim, leading to the military action in Jershon, a new chief commander stepped to the post. Chief Captain Moroni was only 25 when he assumed the top leadership position, but he would quickly implement three important innovations that would change and improve the manner in which the Nephites conducted their wars. The improvements would include: 1) protective equipment (armor), 2) defensive structures, and 3) defensive configurations.

The first innovation (protective equipment) was immediately implemented for the war with the Zoramites in 74 BC and included breastplates, arm-shields, helmets, and thick cloth armor to protect the Nephite soldiers from the blows of the enemy.[563] Within a year, Moroni would introduce a defensive structure known today as the ditch-parapet system, or dry moat system[564] at Noah and Ammonihah and other key cities.[565] Similar earthworks would shortly thereafter be excavated around every Nephite city throughout the entire land.[566] During the following five years (72–68 BC), Moroni would establish widespread defensive configurations, consisting of multiple fortified cities placed at specified intervals along the southern and eastern borders of Nephite lands.[567] The western and northern borders would not be fortified until 66 BC.[568]

THE ZORAMITE WAR

At this time, the Zoramites renounced their affiliation with the Nephites and united with the Lamanites in the wilderness, taking upon themselves the same name.[569] The combined Lamanite/Zoramite army, numbering many thousands, then moved into the land of Antionum. They were led by a man named Zerahemnah,[570] who in organizing the armies placed Amalekites and Zoramites in leadership positions because of their intense hatred for the

Nephites.[571] By so doing, he felt that he could utilize their vengeful and murderous influence to continually bolster the hatred and animosity of his forces and thereby fuel their energy and increase their willingness to fight.[572]

The Lamanite army began moving toward Jershon, but as the Nephite forces came into their view, the Lamanites were instantly intimidated by their appearance. Whereas the Lamanites (with the exception of the Zoramites and Amalekites) were naked except for a loincloth, the Nephites were dressed in thick cloth armor and wore head-plates, arm shields, and breastplates.[573] The Lamanite army immediately turned about and retreated into the wilderness.[574]

Moroni sent spies into the wilderness to follow them. "Knowing of the prophecies of Alma,"[575] he then followed the example of former Chief Captain Zoram and sent messengers to inquire of Alma concerning the Lamanite intentions. The word of the Lord came to Alma, and he sent word to Moroni that the Lamanite army was moving westward through the south wilderness toward the city of Manti at the headwaters of the River Sidon. At Manti, the Lamanites expected to find little resistance.[576]

Leaving a portion of the Nephite army in the land of Jershon, "lest by any means a part of the Lamanites should come into that land and take possession of the city,"[577] Moroni set out for Manti with the remainder of his forces. Likely, there was at least a crude road or well-travelled pathway by this time leading along the most direct course across Nephite lands from the region of Jershon to the city of Manti, whereas the Lamanites were going "round about" through wilderness[578].

MORONI PLANS A PINCER MOVEMENT TO TRAP THE LAMANITES

Arriving in Manti well in advance of the Lamanite army, Moroni gathered the inhabitants from the surrounding region to join with them in the Nephite defense.[579] The entire Nephite army was then moved into a valley on the west side of the Sidon River, in the borders of Manti.[580] To attack the city of Manti, Moroni apparently knew the Lamanites would approach through that valley. He placed spies (scouts) along the anticipated route so that he would know the time of their arrival.[581]

Next, he split the Nephite army into two divisions. One division, led by Chief Captain Lehi, was sent to the east side of the Sidon, where they concealed themselves in the wilderness on the south side of a hill called Riplah.[582] Moroni's division remained on the west side of the river, positioned in the valley between the river and the borders of Manti.[583] His plan was to form a pincer movement in which the Lamanites would unknowingly move between Lehi's and Moroni's divisions and become trapped between the two at the river Sidon. See Map 2.0: Setting the Trap, and Map 3.0: Lamanites Are Trapped.

Everything went according to plan. Unaware of Lehi's army on the south side of the hill Riplah, the Lamanite army approached Manti from the east, apparently being channeled through mountain valleys and/or canyons to arrive on the north side of the hill Riplah (Map 2.0).[584] As they passed by Riplah, Lehi quickly moved his division counterclockwise around the hill and approached them from behind (Map 3.0).[585] Suddenly, the Lamanites saw Lehi's army and turned to engage them.[586] When the two armies clashed, Lehi's army quickly gained the upper hand, and as their casualties mounted quickly, the Lamanites became alarmed. Fleeing westward to the river, they began crossing to the other side, where Moroni's division was waiting to receive them (Map 4.0).[587]

As Moroni's division began to engage them, the Lamanites tried to turn aside and sweep around them toward the city of Manti, but encountered more soldiers blocking the way.[588] Being the forward portion of the army, the Lamanites who came against Moroni's division were apparently the more powerful and ferocious of Zerahemnah's warriors. They began to contend with great energy and strength, and their vicious blows killed many Nephites, in some cases hacking through the Nephite armor.[589]

TROY SMITH

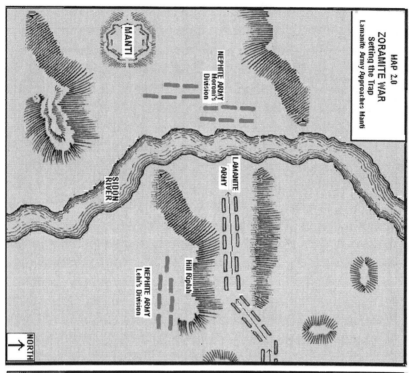

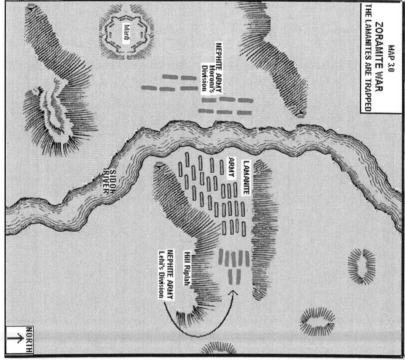

100

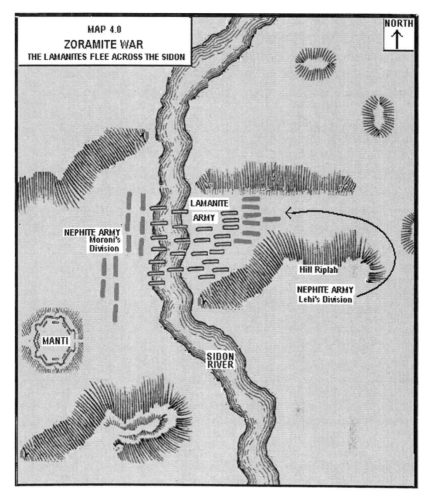

Seeing his men begin to fall back from the ferocity of the Lamanite attack, Moroni urged them to focus upon protecting their wives and children, and the cause of freedom.[590] Taking courage, they began fighting with greater zeal. In time, they began to overpower the Lamanites and drive them back.[591] The Lamanites, having been overwhelmed from both directions, found themselves trapped between the two armies. They became consumed with terror,[592] whereupon Moroni commanded his army to cease the slaughter.[593]

The verbal exchange between Moroni and Zerahemnah that followed accentuated three primary differences between the Christian faith and the pagan cults:

- The Nephites had no desire to kill, or have power over the Lamanites, whereas the Lamanites, especially under Zoramite or order of Nehor influence, were obsessed with destroying or enslaving the Nephites.[594]

- The Nephites had always extended religious freedom to everyone, whereas the pagan cults sought the destruction of the Nephites, specifically because of their religion.[595]

- Moroni believed the Lord had delivered the Lamanites into their hands because of their faith and obedience. He believed the Nephites would always be preserved unless they "should fall into transgression and deny [their] faith."[596] Zerahemnah believed the Nephites had won because of superior strategy and armor, not through the support of a God that he did not believe existed.[597]

Moroni informed Zerahemnah of the conditions by which he would accept their surrender. Each Lamanite warrior would be allowed to depart if he would lay down his weapon and swear with an oath that he would never again attack the Nephites.[598] Zerahemnah was willing to throw down their weapons and depart out of the land, but he refused to swear an oath that he knew they would break.[599] Moroni would not compromise, for as he said, "I cannot recall the words which I have spoken." The Lamanites must swear an oath, or they must take up their swords and resume the battle.[600]

In anger, Zerahemnah took up his sword and lunged at Moroni. Before he could strike a blow, a Nephite soldier slashed out with his sword, knocking Zerahemnah's sword from his hand and breaking it at the hilt. A second swipe of his sword removed Zerahemnah's scalp. Bald and bleeding, Zerahemnah scrambled into a crowd of warriors.[601] The unnamed soldier, of Teancum-like quickness and character,[602] picked up the scalp with the end of his sword, held it high in the air, and shouted to the Lamanite warriors, "Even as this scalp has fallen to the earth, . . . so shall ye fall to the earth except ye deliver up your weapons of war and depart with a covenant of peace."[603]

Many of the Lamanites did as the Nephite soldier commanded.[604] Others followed Zerahemnah's orders. They picked up their swords, and began to contend with the Nephites.[605] Again the

Nephite army prevailed, and many more Lamanites were slain by the sword, until Zerahemnah realized they would all be destroyed if he did not surrender.[606] He and his army threw down their swords and swore the required oath that they would not return against the Nephites.[607] The Lamanites had fought with great ferocity, but in the end, the army of Moroni subdued them, though outnumbered by more than two to one.[608]

PERSISTENCE OF THE ZORAMITE ELEMENT AMONG THE LAMANITES

The period of the Zoramites began in 77 BC. As pertaining to the land of Antionum, or any other Nephite lands, it ended in 74 BC immediately following the Zoramite War when the Zoramites dissented over to the Lamanites and moved to the land of Nephi. During the war, the Lamanite leader Zerahemnah had chosen both Amalekites and Zoramites as his chief captains, because as dissenters from the Nephites, they "were of a more murderous disposition than the Lamanites were."[609] His utilization of leaders from two pagan religions (order of Nehor and Zoramite) demonstrated the momentary overlap of the two religions that was taking place at the time.

The Zoramite lineage, or more specifically the ethno-religious derivative of the people of Antionum, would build on the violent foundation of the Zoramite War. During the following 100-year period (75 BC to AD 25), they would pose a powerful destructive force throughout the land southward. On the other hand, neither the Amalekites, nor the order of Nehor to which they belonged, would ever again be mentioned in the Book of Mormon.

A small number of scriptures provide glimpses of the continued Zoramite involvement in the ongoing conspiracy designed to bring about the destruction of the Christian Nephites. As with the order of Nehor between 200 and 75 BC, the unified nature of this conspiracy through time resulted from the passing of Zoramite religious philosophy from generation to generation until the final defeat of the Gadianton robbers at the end of AD 25. Dissent from the Nephites was naturally engendered by the inherent, unadulterated hatred for Christianity that characterized the pagan cults.

The primary purpose of all pagans throughout Nephite history, whether the order of Nehor or the Zoramites, was the destruction of the Christian Nephite government, for they could obtain power in no other way. The conspiratorial nature of dissent revolved around the secrecy through which the dissenters of necessity operated in their never-ending quest for political power. In 51 BC, this inherent secrecy would be suddenly transformed into an art of deception through the expertise of a man named Gadianton.

During the entire pre-Christ period in the land of Zarahemla (From *ca*. 200 BC until the Great Storm of AD 34), pagan religion was the primary source of intense generational hatred against the Christian Nephites. Indeed, they served as the substrate upon which the conspiracy could be nurtured and thus perpetuate itself across many generations of conspirators. In spite of frequent violent attacks against the Christian Nephites throughout the pre-Christ period, however, the conspirators were unsuccessful in their quest for the elimination of Christianity from the Western Hemisphere.

THE FINAL CHAPTER OF THE ZORAMITES

The account of the Zoramites does not end here. The final chapter of their war against Christianity will be presented in Book 2 of this series. As will be seen in their final offensive as leaders of the reorganized Gadianton robbers, they were never able to reach their diabolical objectives. Their lack of success resulted from the frequent intervention of the Lord on behalf of the righteous element among the Nephites, notwithstanding their continuously diminishing numbers.[610]

CHAPTER 2.5

AMALICKIAH—A NEW MODEL FOR DECEPTION

BRIEFLY REVIEWING NEPHITE HISTORY in Zarahemla to this point in time, it is quite apparent that in more ways than one it can be divided into the period of the kings and the period of the judges. The period of the kings (*ca.* 200–92 BC) was a relatively quiet period of peace and prosperity for the Nephites. In the period of the judges, the stability, so characteristic of the former period, immediately disappeared.

THE CLOSE ASSOCIATION OF LAMANITE ATTACK WITH DISSENTERS

There is no record of dissenters going over to the Lamanites, or of Lamanites attacking the land of Zarahemla during the reigns of Mosiah I or Mosiah II. In fact, throughout the approximately 110-year period of the kings in Zarahemla, there was only one recorded instance of serious internal conflict that resulted in "many dissensions away to the Lamanites,"[611] and one war of defense against Lamanite invasion.[612] Both occurrences took place during the reign of King Benjamin. It is obvious that the two events were interconnected, because, as presented in Words of Mormon, the dissenter uprising[613] and the punishment of the dissenters "according to their crimes"[614] are separated by the war with the Lamanites.[615]

Clear conclusions can be drawn from the above referenced passages in Words of Mormon. First, it seems that a new scenario of dissent was established during King Benjamin's reign, which dissent would be followed shortly by Lamanite invasion. Thereafter, the two events (dissenter rebellion and Lamanite attack) represented two fundamental phases of dissenter rebellion. This new pattern of dissenter behavior became quite common during the period of the judges. As will be seen in this chapter, however, Amalickiah would take the idea of Lamanite assistance to new heights.

THE TURBULENT PERIOD OF THE JUDGES

The end of the period of the kings was also the end of the peace the Nephites had enjoyed for many years.[616] The transition to judges in 91 BC brought an immediate escalation in both political and religious contention.[617] The contention would continue to intensify throughout the pre-Christ period until the Great Storm on the fourth day of AD 34.

The first 18 years of the judges were deeply scarred by serious contention and warfare both from without and within the land of Zarahemla. The Amlicite War in 87 BC[618] was followed in 82 BC by the persecution and murder of Christian converts in the city of Ammonihah.[619] Early in the following year (81 BC), Ammonihah was destroyed by a Lamanite army.[620] Several related battles took place between the Nephites and Nehor-incited Lamanite armies over the next five years, finally concluding in 77 BC with the total defeat of the order of Nehor. Only two years then passed before the Nephites had to defend themselves against the Zoramite-sponsored Lamanite attack in 74 BC.

At the end of the 18th year of the judges, the Nephites could therefore look back on constant internal strife and frequent warfare. However, an even greater threat was yet to come. This ominous threat was already developing even as the Zoramite War came to an end. In 73 BC, when the great prophet Alma the Younger set his affairs in order and exited from the Nephite world,[621] it was looming just below the horizon.

ALMA'S DEPARTURE FROM THE LAND OF ZARAHEMLA

At the end of 74 BC, Alma delivered the Nephite collection of sacred materials to his son Helaman, including the Plates of Brass,[622] the large plate of Nephi,[623] the small plate of Nephi,[624] the twenty-four gold Plates of Ether,[625] the interpreters,[626] and the Liahona,[627] "which were esteemed by Alma and his fathers to be most sacred." He had previously attempted to transfer these items to Nephihah at the time he conferred the office of chief judge upon him, but Nephihah had refused.[628]

In retrospect, it was crucial that Nephihah refuse to take possession of the plates and sacred items from Alma. Through a series of events that soon occurred, Alma's decision became a formal authorized transfer of the records from the Nephite government to his family. It is possible that a new set of records was created at that time and maintained within the government. However, the large plate of Nephi were personally maintained by Alma's descendants from that time forward, even when Helaman II ascended to the judgment seat in 50 BC. It therefore was natural that Alma's family should retain the plates when Helaman's son Nephi relinquished the judgment seat to Cezoram in 30 BC. Had the sacred materials remained in government hands, they might have been destroyed or altered by the Gadianton robbers following the assassination of Cezoram in 26 BC. At the very least, they may have no longer been maintained, being relegated to nothing more than a relic of the past.

Alma emphasized to Helaman the grave importance of protecting and maintaining the records, which God would "keep and preserve for a wise purpose in him, that he may show forth his power unto future generations."[629] He then blessed his three sons, the earth, and the Church and "departed out of the land of Zarahemla as if to go into the land of Melek."[630] He was never seen again. The people in the Church of Christ believed that Alma, like the prophet Moses, was translated—the Lord having "received Alma in the spirit, unto himself."[631]

THE APOSTASY OF AMALICKIAH

It was a constant struggle within the Church to withstand the unending onslaught of dissenters and the consequences of war. It seems that each round of dissent created inroads of wickedness and perversion into the Church of Christ. Just as Alma found it necessary to purge the Church of sinful and unrepentant members after the Amlicite war, and to re-establish the disciplinary regulations of the Church,[632] even so at the end of the Nehor and Zoramite wars, the same was required of Helaman and his brethren.[633] The disruptive influence of war should not be discounted, because in each case the entire land of Zarahemla was affected as the call to arms was issued across the land to defend against a Lamanite attack. The people in all parts of the land were directly affected by the violence, bloodshed, and death.[634]

Likewise, the curse of the Nephite dissenters should not be overlooked. Their involvement in Lamanite aggression likely extended well beyond what was explicitly known to the writers of the Book of Mormon. For instance, the arrival of the Lamanite army during the Amlicite war may have resulted because Amlicite dissenters solicited their support.[635] In their flight from the Valley of Gideon, the Amlicites may have moved in the direction of expected Lamanite assistance.

Even to the extent known, the dissenters posed a continual subversive threat to the Church of Christ and the free government in Zarahemla. Their negative influence was just as great among a large segment of the Nephites (including members of the Church) as it was among the Lamanites. It was not limited to violence, which was merely the final result after dissent reached its maturity.

The incessant chatter of apostates and pagans behind the scenes was an unrelenting cancer in Christian Nephite society. Even before there were robbers in the land, there was secrecy among the apostates as they, many times, moved in clandestine circles while yet disguised as saints of God. They moved among the flock and quietly spread their philosophies of evil and malcontent. As will be discussed in Book 2, the establishment of the secret Gadianton society was a natural evolution of the pagan element that preceded and spawned it.

In like manner as Alma had gone forth in 83 BC, so Helaman went forth with other church leaders in 73 BC to teach the gospel and re-establish the regulations of the Church. They ordained priests and teachers to preside over the Church in every region of the land. As the new leaders took their positions, however, dissent soon rose to the surface when a certain group of church members banded together in rebellion against "the words of Helaman and his brethren."[636]

The greater part of the "people who were wroth . . . were the greater part of them the lower judges of the land and they were seeking power."[637] They picked as their leader a man named Amalickiah, who promised them power if they would make him king. It follows logically that the initial rebellion concerned the individuals that were not chosen for church leadership—apparently much more than it concerned church doctrine.

One might therefore conclude that the desire for power and influence within the government was the root cause of the rebellion. Apparently the dissidents did not think that walking "uprightly before God"[638] should be a requirement for leadership positions within the Church, to advance their political ambitions. Succinctly stated, the leadership choices of Helaman and his brethren, in selecting only from among the humble, righteous, obedient members, raised the ire of the dissidents—wolves that in their rage from being passed over for positions of church leadership could not afterward maintain their disguise in sheep's clothing.

They sought church positions in the same aggressive way one would seek political office, rather than accepting the decisions of the prophet Helaman and other church leaders. Their ultimate goals in seeking positions of leadership within the Church are not provided in the account, but likely they considered such positions as springboards to greater political influence. A second ulterior motive may have been the alteration of church doctrine by subtle means.

The contentious Amalickiah and his followers were in no way amiable; neither were they conciliatory in any sense of the word. It quickly became apparent that, like other dissenters before them, upon their apostasy from the Church, they sought the violent destruction of the Church and the death of its leaders.[639] They gathered together with the intent of murdering Helaman and other leaders of the Church.[640]

Amalickiah was an opportunist. His entire purpose in life was the pursuit of political power. He was a master of deception, and he manipulated the emotions of the people to achieve his sinister goals. His primary goal from the beginning was to become king, and he sought to create a scenario that would enmesh the people's goals with his own. For this purpose, discord within the Church apparently provided a compelling reason—a foundation of discontent, upon which he could build a movement for the overthrow of the free government.[641]

It may seem like a rather extreme twist of logic to transcend from apostasy from the Church to the goal of violently overthrowing the Nephite government. However, once Amalickiah became an open enemy to the Church, his goal of destroying the Church was inextricably tied to destroying the free government that protected it.[642] In a very real sense, it again points to the inseparable connection between the democratic form of government and the very existence of the Church of Christ.

The Christian Nephite government safeguarded the religious rights of all Nephite citizens, both Christian and pagan.[643] In reality, however, Christianity was all that needed protection. The Christian creed of peace and "good will toward men"[644] and the Christian belief that man's agency is a sacred right were not mirrored in the pagan philosophy. Whereas the Christian government would protect pagan organizations, a pagan government would never protect Christian organizations, but to the contrary would itself become a destroyer of anything Christian.

While it may thus appear that Amalickiah's purposes were two-faceted, that is, destroying the Church and obtaining absolute political power through the destruction of the free government, it is actually impossible to separate one from the other. Neither the Church nor the free government could survive without the other. Just as Christianity required a free government (or a Christian king) to exist in a society of both pagan and Christian elements, a free government could not exist without the benevolence of Christian love.

Perhaps it should be emphasized that Amalickiah's dissent was not like leaving the Church today and joining a different Christian denomination. Leaving the Church was equivalent to renouncing Christianity. At that time there was only one Christian church. A person was either a believer in Christ, or an idolater.[645]

Amalickiah's brother, Ammoron, was also a member of the Church of Christ and apostatized with him at the same time, as implied by Moroni in his correspondence to Ammoron during the course of the subsequent war.[646] In his response to Moroni, Ammoron denied the existence of Christ when he said, "And as concerning that God *whom ye say we have rejected*, behold we know not such a being."[647]

Such a statement seems to indicate that Amalickiah and Ammoron never accepted Jesus Christ as their Lord and Savior. Furthermore, the sudden rejection of Christianity by a large number of dissidents that included lower judges seeking power[648] may indicate that their activities were conspiratorial from the beginning and were founded in secrecy—underground operations that surfaced only when their goals of infiltration into the Church, which would lead to political advantage, were frustrated.

Following the pattern of previous apostates,[649] Amalickiah and his co-conspirators joined the ranks of other apostates. Together, they worked tirelessly to convince other prideful church members that were angry over the uncompromising standards and requirements of the Church[650] to join them in their dissent.[651] To everyone they echoed the cry that the only way to achieve their desires was through violence.

Amalickiah also had the support of all the pagan factions, which had never converted to Christianity.[652] During the years that followed the arrival of the people of Alma in Zarahemla, the pagan faction had continuously demonstrated their intense hatred for the Church, which was established at that time. During the period of the judges, their disdain for the Church was a primary underlying factor in their overwhelming desire for a return to monarchy, which would enable them to achieve its destruction. However, notwithstanding the dramatic rate in which these various elements (groups) all rushed to Amalickiah's support, the sword of justice soon hung over them when word of their murderous and seditious actions reached Chief Captain Moroni.[653]

THE TITLE OF LIBERTY

Moroni immediately went into action. He tore a large section of fabric from his coat and made it into a flag. Upon it, he wrote the following words, "In memory of our God, our religion, and freedom, and our peace, our wives, and our children—and he fastened it upon the end of a pole. . . . And he called it the title of liberty."[654] He put on his full armor and, taking the pole into his hands, "he bowed himself to the earth, and he prayed mightily unto his God for the blessings of liberty to rest upon his brethren, so long as there should a band of Christians remain to possess the land."[655]

Moroni "went forth among the people" and called on them to covenant with him to defend "their rights, and their religion, that the Lord God may bless them."[656] As the men from the nearby region (also in full armor) gathered around Moroni, he spoke more concerning the title of liberty. It was, he said, a symbol of the many-colored coat of Joseph. The title of liberty (a remnant of Moroni's coat) represented a remnant of Joseph's coat because the Nephites were a remnant of the seed of Joseph, preserved only by their faith in Jesus Christ.[657]

Moroni sent emissaries into more distant parts of the land to call upon the people to gather to his army.[658] As their numbers began to grow, Amalickiah realized that he could not prevail against them. He therefore gathered all who remained dedicated to his cause and fled into the wilderness toward the land of Nephi, where they believed they would obtain overwhelming support from the Lamanites.

Moroni took his army into the wilderness and was successful in cutting off the people of Amalickiah to prevent them from fleeing to the land of Nephi. His intention was to execute Amalickiah for his treasonous activities.[659] Amalickiah managed to escape, however, with "a small number of his men"[660] and disappeared into the forests of the wilderness.

AMALICKIAH'S WEB OF LIES IN THE LAND OF NEPHI

Amalickiah journeyed up to the land of Nephi and began stirring the Lamanites to anger against the Nephites. With very little effort, he gained the complete support of the Lamanite king.[661] The king sent a proclamation to all the people to gather for battle against the Nephites. Alma chapter 47 contains the account of Amalickiah's overthrow of the Lamanite king, which soon followed, and his takeover of the land of Nephi, all of which occurred before 73 BC came to an end.

He was an evil and murderous man who came swaggering into the land of Nephi with great confidence that he could influence the Lamanites to join his cause. As it turned out, he achieved much more. Helaman's account in the book of Alma[662] describes in detail his precipitous rise to absolute power over the Lamanites through deceit, manipulation, and murder.

It was a great sting operation—an unbelievable scam—mission: impossible! The complexity of what Amalickiah and his partners in crime achieved could not be planned or calculated in advance. It required reckless abandon and total contempt for the Lamanites, as well as complete confidence that they could trick them at every turn. They made their plans on the fly, and the Lamanite kingdom crumbled before them like sand castles in the wind.

Through an incredible chain of events, Amalickiah assassinated the Lamanite king and, in the guise of a good Samaritan, took the Lamanite queen to be his wife. He was fully accepted as the new king of the Lamanites, because he had first ascended through the ranks of the army. He immediately appointed speakers to address the Lamanites from their towers. Before the end of 73 BC, he had succeeded in stirring them to anger and in gathering a large army to go against the Nephites.[663]

The Zoramites had lived in Zarahemla until the previous year. They were appointed as leaders over the Lamanite armies.[664] His purpose was to take advantage of their knowledge of Nephite strengths and weaknesses, as well as their intense hatred for the Christian Nephites.

AMALICKIAH SETS HIS SIGHTS ON ZARAHEMLA

Looking back to 81 BC, it was during that year that the Lamanites, under the influence of the order of Nehor, had their way in the Nephite cities of Ammonihah and Noah.[665] They had found the two cities totally defenseless against military attack. Erupting suddenly from the adjacent west wilderness, they had taken Ammonihah completely by surprise, mercilessly slaughtering men, women, and children—leaving no one alive in the city. As they departed, they brushed across the edge of Noah's boundaries, killing Nephites in their path, with the exception of a few who were impulsively abducted. Though they had paid dearly for that attack,[666] in 73 BC the Lamanites likely looked back on Ammonihah as a great victory. In fact, it was the only victory they had experienced during the entire Nephite period in Zarahemla.[667]

After the fall of Ammonihah, Nephites went to the site to survey the destruction. Due to the sheer magnitude of properly burying thousands of bodies, the remoteness of the site, and the fact that no inhabitants remained to object to the harsh and troubling odors of decay, they had made large piles of the dead Ammonihahites and covered them with a thin layer of soil. The stench of rotting flesh was thereafter so great that the city was left alone for about eight years.[668]

Amalickiah's choice of Ammonihah as the first point of attack seemed completely logical. The city of Manti was the location of the first and only battle of the Zoramite War during the previous year. Manti was a popular Lamanite attack point, perhaps the one most frequently chosen by the Lamanites, lying as it did in such close proximity to the south wilderness, which bordered on the land of Manti.[669] Manti was positioned on the Sidon River, upstream of the capital city of Zarahemla. For these reasons, it would be well-defended, and an attack there would not surprise the Nephites.

The same was true of the land of Jershon for a number of reasons. First, the last great battle of the Nehor Wars had taken place there in 77 BC. Second, the Zoramite War was initiated there, though no fighting had occurred, because the Lamanites were frightened at the first use of Nephite armor and fled into the wilderness. Third, the wilderness south of Jershon was teeming with Lamanites. Amalickiah could be certain that the Nephites would be ready in Jershon.

Ammonihah, on the other hand, had been attacked only once—eight years earlier in 81 BC. In 74 BC, before either Amalickiah or the Zoramites had dissented away to the Lamanites, the city remained in ruins as a consequence of the previous Lamanite attack.[670] Now in 73 BC, making the assumption that the current conditions were the same as in the previous year, Amalickiah was certain Ammonihah would still be the weakest point along the Nephite perimeter. He fully expected to surprise the Nephites just as the Nehor-provoked Lamanites had done in 81 BC.

Amalickiah's intelligence was old and outdated. Earlier in 73 BC, "while [he was] obtaining power by fraud and deceit,"[671] Moroni was employing his army in building fortifications around key cities along the Nephite borders. Moroni found it useful to employ

Ammonihah and the neighboring Noah as defensive cities, because at that moment in time, the two cities still lay at the boundary of the west wilderness. Five years later, after the Nephites claimed all lands north of the narrow strip of wilderness from sea to sea, the two cities would no longer be located at the border of the land of Zarahemla.

LAMANITE ARMOR

The Nephites had first introduced thick cloth armor, head-plates, arm-shields, and breastplates during the Zoramite war of the previous year (74 BC).[672] In 73 BC, when Amalickiah sent his Lamanite army to attack Ammonihah, they had fashioned some armor of their own. The Lamanite warriors carried shields and wore breastplates.[673] They wore thick animal skins in place of the quilted cloth armor of the Nephites. This innovation resulted directly from the Zoramite war, in which many Lamanites (naked except for a loincloth) were cut to ribbons at Manti by the armored Nephite soldiers.[674] Amalickiah was sure that his armies, fighting on equal terms with the Nephites, would have great success. He certainly did not expect the great surprise Moroni—always a step ahead—had in store for them.

MORONI'S FORTIFICATIONS AT AMMONIHAH AND NOAH

In late 73 BC,[675] Nephite scouts discovered a large Lamanite army advancing through the west wilderness toward the city of Ammonihah.[676] No doubt they returned to the city in great haste to warn the Nephite commanders. The alarm was quickly relayed throughout the city.

In nervous anticipation, Nephite soldiers hastily moved to their preassigned posts and readied themselves for the imminent Lamanite arrival. This would be the first test of Chief Captain Moroni's fortifications. There was no precedent for it in the land of Zarahemla, though the Nephites had previously fortified their cities in some manner while they lived within the land of Nephi.[677] Though the high dirt embankment around the city looked formidable, and though they no doubt had drilled frequently in the art of repelling enemy attacks, some may have wondered if it was sufficient to withstand the attack of an army as large, bloodthirsty, and fanatical as dissenter-driven Lamanite armies of the past. However, they likely took courage in the fact that the element of surprise was entirely on their side.

When the Lamanites arrived at the edge of Ammonihah, to their astonishment and disappointment, they found the city had been made into a fortress. A deep ditch had been excavated all the way around a portion of the city,[678] except for one point of access. Their superior numbers would be of little advantage to them on this day, because they could not overrun the city from all sides.

The Lamanites were daunted by the immense scale of the earthen walls. The soil from the encircling ditch was piled on the inner edge, so that upon completion the fortification presented a barrier of twice the depth of the ditch—the depth of the ditch plus the height of the soil piled on its inner lip. For example, digging a ditch to a depth of 15 feet would have created a vertical barrier of 30 feet. When they first approached, it had given the appearance of being only half that size, because half of the height of the barrier was below ground level. As they moved closer, however, and the ditch came into full view, they became aware of its full dimensions.

Assessing the situation, the Zoramite leaders[679] made the field decision to retreat from Ammonihah and seek a more accessible attack point. They turned around and marched into the wilderness, heading in the direction of the nearby city of Noah. The chief captains gathered together and weighed carefully the situation facing them. They knew of the severe consequences waiting for them if they should return to Amalickiah without attacking a Nephite city. Feeling the extreme weight of their leadership responsibility, each of the chief captains stepped forward and swore with an oath that regardless of what they found at Noah, they would attack the city.[680] It was an oath that would cost them their lives.

The above scenario, in which the Lamanites were stymied by Moroni's innovations, was essentially a replay of the scenario in the borders of Jershon one year earlier.[681] In 74 BC, Nephite armor stopped the Lamanites in their tracks and made them turn back into the wilderness[682]—in 73 BC, it was the fortifications.[683]

ATTACK AT NOAH

When the Lamanites arrived at the city of Noah, they found to their surprise and dismay that the city was fortified even more formidably than the city of Ammonihah. There was a second reason for disappointment. Chief Captain Lehi was the commander of the Nephite military unit assigned to that city.[684] Lehi had gained quite a reputation among the Lamanites for his eminence as a military commander and as a powerful warrior.

Likely the son of Zoram,[685] he had been involved in all of the battles over the past ten years, beginning in 83 BC shortly after the first attack at Ammonihah. He was with his father when they pursued the Lamanites and rescued the hostages that had been snatched from the land of Noah.[686] He was involved in the series of battles that followed Ammonihah's destruction.[687] In 74 BC, at the city of Manti, he had solidified his reputation as a man to be feared.[688] Now he was waiting for them in the city of Noah. He would not let them do what they had done in 83 BC, and he had all those marvelous fortifications to support him, which alone gave a tremendous edge to the Nephite army.

In spite of their disturbing discovery, the Lamanite chief captains had sworn their oaths and had no choice but to attack the city. They brought up their armies and attacked the causeway leading into the city. That, of course, was the place where Lehi had stationed his most powerful warriors to strike down any who might try to enter. When they found they could not fight their way into the city, Lamanites climbed down into the ditch and began digging in the freshly excavated soil, hoping to dig their way in. However, at the bottom of the ditch they found themselves directly in harm's way, because the Nephites could very easily hurl down objects upon them, such as spears, axes, stones, boulders, or any manner of debris. An object hurled from the top of the wall (or simply tossed or pushed over the edge) would gain momentum as it plunged downward toward the frantically digging Lamanites, whereas the projectiles hurled or shot by the Lamanites lost most of their force by the time they reached the top of the wall. Before long, more than a thousand Lamanite warriors had been slain, including all of their chief captains who had taken their customary positions at the head of each charge. After all the Lamanite leaders had been slain, the warriors retreated in disorder back into the wilderness and, with much trepidation, made their way back to Nephi to give their report to Amalickiah. When the news came to Amalickiah of the humiliating defeat, he was furious. He swore that he "would drink the blood of Moroni,"[689] his great nemesis.

72-68 BC
THE CALM BEFORE THE STORM

The remarkable defensive innovations Moroni introduced in 73 BC at key cities along the western and southern borders of Zarahemla directly resulted in a six-year period of peace. It was not that Amalickiah did not wish to attack the Nephites during that period. The Lamanite assault at Ammonihah and Noah during the first months of his reign in Nephi had shown that domination of Zarahemla was his top priority.

He realized, however, that the Lamanites were not ready to attack the Nephites. The differences between Nephite and Lamanite military capabilities were so great that he would have to develop a different plan, a new strategy and new techniques to go successfully against the fortified Nephite cities. He must carefully choose the right point of attack. In addition, he must wait for the right political moment in the internal affairs within the Nephite nation. It is likely he had spies in Zarahemla who kept him informed of Nephite political developments, as well as supplying him with information about dissident unrest.

MORONI EXPANDS AND IMPROVES THE DEFENSIVE FORTIFICATIONS

Taking advantage of the six-year hiatus between Lamanite attacks (73–67 BC), Moroni engineered a dramatic improvement of Nephite defensive capabilities through the establishment of an uninterrupted line of fortified cities, placed at regular intervals along the southern and eastern perimeters of the greatly expanded Nephite lands. The southern line of cities was placed along the entire course of the narrow strip of wilderness, which extended from the west sea to the east sea. The eastern line of cities extended northward along the east sea from Moroni at the southeast corner of Nephite lands into the land of Bountiful on the north (See Appendix A, Map A-6). See also Part 3, Chapter 3.4 for a description of these fortified cities, as contained in Alma chapter 50.

68 BC

FLIGHT OF MORIANTON TOWARD THE LAND NORTHWARD

Following a disagreement with the people of the neighboring city of Lehi, the people of the city Morianton decided to flee into the land northward. When news came to Moroni concerning their intentions,[690] he dispatched an army led by a man named Teancum to apprehend them. He knew that if the people of Morianton should unite with the inhabitants of Bountiful, they would threaten the security of the land of Zarahemla.[691] With Amalickiah threatening the southern border, Moroni would not sanction even the possibility of relinquishing control of the narrow neck of land.

Teancum's army headed the people of Morianton "by the narrow pass which led by the sea into the land northward, yea, by the sea, on the west and on the east."[692] In the ensuing confrontation, Morianton urged his people to resist. A battle commenced during which Morianton was slain by Teancum, and his followers were escorted back to the city of Morianton. Peace was re-established between the two cities.[693]

THE PASSING OF CHIEF JUDGE NEPHIHAH

Near the end of 68 BC, Chief Judge Nephihah died after a reign of almost 16 years.[694] He had "filled the judgment-seat with perfect uprightness before God."[695] His son Pahoran "was appointed to fill the judgment-seat, in the stead of his father; yea, he was appointed chief judge and governor over the people, with an oath and sacred ordinance to judge righteously, and to keep the peace and the freedom of the people, and to grant unto them their sacred privileges to worship the Lord their God, yea, to support and maintain the cause of God all his days, and to bring the wicked to justice according to their crime."[696]

67 BC

POLITICAL UNREST

A certain group of dissidents viewed the "changing of the guard" as a new vista of opportunity. They hoped Pahoran could be pressured into making the political changes first sought by Amlici and his followers during Alma's reign.[697] In fact, they were repulsed at the thought of having to endure another endless reign which catered to the Christians, and which denied them their political rights. The time for action had arrived.

After Pahoran began his tenure as the chief judge, an issue of contention was raised by this radical political faction, which was known as the "king-men."[698] They "desired that a few particular points of the law should be altered."[699] This was likely the terminology of their petition, and it reflected the same level of cunning and arrogance as that exhibited by Amlici in his bid to take over the government twenty years previously.[700]

It was a blatant understatement. The "few particular points," if changed, would result in the complete abolishment of the Nephite free government and the establishment of a king over the land.[701] Cutting through the clever rhetoric, it was simply the second attempt to abolish the system of judges and return to monarchy.

The king-men put pressure on Pahoran to authorize the desired changes in the law, which indicates the considerable power held by the chief judge. Their demand was introduced in the form of a written petition, which likely contained a required minimum number of signatures.[702] When Pahoran refused to make or allow the desired changes,[703] the king-men refused to drop the issue. Pahoran's inherent power was such that if he refused to make a change, the only way to proceed further, that is, to overrule him, was to obtain a vote of the people.

To this end, it is likely a second petition was introduced advocating a vote to "dethrone" Pahoran[704] and crown a king. Copies of the new petition were again carried among the people for the required number of signatures. The first petition had been addressed directly to the chief judge, for apparently he alone held the power to act upon it, though to be ratified any changes he should make to the law must then be put to a vote. The second petition was likely addressed to a carefully selected body of lower judges,[705] who ruled that a vote or election must be held to determine if Pahoran should retain his seat, or be replaced by a king.

THE IDENTITY OF THE KING-MEN

The king-men considered themselves to be of royal lineage. They are referred to as "people who professed the blood of nobility."[706] Alma 51:8 states, "Now those who were in favor of kings were those of high birth, and they sought to be kings; and they were supported by those who sought power and authority over the people." This indicates that the political division was drawn along ethnic (tribal) lines.

"Those of high birth" were apparently not descendants of Nephi, Sam, Joseph, or Jacob, for they were all descendants of Lehi, none of which had a unique or prestigious heritage over the present Nephite leaders, unless perhaps they were direct descendants of Mosiah, the most recent king. They were not of Lamanite descent, for other than the righteous people of Ammon, the Lamanites lived in the land of Nephi. The only other ethnic groups in the land of Zarahemla were Zoramites (descendants of the original Zoram) and Mulekites, neither of which were descendants of Lehi. The Mulekites, or a portion thereof,[707], descended from Judah, the kingly tribe of Israel. It can only be speculated from what tribe Zoram descended, though likely it was also Judah.

THE FREE GOVERNMENT HANGS ON THE OUTCOME OF A NEW VOTE

In essence, there was no difference between this latest attempt to return to kings and the previous attempt by Amlici. The king-men may have felt they were being clever by first appealing directly to Pahoran, but his refusal immediately brought the wolves out of the closet. Afterward, they proceeded exactly as before. Though none is mentioned in the text, there was likely a candidate already chosen by the king-men, who ran against Pahoran like Amlici had run against Alma.

Those who wished to maintain the free government were called "freemen"[708] or "people of liberty."[709] When the matter was put to a vote, the freemen obtained a majority, or as stated in the text, "the voice of the people came in favor of the freemen, and Pahoran retained the judgment seat." [710] The king-men were silenced by the results and withdrew their objection, acquiescing to the voice of the people. This was a variation of the Amlici debacle, because Amlici had refused to accept the results and immediately resorted to war.

ONE ADDITIONAL CONSIDERATION

Before these objections to Pahoran were raised, he had taken the judgment seat without a vote of the people. Therefore, the default procedure for the succession of chief judges was the transfer of power by lineage unless a substantial objection was raised, or unless another candidate received support that was sufficient to require a vote.[711] Pahoran had been appointed chief judge simply according to his inherent right as a son of Nephihah.[712]

THE AMALICKIAH AND AMMORON OFFENSIVE

THE EASTERN SEABOARD—THE FIRST BATTLEFRONT OF THE WAR

At the beginning of 67 BC, while the land of Zarahemla was embroiled in this political turmoil, Amalickiah seized the opportunity and moved his armies to a location within the east wilderness immediately southward of the coastal city of Moroni. See Map 5.0 at the end of this chapter. He resumed his war against the Nephites by attacking the city within Jershon that lay at the southeast corner of Nephite lands. When Moroni fell, Amalickiah continued up the east coast, taking control of a line of six cities along the coastal border of Jershon. It looked as though he would take control of the east coast all the way to the narrow neck of land at Desolation. At the city of Bountiful, however, he was suddenly and emphatically stopped by a powerful army led by Teancum, who had previously slain Morianton and brought his followers back to their land in Jershon.[713]

A SECOND BATTLEFRONT—REBELLION OF THE KING-MEN

Amalickiah initiated the east coast invasion as the king-men contention was coming to an end. When the king-men heard the news of his attack, "they were glad in their hearts; and they refused to take up arms."[714] Many, if not most, of them perhaps had stood behind Amalickiah in 73 BC, when he had first risen up against the Church of Christ and the Nephite government. Now, they rose up in defiance of the Nephite military, led by Chief Captain Moroni, notwithstanding the covenant they had previously made with him.[715] Because of the king-men rebellion, Moroni was unable to send reinforcements to the east coast to prevent the fall of so many cities and the loss of many Nephite warriors. The king-men rebellion was put down before the end of 67 BC.

JUSTICE FOR AMALICKIAH

After capturing Mulek, the northernmost city in Jershon, Amalickiah quickly moved to the eastern border of the land of Bountiful, where the city of Bountiful was located.[716] His plan was to take control of the city. He would then continue on to the narrow neck of land and take possession of the narrow pass at Desolation.

By controlling the choke point at Desolation, the Lamanites could cut off any retreat of the Nephites into the land northward.[717] In effect, Amalickiah planned to do to the Nephites the same thing they had done to Morianton and his people,[718] but as an offensive maneuver rather than a defensive one. He would then have them trapped in the land southward. Only then would he turn his attention to the interior of the land and in his own good time take control of Zarahemla.

It was at the eastern border of Bountiful, however, that Teancum and his elite army—a choice unit of some the most powerful and skilled fighters of the Nephites[719]—stopped Amalickiah dead in his tracks. Teancum's army engaged them, quickly overcame them, and then punished and "harassed" them until they fled down to the shores of the east sea, near the city of Mulek.[720]

That night, while the Lamanites were deep in sleep "because of their much fatigue, which was caused by the labors and the heat of the day," Teancum crept forth with a servant into their camp. He slipped into Amalickiah's tent and "put a javelin to his heart," and then returned with his servant to the camp of the Nephites.[721] He awakened his army and informed them of Amalickiah's demise. They stood throughout the remainder of the night, ready for any retaliation. Amalickiah's death marked the end of 67 BC.

A THIRD BATTLEFRONT—THE SOUTHERN BORDER OFFENSIVE

Alma Chapter 51 gives the account of Amalickiah's 67 BC invasion along the east coast and of the simultaneous internal king-men rebellion. Not until Helaman's epistle to Moroni in Chapter 56 is the reader made aware of a third Lamanite campaign, which from the very beginning of the war was being conducted along the southern boundary between Manti and Antiparah.

Between 72 and 67 BC, Moroni had established border cities along the southern border of Nephite lands from Manti to the west sea.[722] Looking westward from the headwaters of the Sidon River, the line of five cities are identified as Manti, Zeezrom, Cumeni, Antiparah,[723] and a city not identified by name, which bordered on the west coast.[724] Prior to the start of the war, Moroni had fortified the five cities along that segment of the narrow strip of wilderness.

In about 67 BC, he had appointed Antipus to command the armies that had been emplaced to defend those cities.[725] In his epistle to Moroni, Helaman describes a very intense conflict that had decimated the army of Antipus.[726] He had discovered their plight upon his arrival in that part of the land with his stripling warriors in 66 BC.

66 BC

EASTERN SEABOARD—AMMORON REPLACES
AMALICKIAH AS KING OF THE LAMANITES

On the first day of 66 BC, King Amalickiah was discovered dead in his own tent. His army was shaken by the discovery. Then, as darkness faded into morning light, they saw Teancum's army, which had overpowered them the previous day, ready to do battle.[727] Consumed by fear, they fled with all their army into Mulek's protective walls.[728]

To perpetuate the dynasty established by Amalickiah, his brother, Ammoron, had been placed second in command. This can be deduced because he could not take Amalickiah's place as king of the Lamanites unless he was authorized by Amalickiah to become the chief commander of the army in the event of Amalickiah's death.[729] It was in essence a parallel to Amalickiah's replacement of the Lamanite king.

In the world of the Lamanites, the rule of military might was a primary determining factor in the transfer of power. By being the "legitimate" head of the Lamanite army, Amalickiah had held the supreme position of power in the Lamanite military at the death of the Lamanite king, a position that was requisite to his ascent to the throne in such circumstances, and more especially if the king had no heir to the throne. His rise to the throne had required three critical steps,[730] whereas Ammoron's ascent was a single step, because Amalickiah was both the king and military leader at the time of his death and had made Ammoron second in command.

A FOURTH BATTLEFRONT—THE WESTERN SEABOARD

After assuming command of the Lamanite forces, Ammoron departed from the eastern campaign and made his way southward along the eastern border, then westward along the southern border. He passed through Antiparah and then turned southward to the city of Nephi, where he informed the queen (his brother's widow) of Amalickiah's death. He then gathered a large number of men, marched to the west coast and attacked there.[731] His stated purpose was "to draw away a part of their forces to that part of the land"[732] to prevent additional reinforcements from being deployed to the battlefronts in the east and south.[733]

At that time the king-men uprising had been put down, and the war along the west sea was intended to continue on where the king-men had left off and thus maintain the distraction from the eastern seaboard and southern border invasions.

FINAL COMMENTS ON THE AMALICKIAH AND AMMORON WAR

The Amalickiah and Ammoron War would be conducted along four separate and independent battlefronts, though never more than three at any one time. It is noted that while there were never more than three battlefronts at any given time, three were active during five of the seven years of the war. See Table 3.0 in Appendix D. Map 6.0 (below) depicts the location where each military thrust was halted.

THE PAGAN ELEMENT IN THE AMALICKIAH
AND AMMORON CONFLICT

The religious affiliation of Amalickiah and Ammoron is not clearly defined following their apostasy from the Church of Christ. The motive, which caused Amalickiah to rise up in rebellion in the land of Zarahemla, was his desire to be king. However, his desire to be king was tied to his desire to achieve a specific goal—to destroy Christianity. Therefore, the first step in his rebellion was apostasy from the Church.

Referring to Alma 1:32, the record indicates that people not in the Church generally practiced idolatry. The term "unbeliever" or "unbelief," as used in the books of Mosiah and Alma,[734] therefore did not refer to a lack of any beliefs, but to specifically not believing in Christ. An example of this is Alma the Younger, who was numbered among the unbelievers, but who practiced idolatry.[735] He thus had pagan beliefs, but was called an unbeliever.

By the same token, Ammoron, when he made his caustic statement to Moroni concerning his non-belief in Jesus Christ, did not mention an opposing religion,[736] but neither did he eliminate a pagan belief as the underlying influence. Furthermore, he retained pagan Zoramites previously chosen by Amalickiah for leadership positions in his army.[737] A close association with the Zoramites is therefore implied and was certainly required in the day-to-day military operations.

A detailed account of the Amalickiah and Ammoron War will not be included in this chapter. For those who are interested, the war is considered in much greater detail in Appendix D, in which the war is divided into one-year periods. The four battlefronts are correlated within each period.

60 BC

MORONI STRENGTHENS THE SOUTHERN BORDER
AND STEPS DOWN FROM HIS POST

The Nephite victory was hard fought, and it came with the loss of many lives and much property. Following the conclusion of the war, Moroni could not rest from his labors until he repaired and further strengthened the defensive cities along the southern border.

[738]Once this work was completed, Moroni handed the leadership of the armies to his son, Moronihah.[739]

At 38 years of age, Moroni had been subjected to continual hardship in the wars, which had been unrelenting and virtually nonstop. He had been seriously wounded—to what extent, we are not told. Now he retired to his home so that he could live out his life in peace. Five years later in 56 BC, he died at the relatively young age of 43.[740]

MORONI'S LEGENDARY ACCOMPLISHMENTS

From the time of his appointment to leadership of all Nephite military operations and throughout his entire career, Moroni had displayed brilliance unequaled in all of Nephite history. His military innovations dramatically raised the standard of Nephite warfare. While Amalickiah was recruiting the forces of evil in his bid to defeat Nephite authority and establish himself as king over the entire land southward, Moroni was expanding the Nephite military presence across the entirety of Nephite lands and establishing a defensive infrastructure throughout for the protection of the armies.

The combination of his superior military talent, exemplary courage, obedience to God, and compassion for his fellowman made Moroni a model for all Nephite citizens, not merely his compatriots in the military. That is exactly how Mormon felt about him near the end of Nephite civilization when he abridged the record of the Nephites.[741] Through his military accomplishments, his total non-compromising obedience to the gospel of Jesus Christ, and his unbending loyalty to the Nephite cause of freedom, Moroni became a true hero of Nephite history—one of the greatest heroes of all.

To label him as a warrior first is to misunderstand his true identity. He was first and foremost a man of God with unwavering integrity and unfailing compassion. Second, he was a great leader of men. Third, he was a military genius. The role he played in Nephite history was dictated by the circumstances of his day, which required that he give the utmost farthing of his ability and dedication in defense of his people. Rising to the mark, he became a Nephite legend.

FINAL REMARKS

The defeat of Amalickiah and Ammoron brought an end to the first of three great challenges against Christian Nephite authority and power in the land of Zarahemla. For a short time, the Nephites would be able to rest and find joy in the peace that thereafter settled upon the land. The following chapter will take advantage of this moment of respite to review the pagan assault that began during the reign of King Benjamin and accelerated rapidly during the period of the judges.

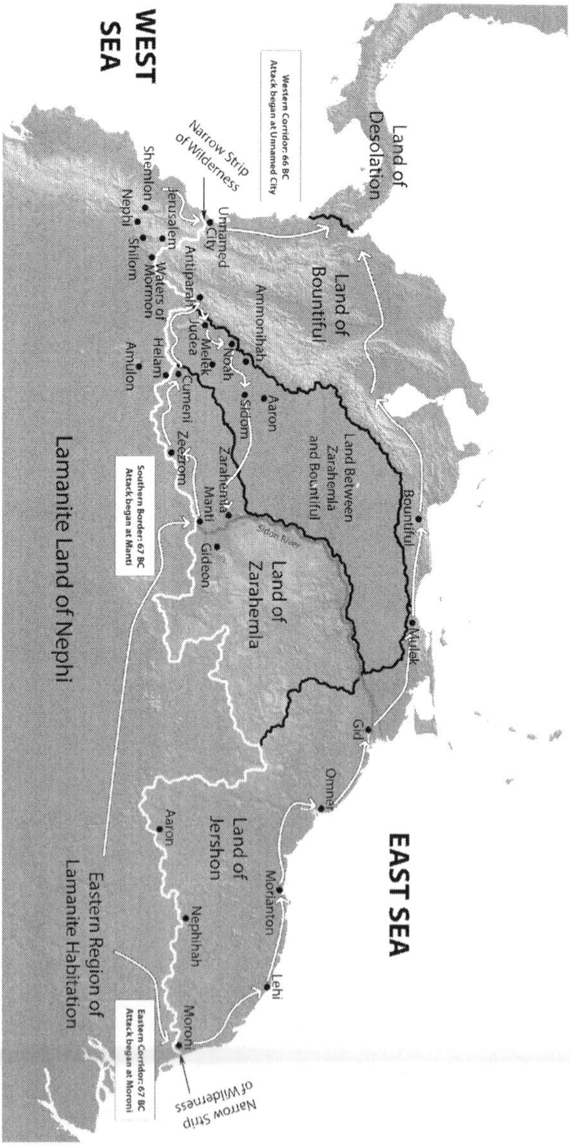

Map 5.0: Amalickiah and Ammoron War. Plan of Attack in 67 BC.

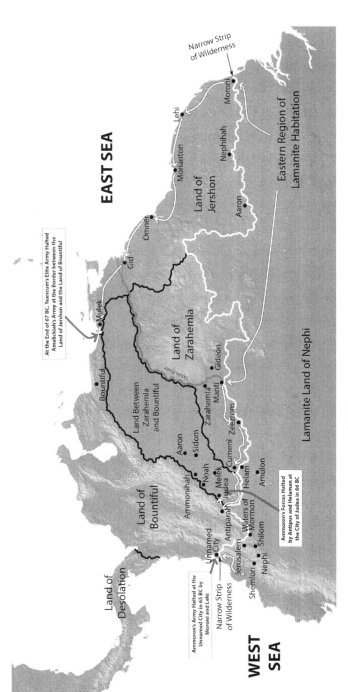

Map 6.0: Amalickiah and Ammoron's Armies. Halted along 3 Lines of Attack between 67 and 65 BC

CHAPTER 2.6

THE HIDDEN WORLD OF THE DISSENTERS

THROUGHOUT THIS BOOK, THE role of dissenters in the frequent Lamanite offensives against the Nephites has been observed. It is quite apparent that Nephite leaders (or in some cases, Mormon as the abridger) may not always have known the full extent of the dissident plots or dissenter interaction with the Lamanites. For example, a Lamanite attack during the reign of King Benjamin occurred at essentially the same time as a serious incident of dissent within the land of Zarahemla.[742] Two other examples are provided in the Book of Mormon of Lamanite armies that arrived at moments of weakness because of internal contention, first during the Amlicite war in 87 BC and later during the king-men disturbance in 67 BC (the invasion of Amalickiah). The Book of Mormon does not link the dissenter and Lamanite factions together in any of the three instances.

ANOTHER REMARKABLE COINCIDENCE

In light of the three previous occurrences, some questions naturally come to mind concerning the series of events that preceded an attack in 51 BC by a Lamanite army sent by Tubaloth, the Lamanite king.[743] The attack took place during the period of political turmoil surrounding the passing of the chief judge Pahoran I. It is apparent that Pahoran died suddenly, because he did not choose a successor. Three of his sons, Pahoran II, Pacumeni, and Paanchi, contended for the judgment seat.

The subsequent election triggered a series of actions and reactions from dissenters, each a little more drastic than the former. When the people had voted to elect Pahoran II as chief judge, Paanchi reacted by attempting to stir up his supporters to rebellion.[744] When the plot was uncovered, the people acted by trying Paanchi and sentencing him to death, whereupon the dissenters reacted by sending a man named Kishkumen to assassinate Pahoran.[745] The people acted again[746] by establishing an investigative probe, which uncovered some of the individuals involved in the assassination, and they were put to death.[747]

In a further action, Pahoran's brother Pacumeni was elected to fill the empty chief judge seat, "and it was according to his right."[748] He was the only remaining son of Pahoran who had sought office. Unlike Paanchi, he had shown respect for the process of law and supported his brother when he was initially appointed.

Certainly at this point, the dissidents were in no position to challenge Pacumeni's right by lineage to the judgment seat for two apparent reasons. First, they had already failed in their bid to win an election, even in support of a legitimate heir to the position. Second, their entire movement was under investigation because of the assassination of Pahoran. Without doubt, they were afraid to draw any attention to themselves for fear of being implicated in the crime.

Though Paanchi had been executed and Pacumeni had taken office, the murder of Pahoran had not been solved. There was considerable tension in the city of Zarahemla, especially considering the fact that the supporters of Paanchi constituted a significant portion of the people of Zarahemla, enough so that they had expected to win the election. The leaders of his supporters were unable to respond to the latest actions of the government, and they were seething with rage, having gained nothing from all their efforts. No doubt they were desperate to find a solution to their dilemma. The immediate resolution came from a most unexpected source.

CORIANTUMR'S ATTACK IN THE CENTER OF THE LAND—COINCIDENCE VERSUS CONSPIRACY

In the beginning of 51 BC, a Lamanite army came down against the Nephites. The army was commanded by one Coriantumr, a dissenter from the Nephites. It was a demonstration of immaculate timing that coincided perfectly with the internal dissent. Coriantumr was sent by Tubaloth, the son of the Nephite dissenter Ammoron, who had succeeded his father as king of the Lamanites.

Coriantumr passed between the fortified cities at the perimeter of the land, where Moronihah[749] had stationed his greatest forces, and marched to the very center of the land of Zarahemla. In other words, he ignored the danger of being trapped inside the land of Zarahemla. He made a beeline for the city of Zarahemla where the contention was taking place.

Because of the internal dissension, and because such a brash move was not anticipated, the city of Zarahemla was not prepared for defense against a Lamanite army. The guards at the entrance into the city[750] were cut down, and Coriantumr took control of the city, killing all who opposed him. Chief Judge Pacumeni fled to the outer wall of the city, where he was trapped and slain by Coriantumr. Many Nephites were cast into prison.[751] To imprison, rather than kill them, seems to suggest a political purpose for the Lamanite attack, likely in concert with Paanchi's supporters.

It is projected that the perfect timing of Coriantumr's attack occurred because intelligence was provided to Tubaloth from inside the land of Zarahemla in a similar fashion to the correspondence in 62 BC between Pachus, the leader of the king-men, and Tubaloth's father, Ammoron.[752] This would explain why Coriantumr would cast caution to the wind and march his army into the center of the land to be surrounded by the Nephite armies. Perhaps he thought there would be more support from the dissenters. Perhaps the dissenters in their desperation were impulsive and reckless in requesting assistance from sending out an invitation to the Lamanites.

CORIANTUMR'S MARCH IDENTIFIES THE DIRECTION OF THE CITY OF BOUNTIFUL FROM THE CITY OF ZARAHEMLA

Placement of the city of Bountiful to the north of Zarahemla is determined by Coriantumr's march northward from the city of Zarahemla in the direction of the city.[753] His army was halted by Lehi's army before they reached the southern border of the land of Bountiful.[754]

LOOKING AT THE LARGER PICTURE

Considering Coriantumr's attack in connection with the three previous coincidences, sufficient evidence has now accumulated to warrant a closer look at the entire history of Lamanite attacks up

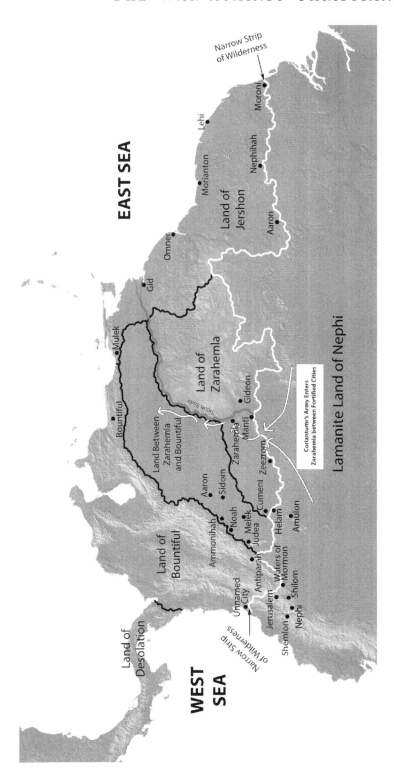

EAST SEA

Narrow Strip of Wilderness

Moroni

Lehi

Morianton

Nephihah

Land of Jershon

Omner

Aaron

Gid

Mulek

Land of Zarahemla

Bountiful

Sidon River

Gideon

Land Between Zarahemla and Bountiful

Manti

Zarahemla

Lamanite Land of Nephi

Cumeni

Zeezrom

Coriantumr's Army Enters Zarahemla between Fortified Cities

Aaron

Sidom

Land of Bountiful

Ammonihah

Noah

Melek

Judea

Helam

Cumeni

Amulon

Antiparah

Waters of Mormon

Shilom

Nephi

Unnamed City

Jerusalem

Shemlon

Narrow Strip of Wilderness

Land of Desolation

WEST SEA

Map 7.0: 51 BC—Coriantumr's Attack In the Center of the Land of Zarahemla to this point in the Book of Mormon. Between *ca.* 200 and 50 BC there were six separate episodes of warfare. Table 3.0 in Appendix D lists each war and supplies an identifying name, the exact or approximate year, and other pertinent information.

Only one Lamanite attack occurred during the entire period of the kings in Zarahemla. The attack occurred during King Benjamin's reign occurred only after many years of peace in the land of Zarahemla. It was followed by a comparable period of peace before the next Lamanite attack, which did not occur until the fifth year of the reign of the judges.[755] Given such long periods between the Lamanite attacks, the mention of dissenters in each case points to a strong likelihood that the two actions were closely related.

It is therefore concluded that in each case the Lamanites attacked the Nephites after being stirred up by the dissenters. If correct, then this tradition of bringing in the Lamanites to achieve dissenter objectives was considered to be the most important weapon in their arsenal, one that they never failed to utilize. Lamanite attack never occurred spontaneously without dissenter involvement. In every case, other than the destruction of the city of Ammonihah,[756] activities were coordinated between dissenters in the land of Zarahemla and Lamanites within the land of Nephi, many times unbeknownst to the Nephite government, or to the writers of the Book of Mormon.

Consider the following:

- Prior to the internal contention and war described in Words of Mormon, there had previously been no warfare during the reign of King Benjamin and no warfare during the reign of his father, King Mosiah I. An approximate 50-year period of peace had preceded the Lamanite attack. Was it a coincidence that the internal dissent and external attack occurred in the same context?

- After the internal contention and war described in Words of Mormon, there were no further attacks during the reign of King Benjamin. There were no attacks during the subsequent 30-year reign of King Mosiah II. Five years into the reign of the judges (87 BC), Amlici rebelled against the new democratic government established by Mosiah II and started a civil war. The Amlicite War thus took place after an approximately 60-year period of peace. Was it a bizarre coincidence that the first Lamanite army to invade the land of Zarahemla in 60 years arrived on the second day of the Amlicite War?

- In 67 BC, when Amalickiah led a Lamanite army down to Zarahemla from the highlands of Nephi, it had been five years since his first attack. Was it purely by chance that his second attack coincided precisely with a change in government leadership and the related unrest of the king-men?

- In 51 BC, when Tubaloth sent Coriantumr into the center of the land, it had been ten years since the previous war with Amalickiah and Ammoron had ended, and two years since a dissenter incited Lamanite army had attacked the southern border of Zarahemla.[757] Was it coincidental that the attack occurred immediately following the execution of Pacumeni for the assassination of Pahoran II?

These corresponding events seem to go far beyond the range of coincidence. It is projected that in all four instances, the initial Lamanite attack against the Nephites was a coordinated effort between dissenters in Zarahemla and their pagan allies in the land of Nephi.

THE FOUNDATIONS OF SECRECY

Looking back to *ca.* 100 BC, King Mosiah issued a proclamation at that time forbidding religious persecution.[758] Afterward, it became a violation of the law to engage in any type of persecution, whether against pagan or Christian religion.[759] As a result, the pagan dissent movement, which had been openly committed to the destruction of the Church of Christ,[760] of necessity became a secretive movement. Prior to their conversion to Christianity, Alma the Younger and the sons of Mosiah were for an undisclosed period of time drawn to the pagan cause and became actively engaged in the secret plan of destruction.[761]

Long before King Mosiah established the unprecedented democratic form of government among the Nephites, the pagan religion of Nehor was already established. As outlined in Chapter 2.3, "The Order of the Nehors" was practiced by the Mulekites when first discovered by the people of Mosiah. Later, it was apparently introduced to the Lamanites by the Amalekites when they dissented away from the Nephites, for they were practicing it in the Lamanite city of Jerusalem when Aaron preached the gospel there in 91 BC.[762]

Its establishment in the land of Zarahemla as a church, only shortly after Alma became the chief judge,[763] signaled a more organized pagan identity—a direct response to the Church of God, which had been introduced into Zarahemla 30 years previously.[764] During the fifth year of the reign of the judges, the order of Nehor, under the leadership of Amlici, launched the first violent pagan attack against the Nephite government since the reign of King Benjamin.[765] Though it began as a legitimate political movement, in reality it was a subversive movement from the very beginning, which merely used the new democratic process as a vehicle to implement their plan to seize control and eliminate the free government that made such activities possible. Their real intent was exposed when they lost the election, and their hatred immediately sprang forth in unrestrained violence.

Once the pagan dissenters focused their attention on the destruction of the new democratic government,[766] largely every activity became criminal in nature. Following the Amlicite War, success depended upon the elements of deceit, secrecy, and surprise. Learning from the Amlici disaster, first the order of Nehor (83 BC) and subsequently the cult of the Zoramites (75 BC) congregated in the borders of Nephite lands, where they could plot the overthrow of the free government in complete secrecy and more easily access the Lamanite military machine.

Generally, dissenters maintained a facade of pretended personal, sacred convictions and grievances, since a man could not be punished for his own beliefs.[767] Presumably, they were dedicated to the pursuit of setting right the wrongs of the established government. In this manner, they worked to attain the support of sympathetic Nephites. However, once an individual was brought into the inner chambers of dissent (as in the case of Alma the Younger and the sons of Mosiah prior to their conversion to the gospel), he became aware of a well-organized movement, of which secrecy was the most important and dominant aspect.

In 91 BC, the first year of the judges, the pagans immediately began to recognize in the democratic form of government an opportunity to attain political power, which would enable them to destroy Christianity. This is illustrated by Amlici's political aspirations only five years into the reign of the judges. By that time the dissenters had already become much more open in their intentions than they had been during the reign of the kings, especially after being forcefully subdued by King Benjamin, and by King Mosiah II near the end when he issued his proclamation.

However, they finally learned, after the defeat of both Amlici and the king-men, that even under the rule of the free government they must return to the more secretive methods employed during the latter part of King Mosiah's reign. The movement quickly evolved in that direction, especially after the king-men debacle, when the people became fully aware of their sinister goals and murderous disposition. Furthermore, following the Amalickiah and Ammoron War, any movement to re-establish monarchy may have been outlawed.[768] Therefore, the dissenters relinquished their monarchist approach and began to give the appearance of working within the framework of the law. By 51 BC, the stage was fully set for the rise of Gadianton, the mastermind who would take dissent secrecy to a new level.

TABLE 2.0

NEPHITE WARS IN ZARAHEMLA THROUGH 51 BC

Number	Name/ Description	Time (BC)	Dissenters Involved	Source of Dissent
1	King Benjamin's Defense	*ca.* 150	Unknown— Possibly Amaleki: order of Nehor	Land of Zarahemla
2	Amlicite War	87	order of Nehor: Amlici	Land of Zarahemla
3	The Nehor War	81–77	order of Nehor: Amulonites, Amalekites	Land of Nephi

Number	Name/ Description	Time (BC)	Dissenters Involved	Source of Dissent
4	Zoramite War	74	Zoramites	Land of Zarahemla
5	Amalickiah/ Ammoron War	73–60	Amalickiah, Ammoron	Land of Zarahemla
6	Tubaloth/ Coriantumr War	51	Supporters of Paanchi	Land of Zarahemla

PART 3

NEPHITE GEOGRAPHY
(589–51 BC)

INTRODUCTION

As DESCRIBED IN THE Book of Mormon, Nephite geography was limited exclusively to the land southward throughout the entire period from 589 to 55 BC. Prior to their *ca.* 200 BC journey from the land of Nephi into the unknown, the Nephites had been completely hemmed in on the north, east, and south by a great wilderness. This wilderness dominated both the Nephites and the Lamanites to the degree that it prevented them from even being aware of the land northward prior to the Nephite merger with the Mulekites.

In contrast, the Mulekites had inhabited the land northward for almost 400 years before they were discovered by the Nephites. This can be seen clearly in the fact that many Mulekites bore Jaredite names and practiced Jaredite idolatry. However, in *ca.* 200 BC, when encountered by the Nephites, they were not in the land northward. Instead, they were distributed along the banks of the Sidon River within the land southward.

Mulekite history and geography within the land northward is never provided in the Book of Mormon. The only provided information about the Mulekite past concerns the fact that Mulek was a descendant of King Zedekiah of Judah, who had journeyed with family and friends to the Western Hemisphere after the fall of Jerusalem. This information is coupled with the fact that they had lived in the Land of Desolation within the land northward and had cared for Coriantumr, the last survivor of the Jaredites, during the last nine months of his life. It follows that after his death, they migrated from the land northward into the land southward. Only after arriving at the Sidon River were they discovered by the people of Mosiah.

It was not until 55 BC, approximately 150 years after the merger of the Mulekite and Nephite cultures that the land northward for the first time became a part of Nephite history. At that time, many Nephites journeyed out of the land southward and lived in the land northward for the last 88 years of the pre-Christ period, (55 BC–AD 34). The Book of Mormon is essentially silent, however, concerning the history of the land northward during that period. Based on the available geographic information, a map of the Nephite pre-Christ period in the land northward cannot be drawn—it is simply a land without form extending northward from the narrow neck of land. On the other hand, the geography of the land southward is provided in great detail, as will be shown in succeeding chapters.

CHAPTER 3.1

THE LAND OF ZARAHEMLA—RECENTLY SETTLED

CA. 200 BC

WHEN THE MULEKITES (THE people of Zarahemla) were discovered by the people of Mosiah, they had arrived at the Sidon River only shortly before the Nephites. This can be concluded from the simple fact that Zarahemla, their current leader, had led them from the land of Desolation into the south wilderness.[769] It was the same wilderness that had been reserved by the Jaredites as a hunting preserve.[770] In the Nephite perspective, it was the same body of wilderness that had bordered the Nephite city of Nephi to the north and east, while they had remained in the land of Nephi (587 to *ca.* 200 BC).

Prior to being settled by the Mulekites and Nephites, this expansive wilderness extended from sea to sea and, in general, was the same region that ultimately would comprise the greater Nephite lands of Zarahemla. However, it also extended southward of future Nephite lands into what would ultimately become Lamanite lands, extending eastward from the city of Nephi until it reached the east sea. The relative brevity of Mulekite habitation in the land of Zarahemla prior to the Nephite arrival is further demonstrated by the following conditions:

THE CITY OF ZARAHEMLA WAS SURROUNDED BY WILDERNESS

Little if any progress had been made in settling and developing the land when the Nephites arrived in *ca.* 200 BC, in spite of the fact that the Mulekites had a large population, outnumbering the Nephites. The account of the Nephite war with the Amlicites in 87 BC[771] reveals the limited extent of settlement of the region surrounding the city of Zarahemla that still existed more than

100 years after the Nephite and Mulekite merger. Other than the city of Zarahemla, no cities are identified in the account. The city of Gideon, which would soon be located less than a day's travel eastward of Zarahemla, had not been established in the valley of Gideon. It is first identified in a subsequent account of Alma's missionary travels four years later (83 BC).[772]

To the south of the city of Zarahemla, none of the perimeter cities[773] had been established. When the Nephites defeated the Amlicites, Alma sent spies to follow them "that he might know of their plans and their plots."[774] They returned the following day in great fear and astonishment to report that the Amlicites had joined with an army of the Lamanites "in the land of Minon," a small farming community "above the land of Zarahemla,[775] in the course of the land Nephi."[776] The land of Manti, which by 81 BC was located at the headwaters of the Sidon River,[777] was not mentioned at that time and apparently was not yet established. By 66 BC, Manti would become a fortified city and the first point of defense against Lamanite armies coming into the land of Zarahemla at the headwaters of the Sidon River.[778]

As the scouts reported to Alma, the Lamanites had come into the land of Minon. They had observed the people of Minon fleeing with their flocks in the direction of "our city."[779] The Nephites immediately "took their tents, and departed out of the valley of Gideon towards their city, which was the city of Zarahemla,"[780] From these observations, it is concluded that Zarahemla was the only city in 87 BC.

The Nephites defeated the combined Amlicite and Lamanite forces and drove them into Hermounts, an expansive wilderness filled with wild and ravenous beasts that bordered the city of Zarahemla, both on the north and west.[781] Thus, more than a century after Mosiah's arrival, settlement remained sparse within less than a day's travel eastward of the city of Zarahemla, and non-existent on the north and west. Nephite settlement at that time was principally along the Sidon River from the city of Zarahemla all the way to the land of Minon at the southern border of the land where the city of Manti would later be located. There was no city to the south of Zarahemla. All was farmland, as described in Alma 3:2.

OTHER REGIONAL NEPHITE LANDS: UNINHABITED WILDERNESS IN 87 BC

The heartland region of Zarahemla was one of four major Nephite regions, which, after 72 BC, would constitute the lands of Zarahemla. As outlined previously, habitation of the land of Zarahemla was remarkably limited in area in 87 BC, though more than 100 years had passed since the arrival of the Nephites. In contrast, however, the other three regional lands, identified in later accounts as Bountiful, Jershon, and the land lying between the lands of Zarahemla and Bountiful, would remain uninhabited wilderness until sudden major changes would take place between 77 and 60 BC. The development of each land, as provided in the Book of Mormon, is outlined below.

Bountiful: The land of Bountiful, comprising the northernmost region of the land southward, was completely uninhabited when the Nephites arrived in Zarahemla. The Mulekites had previously passed through Bountiful when they migrated from the land northward to the location where the Nephites discovered them. In 121 BC, approximately 85 years after the arrival of the Nephites, no change had occurred, as indicated by the travels of the 43 men sent by Limhi to find Zarahemla.[782] The search party became lost and wandered across the land of Bountiful into the land northward and back to the land of Nephi without encountering human habitation.

The first reference to Nephite habitation in the land of Bountiful is found in Alma chapter 22 and is included in the account of Mosiah's sons' mission to the Lamanites,[783] which account was entered into the Nephite record after 77 BC. It is a general geographical comment made by Mormon to describe Bountiful and identify its importance in matters of defense. It does not refer to a specific time or event.

The second reference to the land of Bountiful refers to the period from 72 to 67 BC, during which defensive cities were established at intervals along the east coast to seal off the Lamanites and Nephite dissenters from the land northward,[784] and Nephites were encouraged to occupy the cities and the regions surrounding them. Again, it is a statement of the importance of the land of Bountiful, as pertaining to Nephite military defense. It gives no information concerning the settlement or Nephite habitation of Bountiful.

One other reference to Nephites living in Bountiful is given in connection with the account of Morianton's flight toward the land northward in 68 BC.[785] Alma 50:32 refers to Moroni's fears that the people in the land of Bountiful might be persuaded to join with Morianton in rebellion against the Nephites. It was a cause of great concern to Moroni, particularly at that time, when Amalickiah was threatening to attack from the south. Though a general reference is made to Nephite habitation of Bountiful, no specific statements are provided as to the degree of habitation.

Unnamed Land between Zarahemla and Bountiful: Two references are provided in the Book of Mormon pertaining to a land never identified by name that was sandwiched in between the land of Zarahemla and the land of Bountiful, lying to the northwest of Zarahemla and to the southeast of Bountiful. It is first referenced in 35 BC, when the Lamanites invaded the Nephites with such great force that the Nephites were forced to evacuate all of their lands in the land southward.[786] As they fled in the direction of the narrow neck of land, they passed through the unidentified land and into the land of Bountiful.[787] Its position between the land of Zarahemla and the land of Bountiful places it in essentially the same location as the wilderness of Hermounts, the wilderness that was "infested by wild and ravenous beasts" in 87 BC,[788] when it was identified in the Book of Mormon account during the Amlicite War.

The second reference to the land between Zarahemla and Bountiful occurred in AD 17 when the Nephites congregated in the land southward to defend themselves against the Gadianton robbers. "And the land which was appointed was the land of Zarahemla, and the land which was between the land Zarahemla and the land Bountiful, yea, to the line which was between the land Bountiful and the land Desolation."[789] The three lands likely formed a wide corridor, which extended from the southern boundary of Zarahemla at Manti to the coastal city of Bountiful on the north, and from the cities of Ammonihah and Noah[790] on the west to the city of Gideon on the east.[791] By AD 17, it was located at the center of the most densely populated Nephite region, which Lachoneus I chose for the gathering of Nephites from all across the land southward and from the land northward.

Jershon: The land of Jershon, which stretched southward along the eastern seaboard from Bountiful on the north to the borders of the Lamanite land of Nephi on the south, was not inhabited when the Nephites arrived in Zarahemla in *ca.* 200 BC. It remained uninhabited wilderness until 77 BC, at which time the Nephites allowed the people of Ammon to settle there.[792] Moroni's establishment of a series of fortified cities along the eastern seaboard in 72 BC would encourage Nephites to settle there from that time forward.

THE PEOPLE OF MOSIAH—THE DOMINANT CULTURE

Amaleki listed several important factors in the book of Omni pertaining to the initial interaction of the people of Mosiah and the people of Zarahemla that indicate the people of Zarahemla were absorbed into a dominant Nephite culture:

- They were taught in the language of the Nephites and not vice versa.[793]

- They were illiterate. After learning the Nephite language, Zarahemla gave a genealogy of his ancestors "according to his memory."[794] Thus, for his most important personal information, he had to rely on his memory. The fact that he had no written materials indicates he was illiterate. His genealogy was recorded, not by Zarahemla, but by the Nephites in the large plate of Nephi. The erudition of the Nephites, in sharp contrast to the illiteracy of the Mulekites, alone would elevate the Nephites' status above the people of Zarahemla.

- The people of Zarahemla "denied the being of their Creator."[795] Had there been significant resistance to Nephite dominance, the people of Mosiah would have continued on their journey in search of an uninhabited region. They would never have subjected themselves to the idolatrous people of Zarahemla, who denied the existence of Christ.[796]

- At the merger of the two cultures, Mosiah was appointed to be their king,[797] signifying the initial willingness of the people of Zarahemla to be ruled by the minority party. However, the

Mulekites had no real choice at that time, for Zarahemla was not qualified to be a ruler when compared to the learned and competent Nephite king. Zarahemla's acquiescence to Mosiah's rule may also have resulted from his conversion to the gospel.

The land of Zarahemla became the kingdom of Mosiah I,[798] in spite of the fact that the people of Zarahemla already had possession when he arrived. Thereafter, the people of Zarahemla were "numbered with the Nephites."[799] This, however, was an exclusively political assessment related to their adoption into the Nephite kingdom to become subjects of King Mosiah. Culturally, they remained distinct from the people of Nephi as an ethnic group.

This cultural separation is alluded to approximately 76 years later in 124 BC when the people were gathered to hear King Benjamin's last address.[800] It can also be observed in clarity approximately 80 years later during the reign of Mosiah II, in the public gathering of 120 BC to celebrate the arrival of the people of Limhi and the people of Alma.[801] The Nephites[802] and the Mulekites gathered for the festivities in two separate bodies.[803]

Nephite dominance and control of government continued throughout the reign of the kings and into the period of the judges, as illustrated by the appointment of Alma (a Nephite) as the first chief judge of the Nephites.[804] However, the reign of the judges was not a period of peace and tranquility. Severe challenges to Christian Nephite rule emerged frequently as the countdown continued to the birth of Jesus Christ, and His subsequent appearance among the Nephites.[805]

CHAPTER 3.2

ALMA TEACHES THE GEOGRAPHY OF THE WILDERNESS TO THE LAMANITES

CA. 120 BC

A DENSE AND SEEMINGLY UNENDING wilderness separated the land of Nephi from the land of Helam. As the Lamanites and priests of Noah wandered through the deep forest, they were lost in an incomprehensible tangle of vegetation, which was interrupted only by intermittent streams and perhaps by occasional geologic variation. Perhaps there were frequent marshlands as well, which had to be circumvented so as to travel on dry ground and reduce the danger to the traveler. For the uninformed, the streams and marshland would have presented nothing more than obstacles to travel.

For the informed, rivers and streams might have served as signposts that could direct the traveler to higher and drier ground. Such was the case for Alma, who through revelation from God had deciphered the physical blueprint that lay stretched out between Helam and the Waters of Mormon.

Unlike Mosiah I, who had the benefit of the Liahona when making the first journey from Nephi to Zarahemla,[806] Alma had to appeal directly to the source of the Liahona's power. Whereas Mosiah had simply followed the pointers to find his way to the Lord's appointed location, Alma was likely taught the physical geographical indicators that could be utilized again and again and could be passed on to others. Therefore, when the Lamanites promised peace and liberation to him and his people if he would show them the way to Nephi, he immediately commenced to fulfill his part of the agreement by directing them out of Helam in the direction of city of Nephi.[807]

It is apparent simply in the fact that Alma could find his way through the seemingly trackless wilderness and give concise directions to the Lamanites that the keys to navigating the ambiguous course were observable physical features, which he had previously identified and could teach to others. Undoubtedly, Alma informed the Lamanites of essential observable keys, which they could then utilize to negotiate the wilderness, because they left him in Helam and made the journey without him.

Alma hoped they would honor the agreement they had made with him. However, after he had provided the required information, the Lamanites showed their true character, especially under the influence of dissenters—in this case Amulon and his priests. They failed to honor the agreement, and "set guards round about the land of Helam, over Alma and his brethren."[808] After successfully arriving in Nephi, they sent a part of their army back to Helam. They also sent the families of the guards that had been left in Helam, which plainly revealed the permanency of their intentions.

FURTHER GEOGRAPHICAL CONSIDERATIONS

The geographical implications of the interactions of the Lamanites with the people of Limhi, the Amulonites, and the people of Alma are outlined as follows: In their pursuit of the people of Limhi, the Lamanites had become lost after two days in the wilderness, whereupon they wandered around for an unknown period of time before stumbling upon the Amulonites. They took the Amulonites with them and wandered on. It is recalled that for Alma, Helam was a distance of eight days travel from the land of Nephi. Therefore, when the party of Lamanites and Amulonites arrived in Helam, the Lamanites had traveled at least six days farther from the land of Nephi[809] after becoming lost. While Helam lay along the rather straight course between the Waters of Mormon and the headwaters of the Sidon River, the location of Amulon cannot be ascertained with any certainty. It might have been somewhere between two and eight days away from Nephi, but it was likely in a different direction, or the people of Alma might have encountered the Amulonites when first migrating to Helam.

When the Amulonites had kidnapped the Lamanite daughters, they had simply fled in haste into the wilderness, wandering without any sense of direction until they felt safe from the searches of the Lamanites. They did not know the way from Amulon to the city of Nephi. Therefore, they were as disoriented as the Lamanites. After they joined in the search, nothing changed, and the two parties continued their wanderings. Only after Alma informed them of the route and the essential elements required to travel from Helam to Nephi were they able to navigate the wilderness.

It seems reasonable that by utilizing the sun as their guide, if nothing else, the Lamanite and Amulonite party might have at least traveled in the general direction of Nephi after losing the people of Limhi's trail. However, once lost in the wilderness, they had traveled in exactly the opposite direction. In the morning, for instance, they traveled eastward toward the rising sun, whereas they should have traveled westward away from the sun to move in the direction of Nephi, or toward the west sea.

Their disorientation may be an indication of the density of the forests through which they traveled. It is possible the sun could not be seen overhead due to a thick and unbroken canopy of trees that shrouded the sun and created a world of eternal twilight. Perhaps, however, it was due simply to a perpetual cloud cover that obscured the sun and prevented them from maintaining their orientation. It may have been a combination of both conditions, exacerbated by frequent rainfall, which likely had obliterated the people of Limhi's trail through the wilderness.

THE DISTANCE FROM NEPHI TO ZARAHEMLA

Alma's two-part journey from Nephi to Zarahemla, of which the first leg took place in ca. 145 BC and the second in ca. 120 BC, is the best gauge of the actual distance between the two lands. While it would be easier and more precise to calculate the distance if the rate of travel in units of linear distance per unit of time (for example, miles per hour) and the hours of travel per day were known, there are three general aspects of the journey that enable one to reasonably project the distance involved, if compared to similar documented modes and rates of travel prior to the modern era.[810] These characteristics are listed as follows:

- The precise length of the journey is provided in terms of days, consisting of eight days from Nephi to Helam[811] and 12 days from Helam to Zarahemla,[812] for a total of 20 days.

- The journey of the people of Alma represents the nearest thing to a straight-line route of any such passage that is recorded in the Book of Mormon, which is suggested by the fact that the Lord guided Alma.[813] Their relatively direct route is verified by the fact that Ammon, who had no flocks and no women and children, required 40 days to traverse the same wilderness on his way to find the people of Zeniff.[814]

- It is revealed that the people of Alma moved with all due haste on both legs of the journey because, in each case, an army was in pursuit. On the first leg of the journey, the Lord strengthened them that the army of King Noah could not overtake them.[815] The same is likely true of the second leg, though the army of the Lamanites was stopped by the hand of the Lord in the Valley of Alma, which was only one day out of Helam. [816]

Assuming the people of Alma averaged somewhere between 10 and 30 miles per day in a relatively straight course, the distance between the city of Nephi and the city of Zarahemla was somewhere between 200 and 600 miles. Considering the heightened pace, as described in the book of Mosiah, the rate of travel per day is projected to be closer to the average of 25 miles per day for travel in the pre-modern age,[817] and the total distance is therefore projected to be about 500 miles.

THE WILDERNESS REGIONS OF THE LAND SOUTHWARD

I N CHAPTER 1.3, IT was observed that in about 200 BC, when the people of Mosiah migrated from Nephi to Zarahemla, one of the most dominant aspects of their journey was the dense wilderness through which they traveled.[818] A wilderness hundreds of miles across separated the land of Nephi from the land of Zarahemla, considering the limited highland configuration of Nephi at that time.

When the Nephites arrived, though it is not plainly revealed in the Book of Mormon, Zarahemla consisted of nothing more than a Mulekite settlement on the Sidon River, engulfed on all sides by uninhabited wilderness. Immediately to the north and west of the settlement lay a wilderness called Hermounts, "which was infested by wild and ravenous beasts."[819] Soon the Nephites would learn that beyond Hermounts lay a wilderness called Bountiful, which extended to a narrow neck of land leading into a land northward, where the Mulekites had lived for almost four centuries. The Mulekites had recently passed through Bountiful and Hermounts before arriving at the Sidon River.

As outlined in Chapter 3.1, the land of Zarahemla remained confined to the Sidon River Valley for more than 100 years following the Nephite arrival. (See Appendix A, Maps A-2 and A-3.) Thus, for many years, Nephite perception of the new land would be limited to the immediate vicinity surrounding the city of Zarahemla. When expansion of Nephite lands did occur, however, it would happen quickly. Over a six-year period from 72 to 67 BC, the borders of the land of Zarahemla would be expanded to extend from the east sea to the west sea and encompass all lands between the narrow strip of wilderness on the south and the narrow neck of land on the north. (See Appendix A, Map A-6.)

BOOK OF MORMON GEOGRAPHY—A
SECONDARY TOPIC OF DISCUSSION

The prophet Mormon did not set out to specifically or formally define the geography of Nephite lands, but through the accounts of various migrations, expeditions, wars, and missions, a definite picture begins to emerge. With each account, a new piece of the Zarahemla geographic puzzle is provided. For example, in the account of Alma's mission to the city of Ammonihah in 82 BC, it is stated that Ammonihah was located to the west of the city of Zarahemla and bordered on the west wilderness.[820] In the account of the Nehor Wars,[821] an east wilderness is identified for the first time.[822] Through the 77 BC settlement of the people of Anti-Nephi-Lehi in the land of Zarahemla, Jershon is first identified as occupying the wilderness to the east of Zarahemla and extending along the eastern seaboard from Bountiful on the north to the Lamanite border on the south. Lamanite troop movements in the Zoramite War of 74 BC illustrate the condition that the southern edge of Jershon was lined by wilderness, which was utilized by the combined Zoramite and Lamanite army to move undetected from Jershon on the east to the city of Manti in the center of the land.[823]

On the north, the wilderness of Bountiful stretched from the east sea to the west sea and extended northward to a narrow neck of land that served both to separate the land southward from the land northward, and to provide the only land bridge between the two landmasses.[824] This information is given in relation to Nephite attempts to hem in the Lamanites that they might not gain access to the land northward.[825] Enough information is provided for each of the major components of Nephite geography in the land southward to paint a rather complete picture. In this chapter, information on the primary components is gathered and integrated.

THE ELUSIVE PASSAGEWAY BETWEEN NEPHI AND ZARAHEMLA

Because King Mosiah I was led by the "arm" of God,[826] the Nephites likely took a straight course to Zarahemla. However, notwithstanding the fact that two return expeditions[827] were immediately undertaken, specific physical identifiers of the course between Nephi and Zarahemla were never understood at that time. King Mosiah may have known the identifiers for, like Alma the Elder two generations later,[828] he led the expedition through revelation from God.[829] However, King Mosiah had the Liahona, which pointed the way through the wilderness, whereas Alma did not. Therefore, it was not necessary that Mosiah learn the route—he could simply follow the pointer.

Zeniff participated in both expeditions back to Nephi, the first of which was a round trip that brought his party back to Zarahemla, traveling through the wilderness in both directions.[830] On the second expedition, Zeniff was still uncertain about the way to go, though it was his fourth trip between Nephi and Zarahemla.[831] Only "after many days' wandering in the wilderness"[832] did he and his followers finally arrive back in Nephi.

Zeniff was given permission by Laman, the Lamanite king,[833] to dwell in the land of Nephi. The king ordered his people out of the lands surrounding the cities of Nephi and Shilom. The people of Zeniff took possession of the two cities, immediately commencing the work of repairing the perimeter walls and constructing new buildings.[834] For three generations, they lived in the land of Nephi, maintaining a voluntary separation from the Nephites in Zarahemla. Zeniff had no interest in returning to Zarahemla, and in time (certainly after the passing of the first generation—consisting of those who took part in the journey) even his more or less cursory understanding of the geographical relationship between Nephi and Zarahemla was lost.

Meanwhile in Zarahemla, during the reigns of Mosiah I and King Benjamin, no effort was made to return to the land of Nephi. The Nephites had no desire to reestablish any contact with the Lamanites. In fact, they hoped the wilderness would forever remain a barrier to Lamanite assault. Throughout that period, they avoided learning anything about the wilderness separating them from Nephi.

In 121 BC, more than 80 years after the discovery of Zarahemla, King Mosiah's grandson, also Mosiah, sent an expedition of 16 strong men, led by Ammon, to the land of Nephi.[835] The purpose of the expedition was to learn the fate of the people of Zeniff.[836] Not knowing "the course they should travel in the wilderness," Ammon's party wandered for 40 days before finally arriving in the vicinity of the city of Nephi.[837] The complete isolation between the two regions during the intervening years is vividly illustrated by the fact that neither Ammon's party nor Limhi's party of 43, which only shortly before had failed in an attempt to find the land of Zarahemla,[838] knew the route from one land to the other.

Only through subsequent expeditions between the city of Zarahemla and the city of Nephi[839] did the Nephites finally identify the easiest and most direct course to travel. First, Ammon returned to Zarahemla with the people of Limhi[840] in the latter portion of 121 BC.[841] Next, and more importantly, the people of Alma the Elder took their turn through the same wilderness, arriving in Zarahemla in about 120 BC.[842] The total time required for Alma and his followers to journey from Nephi to Zarahemla was only 20 days, which may have been record time.[843]

AT LAST, THE PASSAGEWAY IS DEFINED! THE NARROW STRIP OF WILDERNESS

In about 90 BC, the sons of Mosiah were the first Nephites to

- Explicitly identify the best route of passage between Nephi and Zarahemla.

- Comprehend the full extent of the geography of the land southward.

- Identify the major geographical feature that physically divided Nephite and Lamanite lands.

This information is recorded in Alma chapter 22. The comprehensive geographic information was assimilated by them, partly through knowledge obtained from former travelers, such as Alma the Elder, Gideon, Limhi, Ammon (a descendant of Zarahemla), and possibly Alma the Younger, who may have been born in the land of Helam. More than likely, however, it came largely from information received through interaction with the Lamanites during their fourteen-year mission, synthesized through personal observation as they moved from city to city and land to land, teaching the gospel.

When the sons of Mosiah journeyed to Nephi at the beginning of their mission, the Lamanites thoroughly understood the geographic keys to the passageway between the two lands. Alma the Elder had first shown them the way from Helam to Nephi only 30 years previously (121 BC).[844] Until then, they had avoided the wilderness due to its inherent dangers and the fact that venturing into it almost certainly meant getting lost.[845] There is only one recorded instance of a Lamanite army coming down to the land of Zarahemla prior to 87 BC,[846] which occurred during King Benjamin's reign.[847] The army's journey to Zarahemla likely resembled Ammon's 40 days of wandering, rather than Alma's relatively straight-line journey of 20 days.

As previously observed in Chapter 3.2, geographical understanding of a discernible route from Nephi to Helam changed the Lamanite perspective of the wilderness. No longer did they see it as an unintelligible mass of vegetation, but a land that could be navigated, likely utilizing the newly acquired geographic indicators.

Their new geographical knowledge of the wilderness was further facilitated and enhanced by the strategic location of Helam. The city was located approximately 40 percent of the distance from Nephi to Zarahemla along the narrow strip of wilderness.[848] After falling into the hands of the Lamanites, Helam likely served as a reference point and place of recourse for Lamanite hunters, explorers, and armies. In time, they would perceive that the narrow strip of wilderness continued eastward from Helam to the headwaters of the Sidon River, and on to the east sea. From that time forth, the route from the city of Nephi to the headwaters of the Sidon River would be fully understood. (See Appendix A, Map A-4.)

The basic knowledge of a specific route through the wilderness from Helam to the Waters of Mormon, initially provided by Alma, thus became the foundation for a growing Lamanite geographic database. During the following 30 years, while the Nephites were content to consider the wilderness an impenetrable barrier, the Lamanites likely became completely engrossed in fully identifying the route to Zarahemla and understanding the geography between the two lands.

The detailed geographical information thus accumulated by the Lamanites did not reach Zarahemla until 44 years later when Mosiah's sons returned from the land of Nephi at the end of their mission in 77 BC.[849] It is included in the account of their mission, which comprises Alma 17–26.

In Alma 22:27–34, the first comprehensive description of Nephite and Lamanite geography is presented, as recorded by the sons of Mosiah.[850] It was provided in describing the geographical distribution of the Lamanites who were in the kingdom of Lamoni's father, the king over all Lamanite lands.[851] According to that description, Lamanite lands extended from sea to sea. The line, which divided Zarahemla from Nephi, was a "narrow strip of wilderness, which ran from the sea east even to the sea west."[852]

In the center of the land, the narrow strip of wilderness bordered on the land of Manti.[853] The narrow strip of wilderness provided east-to-west passage more readily than the body of wilderness that surrounded it. Its use as a terrestrial artery of travel or identifiable land route was demonstrated when the sons of Mosiah, in returning to Zarahemla from the land of Nephi, first entered it, and then used it as a conduit to move eastward with the people of Anti-Nephi-Lehi to the borders of Manti.[854] This point is so important that the four-step progression by which it can be determined must be included:

- According to Alma 27:14, the sons of Mosiah and the people of Anti-Nephi-Lehi "departed out of the land, and came into *the wilderness which divided the land of Nephi from the land of Zarahemla*, and came over near the borders of the land" (emphasis added).

- Alma 22:27 states that the land of Lamoni's father "*was divided from the land of Zarahemla by a narrow strip of wilderness*, which ran from the sea east even to the sea west . . . through the borders of Manti, by the head of the river Sidon, running from the east towards the west—and *thus were the Lamanites and the Nephites divided*" (emphasis added).

Without the information contained in Alma 22:27, one might reasonably conclude from Alma 27:14 that the sons of Mosiah and the people of Anti-Nephi-Lehi wandered through the great wilderness separating Zarahemla from Nephi with no real sense of direction, like the Lamanites before Alma the Elder showed them the way or the party of 16 sent by King Mosiah. Without that key and essential verse in Alma chapter 22, we would know nothing of the narrow strip of wilderness. The wilderness separating Nephi and Zarahemla could only be visualized as large in both compass dimensions—north to south and east to west. However, we do have the benefit of Alma 22:27.

- If the more detailed information from Alma 22:27 is inserted into Alma 27:14, the following is discovered concerning the route of travel: The sons of Mosiah and the people of Anti-Nephi-Lehi departed out of the land of Nephi "and came into the [narrow strip of] wilderness which divided the land of Nephi from the land of Zarahemla, and came over near the borders of the land [of Manti, by the head of the river Sidon]."[855]

- Alma 27:14 does not reveal the actual location of their arrival in the land of Zarahemla. However, the last piece of the puzzle is supplied by Alma 17:1, which informs us that the sons of Mosiah did indeed enter the land of Zarahemla at Manti. When Alma met them, they were "journeying towards the land of Zarahemla" from the land of Manti, having left the people of Anti-Nephi-Lehi in the adjacent wilderness, that is in the narrow strip of wilderness.

STRATEGIC USE OF THE NARROW STRIP OF WILDERNESS

Lamanite armies traveling to the land of Zarahemla could enter the narrow strip of wilderness at any point from east to west. The narrow strip of wilderness would then direct them "straight" to the borders of Manti or elsewhere along the Nephite and Lamanite border.[856] In 81 BC, the Lamanite army that destroyed the city of Ammonihah[857] had departed the land of Nephi,[858] entering the narrow strip of wilderness, and traveled eastward to an arbitrary point to the south of Ammonihah, whereupon they turned northward from the narrow strip of wilderness (through what was, to the Nephites at that time, the west wilderness) to the city of Ammonihah. After they exterminated the people of Ammonihah, they fled southward retracing their steps back to the narrow strip of wilderness, whereupon they turned eastward, rather than turning westward in the direction of the city of Nephi, apparently to remain in the region for the purpose of conducting additional attacks against the Nephites before returning home to Nephi.[859]

Chief Captain Zoram, utilizing the revelation provided by Alma the Younger, first led his army to the east side of the river Sidon. They then moved southward into the narrow strip of wilderness, which lay immediately beyond the borders of Manti.[860] There, the fleeing Lamanite army was intercepted.

THE EXPANDING POLITICAL DIMENSIONS OF NEPHI

When King Mosiah I departed out of Nephi in *ca.* 200 BC, the great body of wilderness bordered the land and city of Nephi, both on the east, and on the north. In *ca.* 145 BC, approximately 65 years later, it still encroached on the borders of Nephi and Shilom when Alma fled to the Waters of Mormon.[861] Nothing had changed in 121 BC when the people of Limhi fled out of the land of Nephi.[862] Consequently, it can be concluded that throughout the period from 200–121 BC, the Lamanites never expanded their lands of habitation eastward or northward into the wilderness. In fact, they seldom entered the wilderness for fear of becoming lost, which is plainly revealed in the Book of Mormon.

Eastward expansion did finally begin in 120 BC through a series of events first set in motion when the people of Limhi fled into the wilderness. The Lamanite army, who fruitlessly pursued them, lost their way and began to wander hopelessly through the wilderness. As outlined in Part 1, Chapter 1.6, the fortuitous discovery of the cities of Amulon and Helam accomplished two things for the Lamanites, in addition to the obvious benefit of aiding them in finding their way home.

First, the Amulonites directly brought about the elevation of the Lamanite culture to a literate society. When the sons of Mosiah journeyed into the land of Nephi 28 years later (92 BC), they found the Lamanites communicating with each other in writing.[863]

Second, though Alma did nothing more than show the Lamanites the way from Helam to Nephi, in so doing he provided them with the geographical keys necessary for navigation through the wilderness along a relatively straight line from sea to sea, that is, along the narrow strip of wilderness. These keys were necessary for the dramatic Lamanite expansion that was about to take place.

Therefore, 120 BC was a pivotal year for the Lamanites because the two beneficial occurrences would directly serve to

- Lift them culturally.

- Lead to a dramatic increase in the amount of real estate they claimed.

In 81 BC, the land of Nephi was temporarily expanded overnight to extend from sea to sea through a series of events first identified in Chapter 2.3, "The Order of the Nehors." They had already begun to expand outward, however, when they established the city of Jerusalem near the Waters of Mormon, after taking possession of the cities of Helam and Amulon in 121 BC. All three cities became intermediate (or interlying) cities between the city of Nephi and the early configuration of Zarahemla.

The Lamanites went from being completely hemmed in by the wilderness bordering to the east and north of the city of Nephi in 121 BC to having a comprehensive knowledge of the geography by 92 BC, or not long thereafter. They first inhabited the east wilderness for about three years beginning in 81 BC. Finally, in 77 BC, they moved permanently into the east wilderness and laid claim to all lands south of Zarahemla from the west sea to the east sea.

Prior to 81 BC, the expanded configuration was little more than a political designation, underscoring their new understanding of a comprehensive geography. In reality, the land of Nephi would still be inhabited only from the highlands of Nephi to the west sea. There was no deliberate eastward expansion from the city of Nephi other than the occupation of the cities of Helam and Amulon and the establishment of the city of Jerusalem.

Furthermore, the permanent occupation of the east wilderness after 77 BC took place only for purposes of aggression against the people of Ammon, who had settled that quarter of Zarahemla. Notwithstanding the reason for the expansion, however, from 77 BC forward, there would be a growing Lamanite population in the east wilderness to the south of Jershon. They would inhabit the eastern seaboard, temporarily both north and south of the narrow strip of wilderness.[864]

TROY SMITH

THE NECESSITY OF THE NEPHITE TERRITORIAL EXPANSION

At the end of 78 BC, when the sons of Mosiah returned from Nephi with the people of Anti-Nephi-Lehi, they brought with them a comprehensive understanding of the geography of the land southward, which they had received from the Lamanites. It marked the first time in which the Nephites had a thorough and complete understanding of the fully expanded configuration of Nephite and Lamanite lands. Nephite understanding of the geography of the entire land southward was thereby instantly increased to a level equal to or greater than that of the Lamanites.

With the increased geographical understanding came a heightened sense of their vulnerability to Lamanite aggression. For the first time they understood the critical importance of expanding their holdings to extend from sea to sea, especially because the Lamanites were already aware of the entire geographic configuration of Lamanite lands. It was the only way the Nephites could secure the land northward to prevent the Lamanites from achieving "power to harass them on every side."[865] The new information was vital for the preservation of Zarahemla against the Lamanite onslaught that would begin in 73 BC through the wicked aspirations of Amalickiah.

THE EXPANDING POLITICAL DIMENSIONS OF ZARAHEMLA

As noted in Chapter 3.1, the wilderness conditions prevalent when the Nephites arrived in Zarahemla persisted across the land of Zarahemla for well over a hundred years throughout the reigns of the three kings of Zarahemla. These prevailing conditions are revealed in the account of the Amlicite War in 87 BC, which took place four years after the transition of Nephite government from kings to judges.[866] Nephite lands during the initial period in Zarahemla, if considered in a sea-to-sea perspective, could be described as a single, continuous body of wilderness, completely uninhabited, except for a narrow band of habitation that extended along the Sidon River valley. This small region of habitation was located near the midpoint of a line drawn from the east sea to the west sea. The land of habitation extended from the land of Minon[867] on the south near the headwaters of the Sidon River to the city of Zarahemla on the north.

162

The Nephites did not comprehend the geography of the new land and made no significant recorded attempts between 200 and 77 BC to determine its boundaries. They defined Zarahemla according to their limited understanding. In fact, the land of Zarahemla was conceptually limited to the lands of Nephite habitation throughout the first approximately 125 years. As they expanded outward, beginning in approximately 100 BC,[868] their perception of the land of Zarahemla grew larger in scope.

Everything changed suddenly in 77 BC upon the return of the sons of Mosiah from the land of Nephi. The most important and perhaps the only physical key to the expanded geographic understanding was the narrow strip of wilderness. After it was identified, the great wilderness could be navigated with confidence by the knowledgeable traveler simply by utilizing its two-fold natural function as

- A permanent and fixed avenue of travel across the entirety of an otherwise unnavigable region.

- A line of demarcation, which entirely divided the land of Zarahemla from the land of Nephi.

Through the expanded geographic knowledge thus acquired by the sons of Mosiah, the Nephites were enabled to comprehend the entire configuration of both Nephite and Lamanite lands for the first time. Zarahemla was immediately redefined as the entire region within the land southward, lying northward of the land of Nephi. It became a greatly expanded region extending from the east sea to the west sea and northward from the narrow strip of wilderness to the narrow neck of land.

As considered in the following chapter, Moroni's expanded configuration of fortified cities, which extended from sea to sea (Part 3, Chapter 3.4), reflected an unprecedented level of comprehension as pertaining to the geography of the land southward. Apparently, the geographic information was unavailable to previous Nephite commanders or to Moroni until the return of the sons of Mosiah from their mission to the Lamanites. The Nephite chief commander simply carried out a program to protect Nephite lands, as they were then perceived for the first time.

While initially there remained many poorly defined regions, eventually all Nephite lands would be fully understood and further subdivided into smaller geographical regions. Each region would become dotted by more and more cities as the population grew, and the people spread across the face of the land—once given the assurance of military support.[869]

THE NARROW STRIP OF WILDERNESS—A NATURAL BORDER BETWEEN THE FULLY EXPANDED LANDS OF ZARAHEMLA AND NEPHI

The narrow strip of wilderness, rather than being an arbitrary line, was presumably a natural boundary separating Lamanite and Nephite lands. Most likely it was a hydrographic divide separating river drainage basins, which idea is supported by the fact that the "head of the river Sidon"[870] coincided with the "narrow strip of wilderness."[871] The Waters of Mormon may have also lain along the divide, though the river flowing out from Mormon more than likely flowed southward from the divide through Lamanite lands. Otherwise, it would have formed a waterway leading directly into the land of Zarahemla.

The idea that Alma and his people followed a generally straight course from Nephi to Zarahemla to traverse the wilderness from the Waters of Mormon to the headwaters of the Sidon in record time was considered earlier. The idea was based purely on the time required for the journey, which was half of the time required by Ammon's party of sixteen to cover the same distance.

Now, in the perspective of the narrow strip of wilderness, this idea is considered further. It seems apparent that the geographical information bequeathed by Alma to the Lamanites, which allowed them to navigate a previously unnavigable wilderness, concerned the narrow strip of wilderness. This conclusion is based on the fact that the narrow strip of wilderness became the single key to a complete understanding of the geography of the land southward. It had to be easily and unmistakably identifiable to be utilized as the border between the lands of Nephi and Zarahemla from sea to sea.

But did the narrow strip of wilderness run in a straight course from the east sea to the west sea? This question is answered by moving through a short series of scriptures in a simple exercise of logic, which is outlined as follows:

- The narrow strip of wilderness divided the land of Zarahemla from the land of Nephi and "ran from the sea east even to the sea west" (Alma 22:27).

- Since Zarahemla was located to the north of Nephi,[872] the narrow strip of wilderness formed the northern border of Nephi and the southern border of Zarahemla.

- In Alma 50:8, it states that "the land of Nephi did run in a straight course from the east sea to the west," which is an obvious reference to the northern border of Nephi, considering the subject being discussed, that is, driving Lamanites across the Lamanite border.

- If the border of Nephi ran in a straight course from sea to sea, then so did the border of Zarahemla and the narrow strip of wilderness that divided them.

MIGRATION OF THE PEOPLE OF ALMA FROM NEPHI TO ZARAHEMLA ALONG THE NARROW STRIP OF WILDERNESS

The following scenario describing the extended migration of the people of Alma from the Waters of Mormon to the land of Zarahemla is projected by applying the idea of the narrow strip of wilderness as a hydrographic divide.

When the people of Alma departed out of the land of Nephi, they were unaware that the Waters of Mormon were located on a hydrographic divide (the narrow strip of wilderness), which would direct them to the headwaters of the Sidon River. By revelation, Alma discerned the observable physical features of the divide, which he utilized as guideposts to negotiate the wilderness. Thus, not only was Alma the first to identify the hydrographic divide, he was also the first to take advantage of it to move along a tangible and discernible pathway through the wilderness. Adjustments to the course of travel could be made any time a stream was encountered by simply moving upstream to the headwaters and then continuing on in the initial direction of travel, whether eastward toward the Sidon River, or westward toward the Waters of Mormon. For Alma, the direction of travel was eastward.

In agreement with the idea that Alma was the first to navigate the divide, and the related idea that Helam was located along the divide, it might also be ventured that the pure water discovered by the people of Alma at Helam issued from natural springs that originated a river.[873] Indeed such a spring would not of necessity be located at the high point of the divide, though neither could the spring known for its pure water emanate from a low-lying, swampy area, inundated by a water table that would continuously encroach on the outflowing water and compromise its purity.

Initially, the pure water in Helam was sufficient in volume for the sustenance of "450 souls"[874] and their domesticated animals.[875] Subsequently, it supported a growing population over the 20-plus years that followed.

There is little or no information provided in the Book of Mormon that would tend to challenge the hypothesis that the narrow strip of wilderness was a hydrographic divide, whereas the above conditions seem to agree with the idea, especially considering the fact that all three identified sites along the route taken by the people of Alma (the Waters of Mormon, Helam, and Manti) were identified specifically by their fountains or by their location at the headwaters of a river or both. The placement of Helam on a hydrographic divide at a location where a natural fountain issued forth abundantly would produce the conditions necessary for habitation, including a pure water source for consumption, well-drained soils for growing crops, and relatively course-grained soils for the support of building structures.

The absence of a waterway, or waterways connecting the lands of Nephi and Zarahemla would explain why the route between them remained obscure for so many years. If the narrow strip of wilderness was a hydrographic divide, it would indeed be more passable than surrounding wilderness. Relatively few streams would be encountered. Streams encountered would be at their smallest dimensions (at or near their source) and would therefore pose the least obstacle to travel. Terrain along a divide would likely be the highest and driest ground in a land of frequent rainfall and abundant marshland.

Uncrossed by watercourses, it would naturally fill the role of a neutral no man's land claimed neither by the Nephites nor the Lamanites.

Anyone capable of negotiating the narrow strip of wilderness could not truly become lost anywhere in either the land of Nephi or the land of Zarahemla. Any stream encountered, either north or south of the divide, could simply be followed to its headwaters (source) to reach the narrow strip of wilderness. The traveler could then turn east or west, depending upon the desired destination.

THE DISTANCE FROM THE CITY OF ZARAHEMLA TO THE NARROW STRIP OF WILDERNESS

In 87 BC, Nephite scouts followed the fleeing Amlicite army to the land of Minon near the southern border of Zarahemla. In the land of Minon, they observed the Amlicites meeting up with a Lamanite army. Alma 2[876] describes a time frame of twenty-four hours for

- The scouts' journey from the valley of Gideon to the southern border of Zarahemla.
- The return trip to the valley of Gideon.
- The frantic rush of the Nephite army to the city of Zarahemla.
- The intense battle with the combined Amlicite and Lamanite army.

Alma did not send the scouts until nightfall on the first day (verse 20). The defeat of the Amlicite/Lamanite army and their flight into the wilderness of Hermounts occurred by the end of the second day (verses 36 and 37).

On the basis of the account of the Amlicite War, the narrow strip of wilderness was located little more than half a day's travel upstream from the city of Zarahemla, as traveled by the scouts, who likely received no sleep during the period. For a normal journey, it may have been a day's travel upstream (south) on the Sidon River from the city of Zarahemla to the borders of the land. By 74 BC, the land of Manti would be situated at the headwaters of the Sidon. It would border on the narrow strip of wilderness and might well have a common border with the land of Minon, considering that both lands were located by or within "the course of the land of Nephi," as interpreted in the following discussion.

THE COURSE OF THE LAND OF NEPHI

The Book of Alma describes the land of Minon as being "above the land of Zarahemla in the course of the land of Nephi."[877] The "course of the land of Nephi," as used in 87 BC, seems to have been a partially understood term used to describe the narrow strip of wilderness, as it would be known after the sons of Mosiah returned from their mission in 77 BC. If so, then Manti, located at the headwaters of the Sidon River, also bordered on the narrow strip of wilderness, or "course of the land of Nephi." Therefore, the two lands were in close proximity to one another.

The "course of the land of Nephi" was a unknown term in *ca.* 200 BC when the people of Mosiah discovered Zarahemla, for, as noted previously, if King Mosiah (the prophet of God who led the Nephites out of Nephi) knew the precise travel route between the two lands, he did not divulge it to his people, and, for a number of years, travel to the land of Nephi was generally avoided. The term would not be utilized with full understanding until Alma the Elder arrived in Zarahemla in 120 BC, for that was the time when the route likely taken previously by the people of Mosiah was rediscovered and in fact understood for the first time.[878] In this case, and perhaps in other instances in the Book of Mormon, a geographical term, as given in a particular verse, may represent a momentary and changing Nephite (or Lamanite) perspective during a specific and limited interval of time. Therefore, consideration must always be given to the precise time in which a geographic statement is made.

In 87 BC, it may not have been known in Zarahemla that the "course of the land of Nephi" extended eastward from the Sidon River to the east sea, and westward to the west sea. Perhaps it was simply considered to be the travel route between the headwaters of the Sidon River and the Waters of Mormon, as identified by Alma the Elder in 121 BC. Such was the limited Nephite geographic perspective in 87 BC because the narrow strip of wilderness had not been fully delineated at that time. Between 121 and 77 BC, the route generally taken by travelers who departed Zarahemla for the land of Nephi, such as the sons of Mosiah in 91 BC, may indeed have been called the "course of the land of Nephi," a reflection of Alma's experience and understanding.

DIMINISHING WILDERNESS WITHIN THE LAND OF ZARAHEMLA

Frequent warfare in Nephite lands between 87 and 60 BC,[879] when combined with the enlarged Nephite understanding of the comprehensive geography of the land southward after 77 BC, contributed greatly to the deliberate settlement pattern that enlarged and fully defined official Nephite boundaries. Much of the settlement of outlying areas was carried out primarily for defensive purposes between 73 and 67 BC. Because of the growing footprint of Nephite habitation, which took place during that period, Nephite awareness of various wilderness areas within and adjacent to the expanding boundaries became more refined. As the settlement of peripheral regions progressed and the Nephite population increased, the pervasive wilderness diminished rapidly. Maps A-3, A-4, and A-5 in Appendix A depict all of the wilderness regions identified below and outline the geographic development that occurred in Zarahemla between 87 and 77 BC.

The East Wilderness: The east wilderness was uninhabited before 81 BC. In that year, the eleventh year of the reign of the judges, following the destruction of Ammonihah, the Lamanites were driven into the east region for the first time, as described in Alma chapter 22.[880] From 81 BC until the permanent settlement of Jershon in 77 BC by the people of Ammon, there was no distinction in that region between the east and south wilderness areas, that is, between Nephite and Lamanite lands. Everywhere in the east region was wilderness during that four-year period, and since all Nephite settlement was in the center of the land in relation to the east and west seas, the future region of Jershon and the adjoining south wilderness in the land of Nephi were simply called the east wilderness,[881] even after the Lamanites were driven there. Lamanite habitation in the east wilderness was temporary at this time, and after a short period of intense suffering,[882] the majority, if not all, returned to the land of Nephi.[883]

The permanent Lamanite settlement of the east wilderness occurred in 77 BC, shortly after the settlement of Jershon by the people of Ammon. A large Lamanite army, which had pursued them from the land of Nephi, was engaged by the Nephite armies. As a result of the ensuing battle, tens of thousands of Lamanites were routed and driven into the surrounding wilderness. Despite their losses, it appeared they were determined to remain in the region to exact vengeance against the people of Ammon and the Nephites who harbored them. Between 77 and 72 BC, the Lamanites were distributed on both sides of the Nephite and Lamanite boundary.[884]

Lamanites occupied the east sea littoral zone, or coastal corridor of Jershon, which is not revealed until they were driven out by Moroni in 72 BC.[885] Their numbers came specifically and almost exclusively from the great battle of 77 BC.[886] This coastal zone lay eastward of the city of Aaron, which was the city of the people of Ammon.[887]

Between 77 and 75 BC, the Zoramites settled the land of Antionum, which was situated to the east of the Nephite city of Aaron, which is projected to be the city initially established by the people of Ammon.[888] It was located near the east sea in the borders of the narrow strip of wilderness.[889] The Lamanite forces for the Zoramite war of 74 BC[890] likely came from the coastal corridor of Jershon, as well as the wilderness lying directly to the south of Jershon in the land of Nephi (see Appendix A, Map A-5). Consequently, the Zoramite war accentuated the danger of allowing the Lamanites to remain in Nephite lands.

Furthermore, in 72 BC, the developing war with Amalickiah placed a sense of urgency on taking action. Therefore, Moroni sent the Nephite armies to drive the Lamanites into their own lands south of the borders of Jershon, that is, south of the narrow strip of wilderness in that region.[891] He then sent Nephites from the land of Zarahemla specifically to settle the eastern coastal portion of Jershon (see Appendix A, Map A-6).[892]

Fully expecting Amalickiah to return after his Lamanite army was defeated at Noah,[893] Moroni established a line of fortified cities along the southern and eastern boundaries of Jershon (see Appendix A, Map A-6). After the fortified cities were in place, it was much easier to persuade Nephites in Zarahemla to move to the peripheral regions, where Lamanite attack was a virtual certainty.[894] Therefore, the fortified cities contributed greatly to the settlement of the land and the diminishment of the east wilderness.

The West Wilderness: Between 200 and 100 BC, the city of Zarahemla and the immediately surrounding countryside comprised all of Nephite settlement and lay in the midst of a virtual sea of wilderness. When the Nephites began to establish other cities after 100 BC,[895] Nephite settlement soon began to spread westward into the wilderness of Hermounts, which in 87 BC still bordered Zarahemla on the north and west.[896] Sometime before 83 BC, the cities of Ammonihah[897] and Noah[898] were likely placed at the western border of Hermounts. The cities of Melek,[899] Aaron,[900] and Sidom[901] were also established in Hermounts at that time.

The relative configurations of both Nephi and Zarahemla during that short period before the borders of Zarahemla were extended to the west sea were indirectly referenced by the sons of Mosiah in Alma 22:28 in relation to the west coastal wilderness: "Now, the more idle part of the Lamanites lived in the wilderness, and dwelt in tents; and they were spread through the wilderness on the west *in* the land of Nephi; yea and also on the west *of* the land of Zarahemla" (emphasis added).

Whereas the land of Nephi under the rule of the Lamanites extended to the west coast and encompassed the land of Lehi's original landing, the land of Zarahemla at that time (91–77 BC) extended only to the west wilderness bordering on Ammonihah and Noah. Therefore, the west coastal wilderness was westward *of* the land of Zarahemla at that time prior to the 72 BC expansion (see Appendix A, Map A-4).

The west wilderness was without internal distinction between 100 and 72 BC (see Appendix A, Maps A-4 and A-5). It simply extended westward from the western border of Hermounts to the west sea. No further settlement toward the west would be attempted until the commencement of 72 BC, following the 73 BC Lamanite attack at Noah.[902] It was at that time that Moroni sent Nephite armies to drive all Lamanites south across the Lamanite border and immediately established the defensive cities along the southern border "from the west sea, running by the head of the river

Sidon."[903] It is likely, however, that the west coast was not fortified until 66 BC, when Ammoron attacked there.[904]

Settlement along the narrow strip of wilderness as Related to the West Wilderness: In about 140 BC, Helam was the first city to be established along the southern border of the west wilderness (see Appendix A, Maps A-3 and A-4). Helam was located along the narrow strip of wilderness eight days travel eastward from the Waters of Mormon.[905] The headwaters of the Sidon River were located twelve days eastward of Helam.[906] As described in 140 BC, the Waters of Mormon lay at the border separating the land of Nephi from the wilderness.[907]

Sometime between 121 and 91 BC, the "great city" of Jerusalem was established near the Waters of Mormon. The city was visited by Aaron in 91 BC at the beginning of his mission.[908] See Jerusalem's projected location in Appendix A, Maps A-4, A-5, and A-6.

Between 87 and 81 BC, the city of Manti was established at the headwaters of the Sidon River.[909] During the Amalickiah and Ammoron Wars (73–60 BC), four additional cities were established along the narrow strip of wilderness between Manti and the west coast.[910] From east to west, the five southern border cities were Manti, Zeezrom, Cumeni, Antiparah, and the unidentified coastal city referenced in Alma 56:31. Antiparah is placed nearest the unnamed city on the west coast, for as described in the account of the Amalickiah and Ammoron Wars, in the line of fortified cities along the narrow strip of wilderness, it "neighbored" the unnamed coastal city.[911] As shown on Map A-6 of Appendix A, according to a uniform spacing of the fortified cities, the city of Cumeni is placed immediately north of the vicinity of Helam, and Antiparah is placed relatively near the Waters of Mormon. In the region extending westward from Cumeni to the west sea, the narrow strip of wilderness marked the southern border of the west wilderness.

Judea is placed within the west wilderness to the north of Antiparah due to the proximity of the two cities, as indicated in Helaman's account of the 2,000 stripling warriors.[912] Lamanites had lived along the west coast of Zarahemla to the north of the narrow strip of wilderness long before King Mosiah I led his people out of Nephi.[913] There is no account of any Lamanite or Nephite settlement or habitation within the heart of the west wilderness. However, it is likely that after 121 BC, many Lamanites were spread throughout the region until they were driven out by Moroni in 72 BC. Once they learned how to negotiate the narrow strip of wilderness, they could no longer become lost. They would simply follow the first stream encountered to its source, and then follow the narrow strip of wilderness to the city of Nephi, or to any other desired destination, according to their knowledge.

The Capital Parts of the Land: After 72 BC, the cities of Ammonihah and Noah no longer delineated the eastern boundary of the west wilderness. From that time forth, the two cities may have instead marked the western edge of the regional land between Zarahemla and Bountiful,[914] as it is identified in the Book of Mormon. They also marked the eastern boundary of the land of Bountiful. The two cities, as well as other fortified cities, may have secured the western border of the region of gathering in AD 19, when Lachoneus gathered the Nephites to defend against the Gadianton robbers.[915]

West Coast Wilderness: A coastal wilderness filled with Lamanites[916] lined the west coast, both north and south of the narrow strip of wilderness, similar to the wilderness along the east coast of Jershon between 77 and 72 BC.[917] It was logical that the Nephites, finding themselves nearly surrounded by Lamanites, on the west as well as the east,[918] with the west and east coastal wilderness strips both extending northward to the narrow neck of land, made it a high priority to guard the narrow neck of land at the northern border of Bountiful,[919] especially as the land northward came more and more to their attention.

As mentioned previously, the west coast region was filled with Lamanites long before the Nephite occupation of Zarahemla. Being the place of the first landing, it was their home from the beginning. They had remained there when Nephi and his followers fled to the highlands of Nephi. Though in time they would have naturally expanded both northward and southward along the coast from the location of the first landing, their northward movement was suddenly accelerated following the discovery of the highland location of the city of Nephi, between 19 and 29 years after Nephi's departure.[920] Without doubt, they immediately settled in the adjacent coastal region directly west of Nephi, where they could launch frequent attacks against the Nephites.

If Nephite armies and fortifications had not blocked the narrow pass, the Lamanites might eventually have moved northward along the coastline into the land northward, creating an ominous threat to Nephite security. In troubled times, especially after the Lamanites had gained an expanded understanding of the geography of the land southward, the narrow neck of land, and the land northward, this inherent geographic vulnerability would also explain the need for a line of fortified cities along the west coast of Bountiful in Zarahemla to prevent Lamanite armies or individuals from freely traveling up the coast.

As referenced previously, specific knowledge of various regions of Nephite lands within the land southward is provided in the Book of Mormon through accounts of historical events. Not many accounts focus on the western border of Nephite lands. However, the account of the war with Amalickiah and Ammoron does refer briefly to the establishment of an army, or armies, to protect the "west borders of the land"[921] by the west sea.

It might, therefore, be projected that during this period of expanding geographical claims, the Nephites established fortified cities along the west coast in the land of Bountiful along the west coast—the counterpart to the east coast land of Jershon. Thereafter, the west coast of Bountiful extended from the narrow strip of wilderness on the south to the land of Desolation on the north. The Book of Mormon, however, never identifies a west coast equivalent of the fortified coastal cities of Jershon. Still, the cities can be logically projected to have extended northward from the unnamed coastal city at the southwest corner of Nephite lands, especially after Ammoron's offensive in 66 BC.[922]

A short series of scriptures outlines a logical sequence of events whereby this line of fortified coastal cities was likely placed by Moroni along the western coastline:

- The first reference to the western littoral zone in Alma 22:28 stresses Nephite concerns for Lamanites inhabiting the coastal region, which lay to the west of the land of Zarahemla.

- In 72 BC, the first fortification of the west coast perimeter was completed, though apparently it was limited to the unnamed city at the southwest corner of Nephite lands, as part of the string of cities along the southern border of the land of Zarahemla (narrow strip of wilderness) from the west sea to the Sidon River.[923]

- As stated in Alma 51:30 and 52:9, Moroni believed that Amalickiah and Ammoron's prime objective was gaining control of the narrow neck of land. It follows that fortifications must be placed along the west coast to provide defense all the way to Desolation.

- It is therefore projected that additional cities, extending northward from the unnamed city along the west sea, were established by Moroni in 66 BC to defend against Ammoron's attack there.[924]

The unnamed west coast city located at the border between Nephi and Zarahemla is referenced only once in the account of the Amalickiah and Ammoron Wars. The reference is purely incidental, as included in the account of Helaman and the 2,000 stripling warriors in 65 BC. Helaman describes the ploy to entice the Lamanites to come out from the city of Antiparah against them: "And we were to march near the city of Antiparah, as if we were going to the city beyond, in the borders by the seashore."[925] This indirect reference provides a foundation for the above projection by specifically identifying one of the fortified coastal cities, which otherwise would not be known.

The Wilderness of Bountiful: The history of the Bountiful wilderness, as it played a role in Book of Mormon history, goes back about a thousand years into the Jaredite era. The Jaredites lived in the land northward. In the days of the wicked Jaredite king Heth, there occurred a long and devastating drought. As a result, large numbers of poisonous snakes were driven from their normal habitats and caused the Jaredite flocks to flee toward the land southward. Many of the animals reached the narrow neck of land and passed over into the land southward. "And it came to pass that the Lord did cause the serpents that they should pursue [the animals] no more, but that they should hedge up the way that the people could not pass."[926]

It was the widespread effect of the drought that generated a prolonged migration toward the land southward. The people followed the trail of the animals, and in desperation for food, they devoured their dead carcasses along the way. At the narrow neck of land, they found such an immense number of poisonous serpents that it was virtually impossible to pass through. This is the first Jaredite reference to the land southward where Lehi landed somewhere between 500 and 1,000 years after the time of Heth.

It was not until the reign of the Jaredite king Lib (eight generations after Heth) that the poisonous serpents were destroyed sufficiently to allow the Jaredites to travel along the narrow neck of land into the land southward. Lib's reign fell fairly close in time to the first landing of the Nephites, though likely their arrival was still a future event at that time. Lib became enamored with the south wilderness, which was filled with game animals of all kinds. He went on many hunting expeditions into the land southward and became renowned among his people as a skilled hunter. He established "a great city by the narrow neck of land, by the place where the sea divides the land,"[927] which was at or near the location of the later Nephite city in the land of Desolation.[928] The city of Lib probably became a commercial center where game from the land southward was processed (likely smoked and/or dried) before shipment to the land northward.[929]

A few years following Lehi's 589 BC arrival in the land southward, the Mulekites landed in the land northward within the land of Desolation just north of the narrow neck of land.[930] At the time of the Mulekite landing, the Jaredites were in their last major cultural period, which would lead to total extinction in a terminal civil war. The land of Desolation was bordered on the south during that period by the Jaredite city of Lib[931] and on the north by the Jaredite land of Moron.[932] It is apparent that the region of Desolation was not inhabited by the Jaredites, for they allowed the Mulekites to settle there. Desolation remained the homeland of the Mulekites until shortly after the Jaredite destruction, at which time Zarahemla led them into the south wilderness.[933] Their departure into the land southward likely came shortly after they cared for Coriantumr (the last Jaredite king) during the nine-month period that ended with his death.[934]

Prior to the migration of the people of Zarahemla into the land southward and their settlement along the banks of the Sidon River, the entire region between the narrow strip of wilderness and the narrow neck of land was uninhabited wilderness.[935] On the basis of Ether's statement that the Jaredites did not inhabit the land southward,[936] the region was apparently uninhabited throughout the entire 2,000 years of Jaredite history. Other than Jaredite hunters from the north and Nephite hunters from the south, the Mulekites were the first humans of the post-flood era to penetrate this great wilderness. They were the first to enter the region with the intention of settling there. They arrived at the Sidon River, however, only shortly before King Mosiah led his people into the same region.

Bountiful was likely the name given by the Mulekites to the northern portion of the south wilderness. Bountiful extended southward from the narrow neck of land an unspecified distance into the land southward. During the Nephite period in Zarahemla, the land of Bountiful ultimately became one of the major divisions of Nephite geography in the land southward as they began to differentiate various regions within Nephite lands. Over the course of Nephite history in the land of Zarahemla, Bountiful evolved from an uninhabited wilderness teeming with wild game into one of the crucial regions in the Nephite defensive configuration. The southeastern portion of Bountiful[937] became part of the "capital parts of the land."[938]

The first Nephite reference to Bountiful is found in the Alma chapter 22. There it is described in terms of how it was perceived by the Mulekites (the people of Zarahemla) when they arrived from the land northward. They called it Bountiful, distinguishing it from their former land of habitation (Desolation). The name given to Desolation likely describes the conditions there, which forced them to flee into the land southward. The detrimental effects of the great Jaredite curse, including drought and disease, which had continued after the war ended, rendering their lands uninhabitable,[939] had spilled over into the land of Desolation.

In the Mulekite perspective, before penetrating into the land southward, all the lands lying south of the narrow neck of land were part of the large wilderness utilized by the Jaredites as a source of wild game.[940] They had no idea of its full dimensions. Sitting on the southern borders of the same wilderness at that time, the Nephites had no idea how far north it extended, or that the land northward lay just beyond and was occupied by the thousands of Mulekites and millions of Jaredites.

The Nephite Settlement of Bountiful: No specific information is provided in the Book of Mormon concerning the initial settlement of Bountiful during the Nephite period in Zarahemla. Certainly it was uninhabited in 121 BC, when Limhi sent the party of 43 in search of Zarahemla.[941] They departed the land of Nephi, became lost in the wilderness, wandered north along the narrow neck of land into the land northward, and returned to Nephi without encountering human habitation.

Alma 22:32–33 refers to habitation in Bountiful "from the east unto the west sea" for the specific purpose of hemming "in the Lamanites on the south, that thereby they should have no more possession on the north, that they might not overrun the land northward." The context of this statement (as contained in the missionary account of Mosiah's sons) is approximately 90 BC, immediately following the conversion of the Lamanite king, when he sent a proclamation to his people commanding them to allow the sons of Mosiah to preach the gospel throughout the land. However, the statement seems to be an editorial comment made by Mormon, referring chronologically (as will be seen) to the period following the destruction of Ammonihah in 81 BC, as presented in Alma 16—the chapter immediately preceding the missionary account.

Bountiful was not inhabited in 91 BC. Based on the chain of events outlined in Alma chapter 50, it was not settled until after 72 BC. In that year, Chief Captain Moroni sent the Nephite armies across the face of the land, into the east wilderness and throughout the region lying between the west sea and the Sidon River.[942] His purpose was to drive the Lamanites southward across the narrow strip of wilderness.[943] Fortified cities were then established at intervals along the narrow strip of wilderness from the city of Moroni on the east coast to the previously referenced unnamed city on the west coast.[944] Through these extensive military actions, the land of Zarahemla was expanded to extend from the east sea to the west sea. Only then did Nephites likely feel secure enough to move outward to remote regions, such as the east coastal wilderness and the wilderness of Bountiful.

Considering the frequent turmoil that took place between 87 and 77 BC, with Lamanite attacks occurring in 87, 81, and 77 BC, the peripheral regions were considered dangerous places to live until 72 BC. As a direct result of the security provided by Moroni's establishment of the fortified cities in that year, it appears that the Nephites began to inhabit the land of Bountiful shortly after 72 BC, but they did not fortify or occupy the border between Bountiful and Desolation at that time.

Both conditions are indicated in the account of the singular event involving the people of Morianton, which took place only four years later in 68 BC.[945] As a result of a clash between the inhabitants of the neighboring cities of Morianton and Lehi, Morianton decided to flee with his followers into the land northward. To reach the narrow neck of land, the people of Morianton of necessity must pass through the land of Bountiful. Moroni's fears surrounding their flight are considered in the following scripture:

> Now behold, the people who were in the land Bountiful, or rather Moroni, feared that [the people in Bountiful] would hearken to the words of Morianton and unite with his people, and thus he would obtain possession of those parts of the land, which would lay a foundation for serious consequences among the people of Nephi, yea, which consequences would lead to the overthrow of their liberty.
>
> Therefore Moroni sent an army, with their camp, to head the people of Morianton, to stop their flight into the land northward.
>
> And it came to pass that they did not head them until they had come to the borders of the land Desolation; and there they did head them, by the narrow pass which led by the sea into the land northward, yea, by the sea, on the west and on the east. (Alma 50:32–34)

On the basis of the above event, it can be concluded that indeed, the Nephites began to inhabit the land of Bountiful shortly after 72 BC. Their numbers were sufficient to be a concern to Moroni by 68

BC, if they should unite with the people of Morianton. The advantage of the narrow neck of land to repel Lamanite attack would be turned against the Nephites if dissenters gained control of Bountiful, and they would quickly find themselves hemmed in between the narrow strip of wilderness on the south and the narrow neck of land on the north.[946]

An army was dispatched to intercept the people of Morianton and prevent them from uniting with the people in Bountiful and from migrating into the land northward. Bountiful's inhabitants had not joined with the people of Morianton. It is apparent, however, that Morianton had passed through Bountiful and into the "borders of the land Desolation" without opposition. No army was stationed there to turn them back. It was therefore necessary for Teancum to overtake them at the "narrow pass" and escort them back to the land of Jershon.[947]

CORRECT TIMELINE FOR THE EXPANSION OF LAMANITE LANDS

The comment in Alma 22:29 concerning the distribution of the Lamanite king's people in the east wilderness "where the Nephites had driven them" is a bit premature, because the king was still alive at that time. It is noted that the passage in Alma 22 describing the king's lands was provided at the time of his conversion to the gospel in about 91 BC. The first Lamanite habitation of the east wilderness by the east sea did not actually take place until after the destruction of Ammonihah in 81 BC,[948] the year following the king's death.[949] The Lamanites and Amalekites did not settle there permanently until the great battle of 77 BC in the land of Jershon.

This was a time, however, when both Nephite and Lamanite lands of habitation were expanding rapidly. Certainly, it became an accurate description of Lamanite distribution immediately after the sons of Mosiah returned with the people of Anti-Nephi-Lehi at the end of 77 BC. The Lamanites followed them and permanently settled the east wilderness at that time. The Nephites, on the other hand, would not expand the boundaries of Zarahemla from sea to sea until 72 BC.[950]

By way of explanation, Mormon had already presented the account of the destruction of Ammonihah and the subsequent flight of the Lamanites into the east wilderness prior to abridging Alma 22.

In that sense, the full Lamanite distribution from sea to sea, which postdated the king's death, had already taken place. The account of Mosiah's sons' mission thus becomes a flashback in the sense that it returned to the previous time when the king was still alive. When this is considered, it becomes obvious that Mormon was referring to the distribution of the Lamanites after Ammonihah was destroyed.

The geography, as presented in Alma 22, is thus an assessment of its full development after 72 BC, though technically, within the missionary account of Mosiah's sons, it was given at a time before the full geographic development actually took place. This discrepancy in the geography, as detected in these verses, results purely from the rapid development of both Nephi and Zarahemla between 87 and 72 BC. It was a period of only 15 years, which witnessed the greatest rate of growth of the entire pre-Christ period (see Appendix A, Maps A-4 through A-6). Unless one is aware of the precise chronology of the geographic development, no ambiguities are noted.

THE GROWTH OF LAMANITE AND NEPHITE LANDS FROM SEA TO SEA—TWO TIMELINES

The first Lamanite occupation of the east wilderness did not take place until 81 BC,[951] shortly after the Lamanite king died.[952] As discussed earlier, the Lamanite and Nephite distribution statement was made near the beginning of the fourteen-year mission of the sons of Mosiah—immediately following the king's conversion, when he sent forth his decree to his people across the land of Nephi to allow the missionaries to teach the gospel.[953] Therefore, the full expansion of Lamanite lands to include the east wilderness, even temporarily in 81 BC, would not take place for almost ten years. The permanent Lamanite occupation of the east wilderness would not take place until 77 BC, almost fourteen years after the time of the distribution statement.

Likewise, the description in Alma 22:29 of Nephite lands as also extending from east to west along the narrow strip of wilderness would not be fulfilled until 72 BC (almost twenty years later) as a response to the Lamanite expansion. Not until then did Chief Captain Moroni drive the Lamanites out of all lands located to the north of the narrow strip of wilderness and establish fortified cities along there to make sure they did not return.[954] At that time, Moroni established fortified cities along the east coast, at least to the city of Mulek.[955] Moroni wouldn't send orders to Teancum to fortify the land Bountiful and secure the narrow neck of land until 66 BC.[956] It thus becomes evident that these geographical statements were descriptions of Lamanite lands after 81 BC and of Nephite lands after 72 BC, not a snapshot of conditions that existed at the time the statement was given while the king was still alive.

EFFECT OF THE AMALICKIAH AND AMMORON WARS ON THE DIMINISHING WILDERNESS

After Amalickiah's initial attack at the city of Noah, the Nephite military fully understood that further attacks were to be expected in the near future. Thus, it was the developing war with Amalickiah that stimulated Moroni to expand the configuration of Nephite fortified cities to encircle the full extent of Nephite holdings in the land southward. There could be no gaps in the defensive wall around Nephite lands.

Furthermore, the subsequent war with Amalickiah was long and at its height required defense along every border. Nephite armies, in moving from the center of the land to perimeter battlefronts[957] and from one perimeter battlefront to another,[958] crisscrossed every region from east to west and north to south. By the war's end, no region was unknown, and habitation, though perhaps sparse in some areas, blanketed the entirety of Nephite lands. By the war's end, the frontier within the land of Zarahemla had virtually disappeared to include all of the territory within the land southward located between the narrow strip of wilderness on the south and the narrow neck of land on the north. (See Appendix A, Maps A-4, A-5, A-6.)

AREAS OF PERPETUAL WILDERNESS

Notwithstanding the settlement of regions throughout the land southward, there were large regions within the land of Nephi that remained wilderness throughout Nephite history, or at least prior to the Nephite Golden Age.[959] These perpetual wilderness regions became the lands of the Gadianton robbers between 12 BC and

AD 25. During that thirty-seven-year period, thousands and tens of thousands of robbers inhabited this wilderness

NO CITY OF DESOLATION IN THE PRE-CHRIST PERIOD

Before leaving the subject of expanding Nephite habitation within the land southward, the extent of Nephite habitation at the northern boundary of Nephite lands[960] during the pre-Christ period is considered. Simply stated, the Book of Mormon provides no indication that the narrow neck of land, at least the portion included in the record, was inhabited at any time during the pre-Christ period. The fact that there is no reference to a city at the southern border of the land Desolation during the entire period preceding the visitation of Jesus Christ is powerful evidence that the Nephites never settled there at any time.

It is possible that after 55 BC, settlement occurred further to the north where the narrow neck of land began to expand in width, but at "the line Bountiful and the land Desolation," it does not appear that any permanent settlement ever occurred during the pre-Christ period. Even in the account of the defense of Desolation in 34–33 BC (one of only two military encounters at Desolation during the pre-Christ period),[961] fortifications are referenced, but no city.[962]

In AD 31, only three years before the great storm brought the pre-Christ period to a sudden and violent conclusion, the dissenter Jacob led his people into the land northward.[963] No Nephite army was posted at the narrow neck of land to stop or retard their northward movement, notwithstanding Teancum's fortification of Desolation in 66 BC during the Amalickiah and Ammoron Wars.[964] It is therefore concluded that though many Nephites passed through the narrow neck of land between 55 BC and AD 31, no one settled there during the pre-Christ period. Furthermore, it does not appear that an army was maintained there after 55 BC, except as required during times of war.[965]

Considering its location along the only path between the land southward and the land northward and the unsavory characters that certainly passed through frequently during that period of time, it would likely have been a relatively dangerous place to live, especially in small numbers. Therefore, given the absence of a city at Desolation, and lacking the continual presence of an army to provide protection for inhabitants along the way, the likelihood of a small settlement or settlements on the narrow neck of land is small.

THE NARROW NECK OF LAND

The narrow neck of land, which connected the land northward to the land southward, is a common topic in the Book of Mormon. It is referred to frequently, even during the period in Zarahemla from *ca.* 200 to 55 BC, which preceded the first Nephite migrations into the land northward.[966]

In the Book of Helaman, the narrow neck of land is described for the third time—a reference to the Lamanite invasion of 35 BC. At that time, the Nephites constructed fortifications across the narrow neck of land "from the west sea, even to the east; it being a day's journey for a Nephite, on the line which they had fortified and stationed their armies to defend their north country."[967]

Some Book of Mormon geographical interpretations work from the assumption that the land southward and the land northward were separated by a narrow pass, which bordered on the west sea and an unmentioned mountain range, swamp, or other impassable region on the east. That idea is completely dispelled, however, by the first and second descriptions of the narrow neck of land.

The first Book of Mormon reference to the narrow neck of land describes in no uncertain terms an isthmus surrounded by ocean on both sides: "Now, it was only the distance of a day and a half's journey for a Nephite, on the line Bountiful and the land Desolation, from the east to the west sea."[968] Without the last half of this verse, it might indeed be concluded that the distance across the narrow neck of land was measured from the west sea to a vague, undefined point lying somewhere to the east.

However, Mormon nullified such a notion when he added the following: "And thus the land of Nephi and the land of Zarahemla were *nearly surrounded* by water, there being a small neck of land between the land northward and the land southward."[969] Simple logic leads inescapably to the conclusion that without the "small neck of land," the lands of Nephi and Zarahemla (the land southward) would have been *completely surrounded* by water.

The second Book of Mormon reference to the narrow neck of land, the account of the Morianton incident, also states clearly that sea bordered the narrow neck of land on both sides, noting that Teancum's army did not head the people of Morianton "until they had come to the borders of the land Desolation; and there they did head them, by the narrow pass which led by the sea into the land northward, yea, by the sea, on the west and on the east."[970]

In summary, Alma 22:32 and 50:34, the first two references to the narrow neck of land in the Book of Mormon, contain clear and unambiguous descriptions of the narrow neck of land as an isthmus, which connected the land southward to the land northward and was bordered on both sides by ocean. The two scriptures thus become the standard by which other somewhat ambiguous descriptions must be interpreted, such as that found in Helaman 4:7.

MANY WATERS

One other passage implies the narrow neck of land was bordered by sea on both sides. The party of 43 sent by Limhi to search for Zarahemla[971] became lost and wandered along the narrow neck of land into the land northward. There, the Jaredite civilization had flourished for 2,000 years before being completely destroyed in a terminal civil war, leaving a land filled with ruins of every kind. Limhi's account tells of the search party's travel "in a land among many waters."[972] All other references to "many waters" in the Book of Mormon refer to sea in a general sense, the first of which is contained within 1 Nephi chapter 13.[973]

The first Nephite direct physical encounter with "many waters" occurred when Lehi's party arrived at Bountiful after eight years of travail in the wilderness situated to the south of Jerusalem, their previous home. In Bountiful, they "beheld the sea, which [they] called Irreantum, which, being interpreted, is many waters."[974] Today, Irreantum is identified as the Indian Ocean.

Another reference to "many waters" is found in the book of Ether.[975] It refers to an inland sea, which the Jaredites crossed in barges as a trial run for the voyage across the "great sea which divideth the lands."[976] Yet another reference to "many waters" is given in Mormon's description of Cumorah,[977] or Ramah, as it was known to the Jaredites.[978] The Hill Ramah (Cumorah) bordered upon "Ripliancum, which by interpretation, is large, or to exceed all."[979] Today, Lake Ontario lies 20 miles to the north of the Hill Cumorah in

Upstate New York, where Joseph Smith retrieved the plates of the Book of Mormon on September 22, 1827. Lake Ontario is one of a series of inland seas that contain one fifth of the world's fresh water. The shorelines of the Great Lakes "extend for more than 10,000 miles, about equivalent to the combined Atlantic and Pacific coasts of the United States."[980] Looking northward from the southern shore of Lake Ontario, nothing is visible except water, as far as the eye can see, broken by an occasional island at some locations.

Given the foregoing, it could well be said that when Limhi's party traveled "in a land among many waters," they were traveling between two oceans or seas. This is a reasonable conclusion if it can be assumed that "many waters" means the same in this passage that it means in every other passage in which it is used in the Book of Mormon.

CHAPTER 3.4

THE FORTICATIONS ESTABLISHED BY CHIEF CAPTAIN MORONI

72–68 BC

THE DISSENTER AMALICKIAH FLED from Moroni's justice in the land of Zarahemla after his attempted takeover of the Nephite government in 73 BC. Somehow, he and a small band of his close associates eluded the Nephite army that pursued them and escaped to the land of Nephi, while the majority of his army was captured by the armies of Moroni and escorted back to Zarahemla.

In Nephi, Amalickiah deposed the Lamanite ruler and took control of the land of Nephi. He immediately sent the Lamanite army to attack Nephite cities along the western border of the land of Zarahemla. The army, however, encountered defensive fortifications in the cities of Ammonihah and Noah, which prevented them from having any success in their quest. All the leaders were slain, and the army returned to the land of Nephi.

Moroni's fortifications resulted in a six-year period of peace. Amalickiah knew the Lamanites must prepare carefully to make an attack on the land Zarahemla. It was necessary that they carefully choose the right point of attack and wait for the right political moment as reported by his spies within Zarahemla and the level of dissident unrest.

SUDDEN EXPANSION OF NEPHITE PROTECTED LANDS—MORONI IMPLEMENTS A COMPREHENSIVE DEFENSIVE CONFIGURATION

Taking advantage of the six-year pause between Lamanite attacks (73–67 BC), Moroni established an uninterrupted line of fortified cities, placed at regular intervals around the entire perimeter of a greatly expanded geographic region (see Appendix A, Map A-6). The fortified cities were designed to serve three purposes:

- To officially claim the expanded territory, which extended possibly from the east sea to the west sea

- To defend Nephite lands along the entire perimeter of the greater land of Zarahemla.

- To prevent the enemy from controlling (or having access to) the narrow pass leading into the land northward.

Alma chapter 50 identifies the following peripheral regions, which were fortified at Moroni's direction.

I. SOUTHERN BORDER—THE NARROW STRIP OF WILDERNESS

As first described in Alma 22:27, the border between Lamanite and Nephite lands was a "narrow strip of wilderness," which formed a generally east-west line[981] spanning the land southward "from the sea east even to the sea west." It defined the northern boundary of Nephi and the southern boundary of Zarahemla. The southern edge of Jershon comprised the eastern portion of this line, extending along the southern Nephite border from the eastern seaboard to the southwest corner of Jershon. The western portion of the narrow strip of wilderness extended from Manti at the head of the river Sidon westward to the west sea.

The Effect of Recent Developments in the East Region

As discussed in Chapter 2.3, with the exception of a temporary period of Lamanite habitation from 81 to 78 BC,[982] Jershon remained uninhabited wilderness until the people of Anti-Nephi-Lehi permanently settled there in 77 BC (see Appendix A, Maps A-4 and A-5).[983] A sudden flurry of Nehor-instigated military activity both led to and followed the arrival of the people of Anti-Nephi-Lehi in Zarahemla before ultimately culminating in the final battle of the Nehor War at the end of that year. This vengeful Lamanite antagonism posed a serious threat to the Nephites. It was one of several underlying factors that led to Moroni's sudden expansion of the Nephite defensive posture in 72 BC.[984] Whereas the southern border of Jershon was unnecessary and insignificant as a strategic point of Nephite defense before 81 BC, it immediately began to gain importance when the Lamanite army fled into the east wilderness after being surprised by Zoram in the south wilderness (narrow strip of wilderness), following their devastating attack on the city of Ammonihah.[985]

They remained in the east wilderness over the following three years, initially utilizing the region as a base for their unsuccessful military campaign against the Nephites[986] until internal strife began to rage out of control.[987] The fact that they were already heading east when intercepted by Zoram belies the fact that even as they departed from Ammonihah and Noah into the wilderness, their intention was to slip into the east wilderness and continue their war with the Nephites. Otherwise, they would have turned west in the narrow strip of wilderness toward the city of Nephi.

Only at the end of the three futile years of violence and warfare did they depart from the east wilderness and return to the land (city) of Nephi, where once again the people of Anti-Nephi-Lehi became the target of their frustrations.[988] The people of Anti-Nephi-Lehi responded to the renewed hostility (through the counsel of Ammon and his brethren) by fleeing out of Nephi into the wilderness.[989] Upon learning of their departure, tens of thousands of Lamanites were gathered and stirred up to anger by the Amalekites. Soon they pursued the people of Anti-Nephi-Lehi through the wilderness to the land of Zarahemla.

In the great battle of 77 BC, which took place in the borders of Jershon,[990] the Nephites defeated the Lamanites. For the second time, the Lamanites fled into the east wilderness. Some fled eastward into unsettled Nephite lands along Jershon's east coast. Many fled into the region lying southward from Jershon. Their habitation along the seaboard in Jershon ended in 72 BC,[991] when Moroni sent his armies to drive them southward across the narrow strip of wilderness.[992] However, that portion of the east wilderness lying to the south of Jershon became a permanent region within the land of Nephi from 77 BC forward.

The east wilderness had been a place of intense suffering and contention in 81 BC,[993] which likely was the prime reason the

Lamanites had remained there only temporarily, opting to return to the city of Nephi after three years.[994] In contrast, their permanent settlement of the east region in 77 BC coincided with the Ammonite occupation of Jershon.[995] More than likely, it was directly related to the long-term purpose of exacting revenge against the people of Anti-Nephi-Lehi.[996] The region became a focal point of Lamanite aggression from that time forward, and therefore, it became necessary for Moroni to fortify the south border of Jershon in 72 BC. (See Appendix A, Map A-6.)

Revisiting the City of Antionum

The Zoramite city of Antionum was most likely established at the southern border of Jershon in or shortly after 76 BC, the year following the permanent arrival of the Lamanites. It is apparent that it was placed next to the Lamanite border to take advantage of the large number of Lamanites, who were there purely as a result of their hostility to the people of Ammon. The Zoramites, who in their hearts were already dissenters,[997] could thus tap into the new reservoir of Lamanite warriors to accomplish their murderous and subversive objectives against the Nephites.

I.A. SOUTHERN BORDER—EASTERN SEGMENT: THREE FORTIFIED CITIES IN JERSHON

In 72 BC, following the Zoramite conflict and Amalickiah's first offensive, Moroni's first order of business was the placement of a line of defensive cities along the southern border of Jershon. Defense of Jershon was perhaps the top priority due to the fact that the Lamanites in that region were currently the most hostile to the Nephites. They had participated in the Zoramite conflict two only years previously.

As referenced above, many Lamanites had settled Nephite lands along the seaboard to the north of the Nephite and Lamanite boundary. Therefore, it was necessary for Moroni to send an army to drive them southward across the border.[998] After the land was cleared of Lamanites, three fortified cities were established along the southern border of Jershon, which from east to west were identified as Moroni, Nephihah, and Aaron.[999]

The city of Moroni was built on the shores of the east sea in that year. The city of Nephihah was also established between Moroni and a previously existing city of Aaron.[1000] As described in Alma 50:13–15, Aaron was the third fortified city from the east coast, but the only one probably established prior to 72 BC. Aaron could not have been in existence for more than five years, however, because the east region of Jershon was uninhabited and known only as the east wilderness[1001] prior to the arrival of the people of Anti-Nephi-Lehi at the end of 77 BC.

The City of Aaron

The identity of Aaron thus becomes a matter of interest. Its establishment prior to 72 BC, the fact that it bore the name of Mosiah's son, and its location near the southern border of Jershon, where it could be utilized by Moroni as a perimeter stronghold, all combined to provide a strong and compelling implication that it was the city of the Ammonites, formerly the people of Anti-Nephi-Lehi. Reference was made earlier in the Book of Mormon to an unnamed Ammonite city, where Moroni stationed a division of his army during the Zoramite War to defend it if "a part of the Lamanites should [return]," lest they should "take possession of the city."[1002] It is concluded that this unnamed city was the city of Aaron.

The identification of Aaron as the unnamed Ammonite city eliminates the apparent ambiguity of poorly referenced cities (for example, an unrelated and previously unnamed city of Aaron) that would otherwise indicate that the record is incomplete, especially concerning a sequence of events for which the Book of Mormon is most detailed. It explains why Mormon would speak of Aaron in Alma 50:14 without introduction. He had already referenced it in Alma 43:25, though not by name.

In Alma's multi-regional perspective when he traveled to Antionum from the city of Zarahemla to preach the gospel in 75 BC, he described Antionum as "nearly bordering upon the seashore" and "south of the land of Jershon, which also bordered upon the wilderness south."[1003] When the eastern Nephite lands were developed for defensive purposes in 72 BC, the geographic perspective was greatly focused in scope and became much more detailed. The city of Aaron became the third city from the east coast, with Moroni and Nephihah both being constructed nearer to the east sea, though all three cities were on the southern border of Jershon.

IB. SOUTHERN BORDER—WEST FROM MANTI TO THE WEST SEA

Of similar if not equal importance to the eastern segment of the Nephite southern border, fortified cities were also placed along the western segment of the southern border.[1004] The strategic placement of cities along the western portion was extremely crucial because, with the exception of the great battle of 77 BC,[1005] and the initial encounter in the Zoramite War,[1006] all of the previous invading Lamanite armies had passed over the southern border at some point along that western interval. There were at least three attacks at Manti and two at Ammonihah and Noah.

The locations of previous Lamanite attacks were a direct consequence of the geographical relationship between the city of Nephi, where most invasions were organized, and the city of Zarahemla, the ultimate focal point of every invasion. Until 77 BC, when the Lamanites permanently settled the east wilderness, the relatively short segment of the narrow strip of wilderness from Manti to a location generally southward of Ammonihah was naturally the point of Lamanite entry into the land of Zarahemla.

The increasing Lamanite focus upon Jershon did not eliminate the critical importance of defending the western segment. It therefore comes as no surprise that in 72 BC, Moroni also secured cities "on the west, fortifying the line between the Nephites and the Lamanites, between the land of Zarahemla and the land of Nephi, *from the west sea running by the head of the river Sidon.*"[1007] As later identified in Alma 56:14, from east to west, these cities were Manti, Zeezrom, Cumeni, Antiparah, and a coastal city not identified by name. (See Appendix A, Map A-6.)

II. EASTERN SEABOARD—FROM MORONI TO DESOLATION

In addition to the cities along the southern border (narrow strip of wilderness) from the east sea to the west sea, fortified cities were placed along the eastern coast of Jershon and Bountiful. The line of cities included six named cities along Jershon's seashore on the east, which extended northward to the eastern border of the land of Bountiful.[1008] The city of Bountiful in the land of Bountiful and potentially other unnamed cities in Bountiful rounded out the eastern seaboard cities.[1009] Therefore, a minimum of seven named cities, plus the fortifications at the boundary between Bountiful and Desolation,[1010] lined the eastern border of Nephite lands from south to north. The line of coastal cities presented a seemingly unending chain of resistance to Lamanite advancement that would necessitate a herculean effort to reach the land of Desolation on the Narrow Neck (Appendix A, Map A-6).

III. WESTERN SEABOARD—FROM UNNAMED CITY TO DESOLATION

Long before 81 BC, the year of the first sporadic settlement of the east wilderness, Lamanites "were spread through the wilderness . . . on the west of the land of Zarahemla, in the borders by the seashore."[1011] Unlike the east coast, which was truly remote wilderness throughout the first five centuries of Nephite New World habitation, the west coast was the "place of their fathers' first inheritance."[1012]

Many Lamanites had never left the west coast, opting to remain there perpetually. The west shoreline was a direct extension of the place of the first landing. Over the centuries, they had naturally drifted northward along the coastline toward the narrow neck of land.

With the sudden expansion of Zarahemla in 72 BC, the west coastal region lying well to the west of the Sidon River was immediately incorporated into Nephite holdings. As a result, it became necessary to expel Lamanites from the region. Only then could the Nephites eliminate their northward movement toward the narrow neck of land.

Moroni would not have failed to drive the Lamanites out of the newly claimed Nephite lands along the west sea and then to fortify the western perimeter in the same way he fortified the eastern perimeter as outlined above. Though unmentioned in the Book of Mormon text, it is likely that, similar to the fortification of the east coast, cities were established at regular intervals along the western border of Nephite territory during the Amalickiah and Ammoron Wars. Scanty though specific information is supplied for the region in Alma chapter 52.

The indication is given that the cities were fortified only as defense became necessary. It appears that the west coast was not fortified until 66 BC, when Ammoron attacked the region.[1013] The city at the southern end of the western seaboard is referenced in the Book of Mormon, as are the fortifications at the northern end.[1014] None of the intermediate cities along the western coastline are directly referenced, though the crucial need for such a line of cities is provided in Alma chapter 52.[1015]

IV. NORTHERN BORDER—THE NARROW NECK OF LAND: DESOLATION

The primary purpose of the eastern and western coastal fortifications was to impede the northward march of Lamanite armies along either of the two peripheral regions. Neither region had significant Nephite population prior to Moroni's establishment of the fortified cities.[1016] Prior to 72 BC, a Lamanite army, if so inclined, could have moved northward largely undetected along either of the two coastal corridors until they reached the narrow neck of land.

Located at the common end of the two coastal lines, the "line Bountiful and the land Desolation"[1017] was the official northern boundary of the land southward and constituted a single location where the Lamanite armies could be halted and prevented from advancing into the land northward. It marked the southern boundary of the land of Desolation, which extended northward all the way to the former land of Moron, the southernmost land of the Jaredites,[1018] with the exception of the previously mentioned outpost city of Lib, which apparently was established for the processing of game before shipment northward.[1019] The fortified length of the northern border was "the distance of a day and a half's travel for a Nephite" at the southern border of Desolation.[1020] The city of Desolation, which was not established until the post-Christ era,[1021] would become the only city required to provide adequate coverage for defense against attacks from the south to maintain control of the narrow neck of land. In the pre-Christ period, fortifications were established at some point, but no city is ever referenced.

The extreme importance placed upon preventing Lamanites (and dissenters during the Amalickiah and Ammoron War) from passing into the land northward is frequently touched upon in the books of

Alma and Helaman.[1022] However, fortifications were apparently not established when Moroni fortified the southern and eastern borders between 72 and 68 BC. This can be ascertained from the account of Morianton's flight toward the land northward in 68 BC, which is discussed below. An army was not already in place to block Morianton's flight. Instead, it was required that Teancum pursue Morianton and overtake him on the narrow neck of land.[1023]

This would suggest that the southern and eastern borders of Jershon (the hotbed of Lamanite aggression at that time) and the southern border from Manti westward to the vicinity of the city of Nephi were the principle areas of focus in 72 BC. The fortification of each region was addressed as it became necessary. The narrow neck of land would not come to the direct attention of the Nephites until Morianton's flight in 68 BC. Extensive fortifications would not be placed there until 66 BC.[1024] Likewise, the west coastal region, never a problem in the past, would become an immediate concern only when Ammoron waged a campaign there, also in about 66 BC. In time, certainly by 35 BC when the first battle at the borders of Desolation occurred,[1025] fortifications would be extended all across the narrow neck of land.

After all the southern perimeter cities were established, the land of Zarahemla became defensible at any point the Lamanites chose to attack. Generally, Lamanite armies dared not pass by a fortified city and move into the interior of Nephite lands or up the coastline for fear that they would become trapped between Nephite armies[1026] and/or have their supply lines cut off. The only reasonable way they could move northward past a city was to first defeat the occupying Nephite army and take control of the city.

FURTHER IMPROVEMENT OF FORTIFICATIONS AT EACH CITY

In addition to establishing this complete system of fortified cities, the defensive works around each city were further developed as well, especially along the southern border, where initial attacks would occur. At the time of the Lamanite attack at Ammonihah and Noah, the fortifications had been basic, involving nothing more than a ditch, an associated ridge of earth lining its interior side, and a causeway, which was simply a break in the ditch (a point where the ditch was not excavated) that provided a walkway into the city.

Given the luxury of time, Moroni was able to further enhance the fortifications by adding a framework of wooden timbers at the top of the ridge of earth circling each city. The vertical height of the ridge circling each city was thus increased by about five or six feet.[1027] It provided a measure of stability for the earthen mound and a vertical barrier at the mound's summit, as well as protective cover for the Nephite defenders.

While the Lamanites were occupied trying to climb the precipitous slope of loose soil, they were vulnerable to attack. The walls could be scaled, if a skilled and athletic climber could ascend undetected,[1028] but it was virtually impossible to contend with enemy soldiers while in the act of climbing. Furthermore, if a Lamanite warrior could somehow manage to scale the mound of earth from the bottom of the ditch to the top of the ridge without being slain by falling objects, he then would find a wall at its summit, with armed Nephite soldiers standing securely behind it, well protected from any incoming projectiles that might reach the summit of the ridge. They would be fresh and ready to give battle, while the Lamanites on the other hand would be fatigued from the exertion of the climb.

FINAL THOUGHTS CONCERNING MORONI'S FORTIFICATIONS

The extensive fortifications surrounding at a minimum the southern and eastern borders of the expanded land of Zarahemla were truly inspired of God. Without them, Amalickiah and Ammoron might have succeeded in defeating the Nephites. But it must be acknowledged that it was the Lord who was in control during this time of Nephite obedience to the gospel of Jesus Christ. It was for that purpose that the Lord raised up Moroni and his fellow patriots at that time to defend the Nephites and preserve Christianity.

CHAPTER 3.5

THE HEMISPHERIC WORLD OF BOOK OF MORMON GEOGRAPHY

THE IDENTIFICATION OF NORTH and South America as the land northward and the land southward of the Book of Mormon—joined together by the Isthmus of Panama—is completely viable. In fact, the greater scope of a hemispheric geography has been deemed necessary in order for the Nephites to have been completely unaware of the Jaredites and Mulekites throughout a 400-year period of cohabitation in the Western Hemisphere.

In the hemispheric perspective, the land of Zarahemla comprised the northern portion of South America. It was surrounded by ocean on the north, east, and west, except for the narrow neck of land. The only viable candidate for the narrow strip of wilderness, which defined the southern border of Zarahemla from sea to sea, is described in Chapter 3.3 previously.

Recently, however, after this book had largely been written, the specific boundaries of the four regional lands that comprised the greater land of Zarahemla were still unresolved. Furthermore, at first consideration, identification of the exact boundaries of the regional lands does not seem plausible, or even possible for that matter. The relative position of each land is clearly described in the Book of Mormon, but none of the information provided enables us to determine a precise configuration for their boundaries.

A number of different geographical scenarios have seemed possible. For instance, the Book of Mormon identifies four regional lands, but was there a fifth regional land, a counterpart to Jershon, which extended from north to south along the borders of the west sea? In the center of the land, were the Hermounts nothing more than a southern extension of the wilderness of Bountiful, or was it a uniquely different body of wilderness, as its name would suggest? The answer to these seemingly unanswerable questions recently came, not from the Book of Mormon, but from the Nephite heartland as identified in this book, and more specifically, as it is known today within the boundaries of Colombia and Venezuela.

Los Llanos (pronounced: [yanos], "the Plains") is a vast, tropical grassland plain situated to the east of the Andes in northwestern South America. It is a region of flooded grasslands and savannas. Accounts of the Spanish conquest of the Americas describe the grasses of *Los Llanos* as standing above the heads of men on horseback. Map 8.0 below depicts the boundaries of *Los Llanos* region in the shaded area, as it exists today within the continent of South America. *Los Llanos* stands in sharp contrast to the forest-covered regions that surround it. It borders the Orinoco River on the west and, after the river swings eastward, on the north.

It is projected that this region, which lies within the greater land of Zarahemla, was initially called the wilderness of Hermounts, which bordered the city of Zarahemla "on the west and on the north."[1029] Later, it is identified as "the land which was between the land Zarahemla and the land Bountiful."[1030] Likely, it was called the land of Hermounts, after it was settled and developed, considering the fact that the wilderness of Bountiful, after settlement by the Nephites, was called the land of Bountiful. The city of Zarahemla was situated on the west bank of the Sidon River, which flowed northward at that location from its headwaters at the city of Manti.

Today, *Los Llanos* is well known because of its distinctive characteristics that set it apart from the surrounding forested regions. Just as remarkable is the fact that it extends toward the southwest precisely to the narrow strip of wilderness. On the northeast, it terminates only a few miles from the coast. By identifying the land between Zarahemla and Bountiful as *Los Llanos*, the entire boundaries of the other three lands can now be delineated. By knowing the precise dimensions of the central regional land of Hermounts as it exists today, the scope and extent of the other three lands can be determined. Listing each land separately as they appear on the maps in this book, their boundaries are defined as follows:

- Bountiful is bordered by ocean on the north and west. It is bordered on the east by Jershon, on the south by the narrow strip of wilderness, and along its entire southeast border by the land of Hermounts.

- Zarahemla is bordered along its entire northwest border by Hermounts. It is bounded on the south by the narrow strip of wilderness. On the east, it is bordered by the land of Jershon and an impassable mountainous region known today as the highlands of Guyana.

- Jershon is bordered by ocean on the north and east. It is bounded on the south by the narrow strip of wilderness. On the west, it is bordered by the land of Hermounts, the land of Zarahemla, and the impassable mountainous region.

If accurate, the above geographical information dramatically raises the degree of correlation between the Book of Mormon account and the archaeological record.

In future publications, the Book of Mormon will be further examined in a hemispheric setting. First, events that occurred between 55 BC and AD 34 will supply additional valuable information pertaining to the history and geography of the Nephites within the land southward during the pre-Christ era. The Book of Mormon narrative then moves dramatically into the land northward for the final deadly struggle, which provides valuable information concerning the geography of the land northward.

APPENDIX A

SETTLEMENT AND HABITATION
OF THE LAND SOUTHWARD

THE FOLLOWING SERIES OF maps is based on geographical
information contained in Mormon's abridgment of the large
plate of Nephi from Mosiah chapter 1 to 3 Nephi chapter 8.
Abundant historical and geographical information pertaining to the
land of Zarahemla is contained in this portion of Mormon's abridgment, which deals almost exclusively with the history of Zarahemla.

The loss of the first 116 pages of Mormon's abridgment has prevented students of the Book of Mormon from likewise having a
clear and comprehensive view of the land of Nephi. The lost portion
deals primarily with nearly four centuries of Nephite habitation in
the land of Nephi.[1031] Given Mormon's focus on history and geography, it is likely that they contain much information pertaining to
cities and regions within the land of Nephi, as well as in Lamanite
lands, which at the time bordered along the west sea.[1032]

Little meaningful geographical information is supplied by the
small plate of Nephi (1 Nephi through the book of Omni). This is in
keeping with Nephi's description of the Small Plates as a spiritual
record and not a historical record.[1033]

200

Map A-1: The Geography of the Land Southward as Identified
In the Book of Mormon between 589 and *ca.* 200 BC

PERIOD 1: 589 BC TO CA. 200 BC (MAP A-1)

During this period, the Nephites resided in the highlands of
Nephi and the Lamanites were distributed to the west of Nephi "in
the place of their fathers' first inheritance, and thus bordering along
by the seashore."[1034] The Lamanites were a constant source of violence against them throughout the period. The region later known
as the land of Zarahemla remained undiscovered during the period
and was part of the great wilderness lying to the north and east of
Nephi.

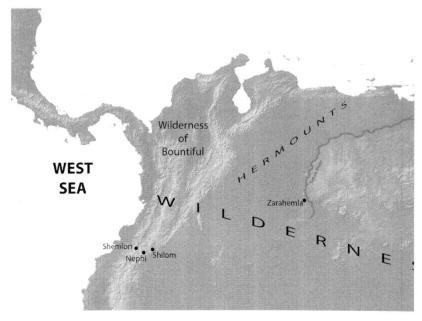

Map A-2: The Geography of the Zarahemla and Nephi as Identified
in the Book of Mormon between *ca.* 200 and 140 BC

PERIOD 2: FROM CA. 200 BC TO CA. 140 BC (MAP A-2)

There were no cities lying between the cities of Zarahemla
and Nephi. The two cities were separated by the great wilderness
region, which was completely undifferentiated at that time. The land
of Zarahemla was nothing more than an isolated settlement zone
along the Sidon River in the midst of the wilderness. This initial
region of expansion extended along the Sidon River valley from the
Sidon's headwaters to the city of Zarahemla (plus the region extending northward from the city of Zarahemla to the city of Bountiful)
would constitute the Nephite heartland throughout the entire pre-
Christ period.[1035]

The city of Nephi was located in a highland region. The land
of Nephi (the region occupied by Lamanites during this period)
extended westward from the great wilderness that bordered on the
cities of Nephi and Shilom all the way to the west sea, the location
of the first landing.

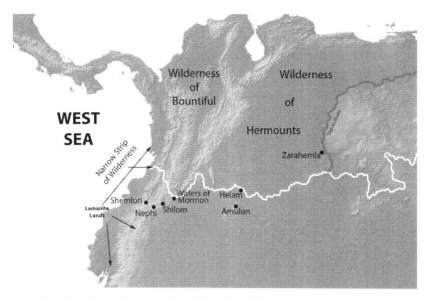

Map A-3: The Geography of the Land Southward as Developed between *ca.* 140 and 87 BC

PERIOD 3: CA. 140 BC TO 87 BC (MAP A-3)

Little change in the settlement of the land southward occurred, except for the establishment of two cities. The city of Helam was established by Alma the Elder and his followers not quite halfway between the city of Nephi and the city of Zarahemla. The city of Amulon was established by the former priests of King Noah, who were led by Amulon. After 121 BC, the two cities were in the hands of the Lamanites.

PERIOD 4: 87 BC TO 77 BC (MAP A-4)

During this period, the Nephites first began to move outward from the city of Zarahemla and establish additional cities. The first Book of Mormon reference to outward expansion is found in Mosiah 27:6. The context of the verse seems to indicate the expansion occurred sometime between 100 and 92 BC during the reign of Mosiah II.

However, it is then implied in Alma chapter 2 that Zarahemla was still the only city in 87 BC during the Amlicite War.[1036] At that time, Gideon on the east and Manti on the south were not yet established. The valley of Gideon was first named by the Nephites in

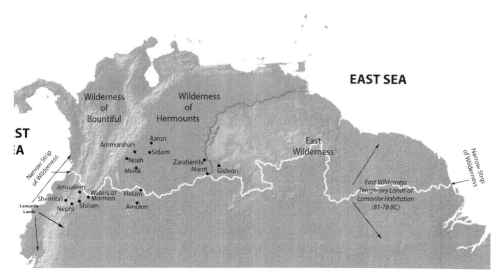

Map A-4: The Geography of the Land Southward as Developed
between 87 and 77 BC

87 BC,[1037] and by 83 BC, a city had been established there.[1038] Manti was established at the headwaters of the Sidon River between 87 and 81 BC.[1039] The wilderness of Hermounts still bordered the city of Zarahemla on the west, where the cities of Ammonihah, Aaron, Sidom, and Melek would be located by the time of Alma's ministry in 82 BC. Hermounts also lay to the north of the city of Zarahemla, where many heartland cities would later by located by 51 BC.[1040] In the land of Nephi, the Lamanites inhabited the east wilderness for the first time during this period, which occurred temporarily from 81 to 78 BC.

PERIOD 5: 77 BC TO 72 BC (MAP A-5)

The Lamanite land of Nephi permanently expanded into the east wilderness in 77 BC, primarily as a Lamanite response to the settlement of the people of Ammon in Jershon. Lamanite antagonism and revenge was the underlying reason for the Lamanite presence in the east wilderness, initially both north and south of the narrow strip of wilderness. In 77 BC, the city of Aaron was likely established by the people of Ammon near the south border of the east wilderness.[1041] In about 76 BC, the city of Antionum was founded by the Zoramites at the south border of the east wilderness.

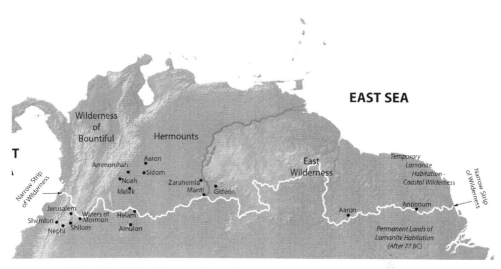

Map A-5: The Geography of the Land Southward as Developed
between 77 and 72 BC

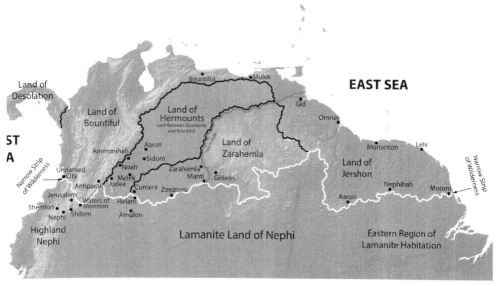

Map A-6: The Geography of the Land Southward as Developed
between 72 and 51 BC

PERIOD 6: 72 BC TO 51 BC (MAP A-6)

This period began in 72 BC when the Nephites identified and
laid official claim to all lands within the land southward lying to
the north of the narrow strip of wilderness, from the west sea to the

east sea. Moroni immediately sent out armies to drive all Lamanites southward across the narrow strip of wilderness before placing defensive cities around the entire perimeter. Eight fortified cities were either established or strengthened along the narrow strip of wilderness. Seven additional cities were placed along the eastern seaboard.

Though never mentioned directly, it is projected that an unknown number of defensive cities were also placed at intervals along the western seaboard. These of necessity would have been placed northward from the unnamed city on the south, when Ammoron threatened the southern border of the land in 66 BC. Once the fortifications were in place, Nephite citizens were then encouraged to move outward from the Sidon River area, both toward the east and the west, to settle the entire land from sea to sea.

There is no indication of fortifications at Desolation or of Nephite occupation prior to 66 BC. In fact, as described in Alma chapter 50, it was necessary in 68 BC for Teancum's army to overtake Morianton at the "narrow pass which led by the sea into the land northward."[1042] He could not rely on an army already in place to stop them at the "line [between] Bountiful and the land Desolation."[1043]

The city of Bountiful, though lying northward from the city of Zarahemla,[1044] was situated by the east sea. Alternatively, the city of Moroni lay southeastward from the city of Zarahemla,[1045] though it too rested on the shore of the east sea. To produce this geographic configuration, the shoreline of the east sea must swing sharply around from the city of Moroni to the city of Bountiful, as depicted on Map A-6.

APPENDIX B

A QUICK SCRIPTURAL GUIDE TO THE GEOGRAPHIC PLACEMENT OF BOOK OF MORMON CITIES

THE CITIES INCLUDED ON Map A-6 in Appendix A comprise all cities identified in the Book of Mormon during the period of maximum growth and development (between 72 BC and AD 34) for which a reasonable geographical location can be ascertained. The cities illustrate the fact that the Nephites had spread across the entire face of the land, from sea to sea. They represent, however, only a small portion of the cities in the land southward during the period.

In the region surrounding the city of Nephi, the cities of Nephi, Shilom, Shemlon, and Jerusalem are included on the map. Other cities are identified in the account of Mosiah's sons' mission to the Lamanites, for which insufficient information is provided to determine their relative geographic location. These five cities have been placed in the lower section of Table B-1 below but are not included on the Appendix A maps.

The cities presented on Map A-6 are listed alphabetically on Table B-1. The verses, which are included within the table, do not necessarily represent all scriptures pertaining to a given city, but establish the relative geographic location, in a regional perspective, with respect to other nearby cities. Verses are omitted with respect to some cities because they do not provide geographical data.

TABLE B-1

SCRIPTURAL REFERENCE GUIDE FOR THE GEOGRAPHIC PLACEMENT OF ALL CITIES ON MAP A-6

CITY	LOCATION	SCRIPTURE
Aaron (southeast)	Southern border of Jershon, the third fortified city from the east sea	Alma 43:25; 50:13–14
Aaron (west)	Near Ammonihah	Alma 8:13
Ammonihah	West of the city of Zarahemla, three days north of Melek	Alma 8:3, 6
Amulon	In the wilderness between the cities of Nephi and Zarahemla	Mosiah 23:30–31
Antionum	Southern border of Jershon	Alma 31:3
Antiparah	Southern border of Zarahemla between Cumeni and the unnamed city along the narrow strip of wilderness	Alma 50:11; 56:13–14, 30–31; 57:1–4
Bountiful	North of city of Zarahemla, bordering on east sea	Alma 51:22–32; 52:16–17; Helaman 1:23
Cumeni	Southern border of Zarahemla between Antiparah and Zeezrom along the narrow strip of wilderness	Alma 50:11; 56:13–14
Desolation	Fortifications only, not a city during the pre-Christ period. Located on the narrow neck of land, at the northern border of Bountiful	Alma 22:31–32; 50:33–34; Helaman 4:4–7
Gid	Situated along the east coast between Omner and Mulek	Alma 51:26
Gideon	Less than one day east of city of Zarahemla	Alma 2:15–20; 6:7
Helam	Eight days eastward from the Waters of Mormon along the narrow strip of wilderness and twelve days westward of the land of Zarahemla, which at that time was limited to the Sidon River valley (see Chapter 3.1, The Land of Zarahemla—Recently settled)	Mosiah 18:30–34; 23:1–5, 20; 24:20–25

CITY	LOCATION	SCRIPTURE
Jerusalem	Near the Waters of Mormon	Alma 21:1
Judea	Northward of Antiparah toward the city of Zarahemla	Alma 50:11; 56:9, 13–15 (1–32)
Lehi	Located between Morianton and Moroni on the coast of the east sea	Alma 50:15, 25; 51:22–32
Omner	Between Gid and Morianton on the borders of the east sea	Alma 51:26
Manti	Located at the headwaters of the Sidon River, less than one day south of the city of Zarahemla	Alma 16:6–7; 22:27; 43:22; 50:11; 56:13–14; 57:22
Melek	Located westward from the city of Zarahemla and three days south of Ammonihah.	Alma 8:3–6
Morianton	Between Omner and Lehi on the borders of the east sea.	Alma 50:25; 51:26
Moroni	At the southeast corner of Jershon on the borders of the east sea	Alma 50:13–14; 51:22–26
Mulek	Between Bountiful and Gid on the borders of the east sea	Alma 51:22–32; 52:2, 16–17
Nephi	Highland Nephi south of the Waters of Mormon	Mosiah 9:8,15; 10:7–8; 11:12–13
Nephihah	On the narrow strip of wilderness between Aaron and Moroni	Alma 50:11, 13–14; 51:24–25
Shilom	Bordered on the city of Nephi in the land of Nephi	Mosiah 9:6–8; 10:7–8; 11:12–13
Shemlon	Located near the cities of Nephi and Shilom in the land of Nephi	Mosiah 10:7–8; 11:12–13
Sidom	Located near the city of Ammonihah	Alma 15:1
Unnamed City	At the southwest corner of the greater land of Zarahemla on the borders of the west sea	Alma 50:11; 56:30–33
Waters of Mormon	Near the city of Nephi in the borders of the land of Nephi	Mosiah 18:1–5, 16, 30–31

City	Location	Scripture
Zarahemla	In the center of Nephite lands after 200 BC, located on the west side of the Sidon River, less than one day north of Manti, less than one day west of Gideon	Omni 1:12–13; Alma 2:21–26; Alma 17:1
Zeezrom	Southern border of Zarahemla between Manti and Cumeni along the narrow strip of wilderness	Alma 50:11; 56:14
Cities with Insufficient Information for Relative Placement of Map		
Ishmael	Possibly not far from the city of Nephi—the first stop of Ammon after he separated from his brethren	Alma 17:20
Lemuel	Not far from the cities of Nephi, Shilom, and Shemlon	Alma 23:12–13
Midian	Near the land of Ishmael	Alma 24:5
Middoni	Near the land of Ishmael	Alma 21:18
Shimnilom	Near the cities of Nephi and Shilom	Alma 23:8, 12

APPENDIX C

A LIST OF HYPOTHESES PROPOSED IN THIS BOOK

IVE HYPOTHESES HAVE BEEN set forth during the course of this book, each of which concerns cultural relationships, physical geography, and events that significantly shaped the Nephite cultural experience. Due to the fact that they are embedded within chapters, they are gathered together in this appendix to provide a quick listing that is easy to find.

Some well-developed ideas are not labeled hypotheses, such as the identification of

- Two pagan periods during the pre-Christ period
- The account of a pagan conspiracy

In such cases, all of the information necessary to reach a logical conclusion is contained in the Book of Mormon. However, with respect to the two major periods of pagan religion, Mormon did not clearly identify the divisions.

The five hypotheses and their location in this book are identified as follows.

HYPOTHESIS 1: THE TIME AND SCOPE OF THE NEPHITE "TRANSGRESSION" (3 NEPHI 5:12)

(As inferred from Part 1, Chapters 1.2–1.6)

Alma was endowed with power and authority from heaven to reestablish the Church of Jesus Christ, not only among the people of Alma, but within the land of Zarahemla as well. The Church had been broken up at the time of "their transgression," which likely took place many years before King Mosiah led his people from Nephi to Zarahemla. The "transgression" may have taken place around 279

BC,[1046] approximately 80 years before the people of Mosiah departed from the land of Nephi. It was during that time that the Nephites had many seasons of war, which resulted in the destruction of the more wicked part of the people.

In 399 BC, during a time of righteousness, Jarom had referenced Nephite prophecies of warning.[1047] From the beginning the prophets had warned the people of Nephi that if they "should fall into transgression, they should be destroyed from off the face of the land."[1048] The prophecies pertained to the Nephites throughout their history, but most poignantly of all to the destruction at Cumorah, for that was the time of their ultimate and final fulfillment. Still, they were in effect at all times and many times spurred the Nephites to repentance. During the days of Omni, approximately 120 years after Jarom's reference, transgression[1049] resulted in the destruction of the wicked part of the people, though the righteous were spared.

While acknowledging the severely limited historical record throughout the Nephite era in the land of Nephi (as contained in the small plate of Nephi), it is submitted herein that this appears to be the most logical time for the breakup of the Church. There was no subsequent period of peace in the land of Nephi, during which the Church could be restored.[1050] War continued from that time until Mosiah gathered up the righteous and departed into the wilderness.[1051]

Alma the Elder was chosen by God as a prophet to reestablish the Church. It was not a restoration of gospel truths, for they had never been lost.[1052] It was a restoration of the Church of Christ and of the saving ordinance of baptism, neither of which were available to the people of King Benjamin at the time they made a covenant with God to bear the name of Christ.[1053] The Church and the ordinance of baptism were immediately reestablished among the Nephites in the land of Zarahemla upon Alma's arrival.

HYPOTHESIS 2: THE ORIGIN OF THE ORDER OF NEHOR

(Part 2, Chapter 2.3)

The religious order of Nehor was practiced by Nehor, the Amlicites, and the people of Ammonihah in the land of Zarahemla. It was practiced by the Amalekites and Amulonites in the land of Nephi.

The religion originated in the Jaredite city of Nehor, the birthplace of Jaredite idolatry during the third generation of Jaredite kings.[1054] The Mulekites practiced a primitive form of the Jaredite pagan religion when they migrated southward from the land of Desolation in the land northward.

As a result, the order of Nehor and the Zoramite pagan religions (Chapter 2.3) divide the history of Zarahemla into two discrete (nonoverlapping) pagan periods, which cover the entire Zarahemla period in the pre-Christ period. The period of the Nehors in the land southward began with the arrival of the Mulekites from the land of Desolation. As pertaining to Nephite history, it began with the arrival of the people of Mosiah in Zarahemla and their merger with the people of Zarahemla. The period of the Nehors is projected to have begun in *ca.* 200 BC and to have ended in *ca.* 75 BC. The period of the Zoramites lasted from *ca.* 75 BC to the defeat of the Gadianton robbers in AD 25. Though it is not stated in the Book of Mormon, the Zoramite religion may still have been practiced in the pagan cities at the time they were destroyed by the Great Storm of AD 34.

HYPOTHESIS 3: THE MULEKITE TRANSFER OF THE ORDER OF NEHOR FROM THE JAREDITES TO THE NEPHITES

(Part 2, Chapter 2.3)

- The Mulekites were not drawn into the final Jaredite war. Though they occupied adjacent land to the south of the Jaredites, they were far enough removed from the Jaredites, geographically as well as culturally, to avoid the destruction but near enough to encounter King Coriantumr, following the war, after he wandered back to his homeland in the city of Moron.[1055]

- It is obvious the Mulekites embraced the Jaredite pagan religion. This can be seen in the fact that "they denied the being of their Creator" when discovered by the Nephites,[1056] in combination with the facts that they had come from the land northward[1057] and many bore Jaredite names. When Alma the Younger, a Nephite, joined the religion prior to his conversion to Christianity, he also gave his children Jaredite names.[1058]

- When the Mulekites fled into the land southward, they nurtured the seed of Jaredite idolatry, though it had been the direct cause of the Jaredite extinction (in direct association with the secret combinations). When they were discovered by the people of Mosiah, they were largely under its influence and ultimately, the Mulekite pagan religion is identified as the order of the Nehors, that is, the order of the people of the Jaredite land of Nehor—the land of its origination.

HYPOTHESIS 4: AMALEKITE TRANSFER OF THE ORDER OF NEHOR FROM NEPHITES TO LAMANITES AND HISTORY OF THE AMALEKITES

(Part 2, Chapter 2.3)

- The Amalekites likely originally lived in the land of Zarahemla, where they embraced the Mulekite variant of the Jaredite religion of Nehor.

- The Amalekites were probably the dissenters who fled to the land of Nephi to escape from King Benjamin's judgment for their insurrection.

- The Amalekites introduced the religion of Nehor to the Lamanites in the land of Nephi and built temples after the order of Nehor. After the Amulonites united with the Lamanites, they too embraced the religion of Nehor. The religion may or may not have been known by that appellation before 91 BC (Alma chapter 1), though it was referenced as such in Alma 21:4, which is part of the account of the mission of the sons of Mosiah in the land of Nephi that takes place at essentially the same time in which Alma became the chief judge in the land of Zarahemla.

HYPOTHESIS 5: THE NARROW STRIP OF WILDERNESS

(Part 3, Chapters 3.2–3.3)

Alma the Elder was the first to discover the narrow strip of wilderness. The Waters of Mormon, the city of Helam (with its pure water source), and the headwaters of the Sidon were all located along the narrow strip of wilderness, likely a hydrologic divide, which separated river drainage basins and naturally delineated the boundaries between the land of Nephi and the land of Zarahemla. As a result, the two nations were not connected by waterways. The divide enabled east and west navigation along the Nephite and Lamanite boundary in an otherwise unnavigable wilderness. It provided the most passable route of travel—largely unimpeded by swamps, bogs, and water streams.

APPENDIX D

THE AMALICKIAH AND AMMORON OFFENSIVE—A YEAR-BY-YEAR ACCOUNT

IN CHAPTER 2.5, THE Amalickiah and Ammoron offensive was introduced and the battlefronts were identified, but a detailed account of the war was not included. Those details are included herein for those who are interested in a year-by-year chronicle of the war, as it occurred within four regions in the greater land of Zarahemla.

THE AMALICKIAH AND AMMORON WARS BEGIN

In 67 BC, shortly after the five-year anniversary of the attack at Noah, all of the critical elements for success seemed to Amalickiah to have fallen into line. The battle plan had been fully developed. Lamanites had been gathered from across the land of Nephi. The land of Zarahemla was embroiled in political turmoil. Therefore, Amalickiah seized the opportunity and moved his armies into place in the east wilderness that bordered the coastal city of Moroni on the south. (See Map 5.0 in Chapter 2.5.)

As presented below, the war would be conducted along four separate and independent battlefronts:

- Eastern seaboard (Amalickiah's first and primary point of attack)

- Center of the land (king-men rebellion—considered a battle-front because of its effect)

- Southern border (one of the initial battlefronts, but not identi-fied until Helaman's epistle)[1059]

- Western seaboard (a diversionary front to replace the king-men rebellion)

The western seaboard would not become a factor until 66 BC. Initially, the Center of the Land would become the second battle-front through the rebellion of the king-men, later to be replaced by the western seaboard offensive when Ammoron attacked there. The war is divided into one-year periods, and the four battlefronts are correlated within each period. The active battlefronts during each year of the war are presented in Table 3.0, which is included at the end of this appendix. It is noted that while there were never more than three battlefronts at any given time, three were active during five of the seven years of the war.

67 BC

EASTERN SEABOARD

THE FIRST BATTLEFRONT—THE EAST COAST OFFENSIVE

According to a carefully organized battle plan, the first attack took place at the city of Moroni on the southern border by the east sea. News of the attack traveled quickly. Soon, it reached the city of Zarahemla.

CENTER OF THE LAND

A SECOND BATTLEFRONT—REBELLION OF THE KING-MEN

When Amalickiah initiated the invasion, the king-men issue was coming to a close. When the king-men heard the news of his attack, "they were glad in their hearts; and they refused to take up arms."[1060] Though they claimed to be of royal stock, they were quite willing to be ruled by Amalickiah, a descendant of Zoram.[1061] The king-men's alliance to Amalickiah, possibly established while he had lived in Zarahemla,[1062] virtually eliminates the possibility that their claimed "nobility" was through descent from Mosiah, or any other descendant of Lehi. Likely, the king-men were Mulekites, descendants of Judah, the kingly tribe of Israel. Their acceptance of Amalickiah as king is a powerful indication that he was also of the tribe of Judah.

Chief Captain Moroni, upon hearing of the dissenters' refusal to defend their country was "exceedingly wroth."[1063] Showing tremen-dous restraint through his respect for the process of law, he sent a petition to Pahoran asking for the power to take his armies against the king-men to compel them to either fight for their country or be put to death. He received the desired authority "according to the voice of the people" and with no time to spare, he went against the king-men "to pull down their pride and nobility" and enlist them in the army.[1064]

To refuse meant death, and about 4,000 king-men were slain by Moroni's army as they raised "their weapons of war" in rebellion. The leaders were cast into prison, for there was no time for their trials.[1065] The remainder, not wanting to die, joined in the cause of freedom. Moroni thus "put an end to those king-men, that there were not any known by the appellation of king-men."[1066]

The king-men insurrection was the full equivalent of an attack by Amalickiah in the heart of Zarahemla. They were just as much an enemy to the Christian Nephite government as was Amalickiah and for all intents, purposes, and effects were an extension of the Lamanite forces. Many, if not most of them, had stood behind Amalickiah in 73 BC when he had first risen up against the Church of Christ. Now, six years later, they saw Amalickiah as an ally in an eternal war against the Christian Nephites. With the help of their internal resistance, the Amalickiah and Ammoron offensive would soon drive the Nephites to the very gates of destruction.

EASTERN SEABOARD

CAPTURE OF SIX CITIES ALONG THE EASTERN SEABOARD:
MORONI, LEHI, MORIANTON, OMNER, GID, AND MULEK

Considering the intensity of the king-men rebellion, it appears that Amalickiah indicated his intent to invade the city of Moroni well before the attack took place.[1067] Likely, his posturing at the borders of the land was designed for the effect he achieved. Because of the king-men rebellion, Moroni was unable to send reinforcements to the city.[1068]

As a result, when Amalickiah attacked the city of Moroni, he was able to storm the city and overwhelm the relatively small number of defenders with hordes of Lamanites. Although a large number of Lamanite warriors died in the attack,[1069] it was a matter of little concern to Amalickiah. They were considered expendable, "for behold, he did care not for the blood of [the Lamanites]."[1070]

After the city of Moroni fell, its inhabitants fled inland to the neighboring city of Nephihah and braced themselves for the next attack, which they expected to follow shortly.[1071]

Amalickiah, however, did not find it expedient to move westward away from the coast to attack Nephihah. Instead, according to his three-phased plan, he moved northward along the eastern seashore in the direction of Desolation.[1072] One by one, the coastal cities were captured—first Lehi,[1073] then Morianton, Omner, Gid, and finally Mulek, the northernmost coastal city of Jershon, [1074] which bordered on the land of Bountiful.[1075] In each city, he left Lamanite warriors, "to maintain and defend"[1076] them against Nephite retaliation.

AMALICKIAH IS SLAIN BY TEANCUM

As previously considered in Chapter 2.5, following the fall of Mulek, Amalickiah immediately moved his armies into position at the eastern border of the land of Bountiful.[1077] His plan was to take control of the city of Bountiful and then continue on to the narrow neck of land and take possession of the narrow pass at Desolation. By controlling the choke point at Desolation, the Lamanites would have the Nephites trapped in the land southward.

At the eastern border of Bountiful, however, he was stopped by Teancum and his elite army,[1078] who drove them down to the shores of the east sea, near the city of Mulek.[1079] That night, when the Lamanites were deep in sleep "because of their much fatigue," Teancum slipped into their camp and slew the Lamanite king. Amalickiah's death took place as the year 67 BC came to an end.[1080] Teancum awakened his army and informed them of Amalickiah's demise. They waited throughout the night, ready for any Lamanite retaliation.

SOUTHERN BORDER—FROM MANTI WESTWARD TO ANTIPARAH

A THIRD BATTLEFRONT—THE SOUTHERN BORDER OFFENSIVE

The account of the Amalickiah and Ammoron Wars, which begins in Alma 51, describes Amalickiah's campaign along the east coast of Jershon, which apparently was coordinated with a king-men rebellion in the center of the land. A simultaneous attack, conducted along the southern border of Zarahemla between the cities of Manti and Antiparah, is not mentioned in the chapter. This important information, which identifies a much more intense and widespread conflict, was not revealed until the epistle of Helaman was introduced into the record (see Alma 56).

As discussed in Part 3, Chapter 3.4, in 72 BC, Moroni began to establish fortified border cities along the southern border of Nephite lands from Manti to the west sea.[1081] Looking westward from the headwaters of the Sidon River, the line of five cities are identified as Manti, Zeezrom, Cumeni, Antiparah, and a city not identified by name, located on the west coast. The fortifications in each city were further improved between 72 and 68 BC.

In 67 BC, Moroni had appointed Antipus as leader over the armies in that region.[1082] Some or all of four southern border cities fell to the Lamanites in the same year because of the internal dissensions of the king-men. This can be concluded from Alma 53:8, which states that by 66 BC,[1083] a number of cities along the western segment of the south border[1084] had already fallen because of internal intrigue and dissensions. Those "dissensions" could be a reference to the king-men rebellion, which according to Alma 51:12–22, occurred when Amalickiah first invaded the land of Zarahemla in 67 BC. The king-men rebellion was put down during 67 BC. It is possible, however, that at least one of the four cities did not fall until the early part of 66 BC,[1085] shortly before Helaman arrived at the city of Judea with the 2,000 stripling warriors.

66 BC

EASTERN SEABOARD

AMMORON REPLACES AMALICKIAH AS KING OF THE LAMANITES

On the first day of 66 BC, King Amalickiah was discovered dead in his own tent. His army was shaken by the discovery. Then, as darkness faded into morning light, they saw Teancum's army, which had overpowered them the previous day, ready to do battle.[1086] Consumed by fear, they fled with all their army into Mulek's protective walls.[1087]

Ammoron immediately left Mulek en route to the land of Nephi. Before leaving, he instructed his army to maintain the cities they had taken,[1088] harass the Nephites on the east coast, and attempt to "take possession" of other Nephite lands if possible.[1089] As he moved southward along the coast of Jershon, then westward along the southern boundary, the same general orders were given to the Lamanite defenders in each city.

For Teancum's army, the year 66 BC became a year of waiting in the land of Bountiful. Moroni sent orders for him to "retain all the prisoners who fell into his hands,"[1090] guard the narrow neck, maintain that quarter of the land, and seek every opportunity to take back the captured cities. Due to the "enormity of the [Lamanite numbers] . . . it was not expedient . . . to attack them in their forts."[1091] He maintained the appearance of "making preparations" to attack the city of Mulek, though in reality he employed his men in building walls and fortifications to defend against Lamanite assault.[1092] Ultimately, reinforcements were sent to Teancum,[1093] though only enough to maintain their position and prevent any further Lamanite advancement toward Desolation.

SOUTHERN BORDER—FROM MANTI WESTWARD TO ANTIPARAH: DEFENSE OF THE SOUTHERN BORDER

ANTIPUS AND HELAMAN LEAD THE NEPHITES

While Teancum prepared the land of Bountiful for defense, Helaman marched with 2,000 young Ammonite warriors[1094] to the assistance of Antipus in the southwestern region.[1095] The Lamanites had made significant advances in that region during the previous year, facilitated primarily by the king-men rebellion.[1096] Moroni was occupied in putting down the rebellion and therefore was unable to join Antipus or send reinforcements to defend that quarter of the land. News of the precarious situation had spread across the land of Zarahemla, soon reaching the people of Ammon.

The Book of Mormon describes the young men who accompanied Helaman as "his two thousand stripling soldiers."[1097] Of Lamanite descent, their parents had been converted through the missionary efforts of King Mosiah's four sons in the land of Nephi. After being converted, their fathers had buried their weapons of war and had sworn an oath to God that they would never again take the life of a fellow human being even in defense, because of their previous murders. Because of their vulnerability to attack from other Lamanites, the sons of Mosiah had escorted the people of Ammon[1098] from Nephi to the land of Zarahemla. The Nephites had given the land of Jershon to them and had set their armies between them and the Lamanites so they could honor their oath without being destroyed.[1099]

Due to the perilous circumstances of the Amalickiah and Ammoron Wars, the Ammonite fathers were considering joining the war in defense of Zarahemla. However, as they prepared to take up arms, "Helaman and his brethren" urged them not to violate their sacred vow; Helaman was afraid that if they did so, "they should lose their souls."[1100] At that time, their young sons came forward and made a covenant that they would fight in the place of their fathers.[1101] They asked Helaman to be their leader.[1102]

FOUR CITIES ALONG THE SOUTHERN BORDER HAVE FALLEN

When Helaman and the 2000 stripling warriors marched to the city of Judea in 66 BC, four cities along the southern perimeter had already been captured by the Lamanites. In his correspondence to Moroni,[1103] Helaman identified the fallen cities as Manti, Zeezrom, Cumeni, and Antiparah,[1104] which were in Lamanite hands at the time of his arrival. The westernmost of the four was Antiparah, which (with respect to the southern line of fortified cities) bordered on an "un-named city" lying on the west coast.[1105] Antiparah held the greatest concentration of Lamanite warriors along the southern border.[1106]

This may be seen as resulting from its location near the city of Nephi in the Lamanite heartland. However, at that particular time, Antiparah represented the leading edge of the Lamanite assault of the Nephite southern border, which had begun at the city of Manti. The greatest number of warriors was required at that location, where the Nephite armies were engaged.

Judea,[1107] an interior city lying near the city of Antiparah[1108] in the direction of Zarahemla, was the focus of the Nephite defensive efforts. Because Judea was not a perimeter city, it (like other cities lying northward of the perimeter line of cities[1109]) had not been fortified prior to the war.[1110] Once fortified,[1111] it would become part of a second tier of defense against Lamanite advancement toward the city of Zarahemla—a new obstacle that the Lamanites must then conquer before they could move on in the direction of the capital city.[1112]

When Helaman arrived, "Antipus and his men [were] toiling with their might to fortify the city."[1113] The Lamanites were intimidated by the arrival of the 2000, and Ammoron, who had arrived from the east coast on his way to visit the Lamanite queen,[1114] decided not to attack.[1115] Helaman felt that Ammoron's decision reflected the direct intervention of Deity. Indeed, they were favored and protected by the Lord.[1116] As a result, they were preserved at a time when neither the city nor the young soldiers were capable of defending against a seasoned Lamanite army. By the end of 66 BC, the fortifications around Judea had been completed and the city was prepared for defense.[1117] It is noted that not only were the fortifications around the city prepared for battle, but also the stripling warriors, who likely went through intensive training in the art and skills of warfare during the same period.[1118]

WESTERN SEABOARD

FURTHER EXPANSION OF THE WAR

As outlined above, after assuming command of the Lamanite forces, Ammoron departed from the eastern campaign and made his way southward along the eastern border, and then westward along the southern border. He passed through Antiparah and turned southward to the city of Nephi, where he informed the queen (his brother's widow) of Amalickiah's death. He then gathered a large number of men, marched to the west coast, and attacked there.[1119] His stated purpose was "to draw away a part of their forces to that part of the land"[1120] to prevent additional reinforcements from being deployed to the battlefronts in the east and south.[1121]

At that time, the king-men uprising had been put down, and the war along the west sea was intended to continue on where the king-men had left off and thus maintain the distraction from the eastern seaboard and southern border invasions. Chief Captain Moroni's absence in the eastern coastal region and along the southern border is apparent during a significant portion of the Amalickiah and Ammoron Wars (67–65 BC), while he was engaged first in putting down the king-men revolt,[1122] and then in defending against

Ammoron's army on the west coast. [1123] In his orders to Teancum in late 66 BC, he stated that he was currently defending against an attack by Ammoron in the borders by the west sea.[1124] At that time,[1125] he placed armies in the unnamed city on the west coast[1126] and in other strategically placed cities further to the north along the coast[1127] in response to Ammoron's attacks.

The western coastal region, which was defended by Moroni's army in 66 BC, was separate from the southern border region where Antipus and Helaman engaged the Lamanites. The closest the southern army would come to the west coast was the land of Antiparah,[1128] whose western boundary touched the eastern boundary of the unnamed coastal land referred to in the same verse. From Helaman's reference to the coastal city, it can be inferred that the Nephites still controlled the city during the seventh month of 65 BC,[1129] because Helaman's army at that time pretended to carry supplies in that direction for the support of Nephite troops stationed there. The unnamed city was the western equivalent of the city of Moroni.[1130]

65 BC

EASTERN SEABOARD

A TIME OF WAITING

For Teancum's army on the eastern seaboard, 65 BC was the second year of waiting for assistance from Moroni. They spent the time maintaining the lands from the city of Bountiful northward, which were still in their possession, and fortifying the land of Bountiful and the narrow pass to prevent any further Lamanite advancement toward Desolation and the land northward. Moroni and Lehi arrived in the land of Bountiful at the end of the year to join forces with Teancum.[1131]

SOUTHERN BORDER

DANGEROUS CIRCUMSTANCES[1132]

During 65 BC, the region of greatest recorded activity was along the southern border. Had Mormon not included Helaman's 62 BC epistle to Moroni,[1133] the account of this twenty-seventh year of the judges would have been limited to just four verses,[1134] largely because no advancement was made on either side. The same was also true on the southern border, where no cities changed hands that year. However, Helaman told the following story that was inspirational to the Nephites and is equally inspiring to us today, which concerned a serious battle in which the Nephites were victorious.

Having prepared themselves for battle by the end of 66 BC, the Nephites under the command of Antipus waited for the Lamanites to make the next move. Not willing to attack the stronghold of Antiparah, they waited patiently during the first two months of 65 BC[1135] for any opportunity to meet the Lamanites on even terms. They kept spies out by day and by night so as to detect any new offensive against them in Judea or against other cities on the north. Ultimately, it became clear that the Lamanites were content to hold the cities they had taken possession of and make no other advances, according to Ammoron's orders.[1136] Though he had departed for Nephi and the west coast, his orders were still in effect. In essence, they were awaiting the outcome of the west coast attack.

At the end of the second month, the fathers of the stripling warriors brought provisions to the army of Antipus, along with an additional 2,000 men. This brought the total number of troops in Judea to ten thousand, and there were enough provisions for the troops and their wives and children. The Lamanites in Antiparah began to grow uneasy. They began sending out detachments seeking to intercept any additional shipments of provisions.

When the Nephites saw their apprehension and unrest, they made a plan to lure the Lamanite army away from the city. The plan called for Helaman and his "two thousand sons"[1137] to head in a westward direction, passing by the northern edge of Antiparah as if delivering supplies to the unnamed coastal city at the southwest corner of Nephite lands.[1138] Antipus likely hid his army in the wilderness near Antiparah to be ready when the sons of Helaman should pass by. If the Lamanite army went after the bait, then the army of Antipus would slip in between them and the city of Antiparah, blocking their return to the safety of Antiparah's fortifications.

This foray was initiated on the first day of the seventh month of 65 BC.[1139] As anticipated, the Lamanite army moved out to intercept Helaman and his 2,000. Helaman turned his sons northward, retreating in full flight, with the Lamanite army hot on their tail. Antipus moved in behind, following in close pursuit. Antipus had only meant to use Helaman's army as a decoy, but now he felt they were in great peril, as the Lamanite army continued ahead at full speed, trying to overtake them before being overtaken by Antipus. All day long the race continued. At nightfall, the three armies stopped for the night. Then at daybreak the race was resumed.

Antipus stopped only briefly at nightfall on the second day, then proceeded on to catch up with the Lamanites early on the third day, for shortly after they began to move, Helaman and his young men observed that the Lamanite army had suddenly halted. What he did not know was that, in his desire to protect the stripling warriors, Antipus had pushed ahead too hard. When they engaged the Lamanite army, he and his army were too exhausted to fight for long.[1140] Many, including Antipus, fell by the sword. Without any direct information, Helaman knew the army of Antipus had overtaken the Lamanites. He felt that they could be in trouble. He realized the time had come when his young sons would have to engage the enemy.

THE TWO THOUSAND STRIPLING WARRIORS

As the stripling warriors were finally called upon to stand and fight, they did so without fear. Quoting from Helaman's account at the point when the pursuing Lamanite army had turned about to contend with the army of Antipus:

> Therefore what say ye, my sons, will ye go against them to battle?
>
> And now I say unto you, my beloved brother Moroni, that never had I seen so great courage, nay, not amongst all the Nephites.
>
> For as I had ever called them my sons (for they were all of them very young) even so they said unto me: Father, behold our God is with us, and he will not suffer that we should fall; then let us go forth; we would not slay our brethren if they would let us alone; therefore let us go, lest they should overpower the army of Antipus.
>
> Now they had never fought, yet they did not fear death; and they did think more upon the liberty of their fathers than they did upon their own lives; yea they had been taught by their mothers that if they did not doubt, God would deliver them.

And they rehearsed unto me the words of their mothers, saying: We do not doubt our mothers knew it. (Alma 56:44–48)

When the young men engaged the Lamanites, their faith in God was rewarded. The Lord gave them great strength, and they quickly overcame the Lamanites, who were compelled to surrender:

> And now it came to pass that when they had surrendered themselves up unto us, behold, I numbered those young men who had fought with me, fearing lest there were many of them slain.
>
> But behold, to my great joy, there had not one soul of them fallen to the earth; yea, and they had fought as if with the strength of God; yea, never were men known to have fought with such miraculous strength; and with such mighty power did they fall upon the Lamanites, that they did frighten them; and for this cause did the Lamanites deliver themselves up as prisoners of war. (Alma 56:55–56)

The story of the stripling warriors is one of the greatest tributes to motherhood in all of the scriptures. In this passage we see the power of their mothers' influence. Their faith was an extension of their mothers' faith. They had been taught by their mothers to exercise faith in God in even the most dire of circumstances, and God would protect them and bring to pass their righteous desires. The Lord blessed them and the Nephite nation because of their faith and their righteousness. As a result, they were all spared (including 60 more who joined them later) throughout the long and bloody conflict. Without the support of the 2,060 stripling warriors along the southern battlefront, the Lamanites would have defeated the Nephites in that region.

The Nephites had no place to guard the large number of Lamanites who gave themselves up as prisoners of war, and they could not keep them from returning to the Lamanites. Therefore, they were transported to the land of Zarahemla by a portion of Antipus's army who had survived the previous battle.[1141] In spite of the Nephite victory over the Lamanite army, the city of Antiparah remained in the hands of the Lamanites.

This speaks volumes for the large number of Lamanites occupying Antiparah.[1142] Though a large army had been sent out in hopes of intercepting Helaman and his 2,000, which was sufficient in number to contend with the army of Antipus as well, there remained in Antiparah an adequate number of Lamanite warriors to defend the city. As the end of 65 BC approached, there was little or no change in the standoff.

WESTERN SEABOARD

MORONI AND LEHI SUCCESSFULLY DEFEND
THE WEST COAST REGION

In 65 BC, Moroni continued the work he had begun in 66 BC in fortifying and defending the cities along the western perimeter. The unnamed coastal city (the southernmost point on the west coastal border of Nephite lands, was not under Lamanite control in 65 BC when Helaman led his warriors in that direction as if delivering supplies.[1143] Moroni and Lehi in all probability were currently defending against the Lamanites (personally led by Ammoron) in that city, because it was on the coast where Moroni was still engaged in 65 BC. He did not depart from that region until near the end of that year.[1144] Since the city must have been in Nephite hands for Helaman's ploy to work,[1145] it can be assumed that it was indeed the location of Ammoron's west coast attack, for he would never move northward without conquering it.

It can also be concluded that Ammoron had no success on the west coast because it (the southernmost city on the coast) remained in Nephite hands. Moroni thus repelled Ammoron's attack and secured the western seaboard (no doubt to include establishing and strengthening other fortified cities lying to the north along the west coast). Near the end of 65 BC, he and Lehi departed with their armies toward to the eastern front to join forces with Teancum.[1146] They arrived at the city of Bountiful at the end of the year.

Moroni's repulsion of Ammoron from the western seaboard marked a major turning point in the Amalickiah and Ammoron Wars. When Ammoron turned away from the west coast, the final corridor of attack had been sealed off to the Lamanites, as illustrated in Map 6.0 in Chapter 2.5.

64 BC

EASTERN SEABOARD

THE TIDE OF THE WAR TURNS DRAMATICALLY

The stalemate between Nephite and Lamanite forces in the eastern coastal region had continued since the latter part of 67 BC. Now, upon the arrival of Moroni and Lehi with additional forces, it was time to take back the city of Mulek. A council of war was immediately called as 64 BC began, in which Moroni, Lehi, Teancum, and other chief captains contemplated how they might lure the Lamanites out of Mulek.[1147] Following the war council, "they sent embassies" to the Lamanite army in Mulek, which was led by a Zoramite named Jacob.[1148] They petitioned Jacob to meet them in open battle on the coastal plain near the city, but he refused. As long as the Lamanites remained within Mulek's fortifications, they had a great advantage. Jacob did not find it expedient to leave the fortifications and fight on in the open.

Moroni devised a strategy to lure the Lamanites out of Mulek.[1149] Under the cover of darkness, he moved a portion of the Nephite army into the wilderness on the west side of Mulek. Teancum led a small detachment down to the seashore on the east side of the city to entice the Lamanites out of the city. The following morning, when the Lamanite scouts discovered Teancum's small unit by the seashore, they alerted Jacob, who jumped at the chance of engaging his troops when they far outnumbered their opponents. They quickly came out against Teancum, hoping to corner him against the seashore, where he would have no place to retreat.

However, as the Lamanites came out, Teancum began retreating northward along the seashore in the direction of Bountiful, staying just outside of their reach. No doubt Teancum and his detachment were among the fastest runners among the Nephites, who could therefore toy with the Lamanite army and always stay just barely ahead of them to lure them toward the city of Bountiful.

Meanwhile, Moroni brought his army out of the wilderness and stormed the city of Mulek, killing those guards who refused to surrender. They took possession of Mulek and then followed after the Lamanite army, which ultimately approached the city of Bountiful in hot pursuit of Teancum's small unit. The stage was now set, and though they did not yet know it, the Lamanites were trapped between the armies of Moroni and Lehi—an exact replay of the battle at Manti in the Zoramite War.[1150]

At Bountiful, the Lamanites "were met by Lehi and a small army, which had been left to protect the city Bountiful. And now, behold when the chief captains of the Lamanites had beheld Lehi with his army coming against them, they fled in much confusion, lest perhaps they should not obtain the city Mulek before Lehi should overtake them; for they were wearied because of their march, and the men of Lehi were fresh."[1151]

It was not long before the Lamanite army realized that Moroni and his army were positioned between them and the fortifications of Mulek. Continuing with the account,

> And Moroni commanded his men that they should fall upon them until they had given up their weapons of war.
>
> And it came to pass that Jacob, being their leader, being also a Zoramite, and having an unconquerable spirit, he led the Lamanites forth to battle with exceeding fury against Moroni.
>
> Moroni, being in their course of march, therefore Jacob was determined to slay them and cut his way through to the city of Mulek. But behold, Moroni and his men were more powerful; therefore they did not give way before the Lamanites.
>
> And it came to pass that they fought on both hands with exceeding fury; and there were many slain on both sides; yea, and Moroni was wounded, and Jacob was killed.
>
> And Lehi pressed upon their rear with such fury with his strong men, that the Lamanites in the rear delivered up their weapons of war; and the remainder of them, being much confused, knew not whether to go or to strike. (Alma 52:32–36)

At this point, Moroni called for them to surrender, and with little further resistance, they delivered up their weapons of war. The number of Lamanite prisoners was greater than the number of the Lamanites and Nephites slain in the battle. They were put to work burying the dead from both sides. They were then taken to the city of Bountiful. There they were put to work fortifying the city with a deep ditch and high framework of timbers placed on the inner ridge of earth. The city had not been fortified before the war, and until the

Lamanite prisoners were available to accomplish the work, sufficient fortifications had not previously been erected.

Moroni thus employed the Lamanite prisoners for a three-fold purpose:

- They would complete an important project by fortifying the city of Bountiful against future Lamanite attacks.

- "It was easy to guard the Lamanite prisoners while at their labor."[1152]

- Moroni could utilize his entire army when he would make an attack upon the cities of Gid, Omner, and Morianton, which, during the following year (63 BC), would become the main focus of attention.

The Nephites did not attempt to take back any additional cities in 64 BC. Instead they focused upon fortifying the region and securing provisions for the soldiers and their families in that region, which had suffered greatly over the previous two years of warfare with its associated deprivation.

SOUTHERN BORDER

NEPHITE SUCCESS ON THE SOUTHERN BORDER—ANTIPARAH RETAKEN

Sometime during late 65 or early 64 BC, Ammoron departed from the west coast. He had been repelled by Moroni's and Lehi's armies. At length, he passed through the city of Antiparah on the southeastern battlefront. During 64 BC, Ammoron sent an epistle to Helaman, offering to abandon Antiparah if Helaman would release the prisoners of war that had been transported to the city of Zarahemla the previous year. Helaman responded that he would release prisoners only upon exchange for Nephite prisoners of war. Ammoron refused to exchange prisoners, and "therefore [Helaman's army] began to make preparations to go against the city of Antiparah."[1153]

The Lamanites in Antiparah became alarmed and abandoned the city at the end of 64 BC, fleeing to other Nephite cities still under Lamanite control.[1154] It is likely Cumeni was the primary city to which the Lamanites then fled, for it was the next city in line along the southern border. Some may have moved on to Zeezrom and Manti, for that was the general direction of the Lamanite retreat at that time. Ultimately, Manti would have been the location at which all of the Lamanites involved in the southwestern campaign would congregate in a final attempt to maintain a toehold in the region.

63 BC

EASTERN SEABOARD

CITY OF GID RETAKEN BY STRATAGEM

After refusing to exchange prisoners with Helaman, Ammoron departed from the southern border campaign at Antiparah and returned to the eastern campaign. At the beginning of 63 BC, having learned from his mistake with Helaman,[1155] he petitioned Moroni for an exchange of prisoners, to which Moroni further stipulated that the exchange must include one Nephite prisoner with his wife and children for each Lamanite prisoner. However, in his exchange of letters with Moroni, though Ammoron agreed to the exchange, he angered Moroni by proclaiming justification for the war. Moroni "knew that Ammoron had a perfect knowledge of his fraud."[1156] Therefore, he decided not to exchange prisoners, not willing to let them have any more strength than they already had.[1157] Knowing the Nephite prisoners were guarded in the city of Gid, he laid a plan to retake the city of Gid by stratagem.

Searching for a Lamanite among his troops, he found a man named Laman, who had been "one of the servants of the [Lamanite] king who had been murdered by Amalickiah."[1158] He sent Laman with "a small number of men" to the city of Gid.[1159] In the evening, Laman went to the Lamanite guards stationed outside the city. The guards saw him as he approached and "hailed him."[1160] He told them he was a Lamanite who had escaped from the Nephites. He said that he had taken some of the wine from the Nephites. Using reverse psychology, he enticed them to drink of it by feigning to resist when they asked for it, arguing that it should be available when the Lamanites should go against the Nephites. The guards countered with the argument that they would receive more with their rations. They insisted that he give the wine to them and they drank deeply. The wine had been "prepared in its strength"[1161] and had an immediate powerful effect. When they passed out in their intoxication, Laman went and informed Moroni.

Moroni had previously ordered his men to prepare a cache of weapons.[1162] In dead silence, they crept past the sleeping guards to the wall of the city, whereupon Moroni tossed the weapons over the wall to the Nephite prisoners inside. Soon, every man, woman, and child who could bear a sword was armed.[1163] Moroni then had his men move out a distance from the guards and surround the city. This would allow the Lamanites to realize their predicament at daybreak without feeling compelled to strike out in panic.

When the Lamanites awoke the following morning, they quickly discovered that they were surrounded by the Nephites both outside and inside the city. They decided it was wise to surrender and give up their weapons. In this way, the city of Gid was taken without a struggle.

CITIES OF OMNER AND MORIANTON

After the capture of Gid, there remained four cities to be recaptured before the Lamanites could be driven out of the land. From north to south these cities were Omner (which bordered on Gid), then Morianton, Lehi, and Moroni. Though little is included in Mormon's abridgement concerning the recovery of Omner and Morianton, it is logical to assume that the Nephites were successful in retaking the two cities during 63 BC following the seizure of Gid. Alma 55:28–32 likely refers to events that took place during the recapture of the city of Omner, though the city is not mentioned by name. Omner was the next city in the line of cities after Gid, though the account of its recapture is never given in the Book of Mormon.

However, the Nephites would not consider going against Morianton, as referenced in the following verse, until they first regained Omner, which was located between Gid and Morianton. Otherwise, they would be surrounded by Lamanites. The Lamanites in all of the cities had to be driven out of the land. It is also possible that the Lamanites fled from the two cities.

The recapture of Morianton is never presented, though Mormon laid the groundwork for its recapture by stating that due to its role as a Lamanite stronghold and supply center, "it was expedient for Moroni to make preparations to attack the city."[1164] His account of what was likely the siege of Morianton at the end of 63 BC[1165] was suddenly interrupted, however, by a dramatic series of events, which began with the arrival of Helaman's epistle to Moroni on the second day of the following year (62 BC).[1166]

Helaman's epistle likely captured Mormon's full attention, once he saw its overwhelming spiritual significance, coupled with the integral role of Helaman's army in the overall success of the Nephite defensive effort. The dramatic chain of events, which immediately followed Moroni's reading of Helaman's epistle,[1167] precluded any return to the account of Morianton's recapture, for it would then have been out of place and anticlimactic. The unforgiving nature of the plates, with respect to corrections, made it impossible for Mormon to rewrite the account, especially considering what was happening in his own life as he abridged the record. Likely, that is why nothing more was written concerning the Nephite acquisition of Morianton, which is learned later by default.[1168]

SOUTHERN BORDER

LAMANITES IN CUMENI SURRENDER TO HELAMAN'S ARMY

In the commencement of 63 BC, Helaman's army, now in control of Antiparah and Judea, received supplies and an additional 6,000 troops from Zarahemla and the surrounding regions. Furthermore, sixty additional stripling warriors joined the 2,000. Bolstered by the increase in troops, they devised a plan to lay siege to Cumeni. They began surrounding the city by night for the purpose of intercepting provisions en route to the city. The Lamanites, realizing their intentions, began to harass them with frequent small attacks in the night, but the Nephites kept guards posted and repelled each attack. Ultimately, a shipment arrived and the Nephites intercepted it and sent the provisions to the Nephites in Judea.[1169] The Lamanites stubbornly continued to hold out in Cumeni until they ran completely out of supplies, and then they surrendered the city to Helaman and his army without a fight.[1170] Thus, depriving them of supplies paved the way for a great Nephite victory.

Afterward, with the large increase in the number of Lamanite prisoners of war (2,000 of which were slain in numerous attempts to escape[1171]) the Nephites were compelled once again to transport them down to the land of Zarahemla. Subsequently, Ammoron sent supplies and a large number of men to a Lamanite army near Cumeni,[1172] which immediately mounted an attack against Helaman's army in the city of Cumeni. Nephite scouts, upon seeing the advancing Lamanite armies, rushed to alert the army of Gid, who had departed Cumeni to transport the prisoners down to Zarahemla. Upon hearing of the Lamanite attack, the prisoners took courage and rebelled, running in mass upon the swords of Gid's army, whereupon most were killed and the remainder escaped.[1173] Unable to catch the fleeing prisoners and having more pressing matters, Gid then turned his army back to the city of Cumeni, arriving as the Lamanites were about to overrun the city.[1174] Had they not arrived at that time, the city would have fallen. Instead, the attack was repulsed, and the city remained in Nephite hands.

Helaman's response to Gid's account of the chain of events that led to his return at the exact moment to save Helaman's army and the city of Cumeni is similar to ours today when we read the account: "Now it came to pass that when I, Helaman, had heard these words of Gid, I was filled with exceeding joy because of the goodness of God in preserving us, that we might not all perish."[1175] What a marvelous feeling of security it is to know that God will protect His people when they are righteous and call upon Him for deliverance from the forces of evil.

However, the city had not been defended without much loss on the part of the Nephites. About a thousand Nephite soldiers had died in the battle.[1176] Therefore, Helaman and his army were astonished when they found that not even one of the stripling warriors had been killed. This miraculous story is found in Alma 57:

> And it came to pass that after the Lamanites had fled, I immediately gave orders that my men who had been wounded should be taken from among the dead, and caused that their wounds should be dressed.
>
> And it came to pass that there were two hundred out of my two thousand and sixty, who had fainted because of the loss of blood; nevertheless, according to the goodness of God, and to our great

astonishment, and also the joy of our whole army, there was not one soul of them who did perish; yea, and neither was there one soul among them who had not received many wounds. (Alma 57:24–25)

MANTI IS RETAKEN BY STRATAGEM

Perhaps the greatest miracle of the Amalickiah and Ammoron Wars were in the military action surrounding Helaman and the 2,060 stripling warriors. The miracle was not limited to a single event, but involved the entire defensive effort on the southwestern battlefront from 66 to 62 BC, as described in Helaman's epistle to Moroni.[1177] Again and again, they fought against insurmountable odds and came away victorious. Initially under the leadership of Antipus and later under Helaman, the Nephites recaptured, one by one, the cities that had fallen to the Lamanites. In each battle, timing was a huge factor, which in virtually every case went against the Lamanites. With each victory, the number of Lamanites seemed to increase, because they became more and more concentrated within a continually diminishing region, but it made no difference.

After the Lamanites surrendered the city of Cumeni to the Nephites, all of the Lamanite forces in the southern region gathered in the city of Manti, the only city along the southwestern border still in their hands.[1178] They far outnumbered the army of Helaman and received "great strength from day to day, and also many provisions."[1179] Helaman petitioned the governor (Pahoran) for additional soldiers and supplies, but he received nothing "for the space of many months, even until we were about to perish for the want of food."[1180] Finally, they received a single shipment of food that was brought to them by an army of 2,000.[1181]

Helaman, as he wrote in his epistle to Moroni, was frustrated because of the grievous lack of support from the government in the city of Zarahemla. He feared that it could result in the overthrow of the land. They prayed earnestly to the Lord "that he would strengthen us and deliver us out of the hands of our enemies, yea, and also give us strength that we might retain our cities, and our lands, and our possessions, for the support of our people. Yea, and it came to pass that the Lord our God did visit us with assurances that he would deliver us; yea insomuch that he did speak peace to our souls, and did grant unto us great faith, and did cause us that we should hope for our deliverance in him."[1182]

From the whisperings of the Spirit, they took courage, knowing that with the Lord's help and strength, they would be successful in driving the Lamanites out of the land. They immediately devised a plan to go against Manti, knowing that God would provide a way for them to retake the city. Soon they set their plan in motion by moving their army into position. They pitched their "tents by the wilderness side, which was near to the city."[1183]

The "wilderness side" referred to the narrow strip of wilderness, which separated the land of Nephi from the land of Zarahemla, as well as the wilderness bordering the narrow strip of wilderness to the south of Manti.[1184]

The Lamanites in Manti became concerned that Helaman's army would "cut them off from their support except they should come out to battle against [them] and kill [them]."[1185] Seeing that the Lamanites began to make preparations to attack, Helaman dispatched Gid with a small unit of men to hide in the wilderness on the right (or to the north) of his army, while Teomner with a second unit hid on the left (or to the south). Helaman's army remained in the same place where they had first pitched their tents.[1186] Soon the entire Lamanite army began moving toward Helaman's army at full speed. As they came close, Helaman fled west with his army into the wilderness, and the Lamanite army followed in close pursuit, passing by Gid and Teomner without any suspicion that they waited there. Gid and Teomner then converged on the city of Manti, cutting off their spies to prevent them from warning the Lamanite army of their maneuver. They overwhelmed the few guards left to secure the entrance. Taking control of the city, they waited for Helaman to return.

The Lamanites continued to pursue Helaman's army until they realized the path had swung around from a westward direction toward the north in the direction of Zarahemla. Immediately, they halted their pursuit and turned back toward the city of Manti, following the same circular path they had followed in pursuing the army of Helaman. At dusk, they stopped for the night, having no idea that Gid and Teomner had retaken the city of Manti. Helaman did not stop his army for the night, but, giving a wide berth to the

Lamanite army, they traveled through the night by a more direct route, arriving at Manti well in advance of the Lamanites.

When the Lamanite army arrived at Manti the following morning, they were "astonished" to find the Nephites had taken possession of the city. Likely, their first impression—and perhaps their only impression—was that this was another army in addition to the one they had been chasing. Thus fearing they would be caught in between two armies with numbers approaching their own, they fled into the narrow strip of wilderness, leaving Helaman and his army relieved yet feeling quite vulnerable because of their distressed physical and mental state. They attributed it to God that they had emerged victorious in the face of overwhelming odds and with little support from the government in Zarahemla.

For Helaman's army on the southern border, the war had come to an end. The fighting would move to the eastern seaboard, never to return. Reflecting once again on the miraculous conclusion of the southern campaign, it is apparent that the greatest miracle of the entire war was in the account of the stripling warriors. Throughout the entire conflict, not one of them had fallen, while all around them thousands of Nephites had died.[1187]

CENTER OF THE LAND

CHIEF JUDGE PAHORAN IS DEPOSED AND
FORCED TO FLEE ZARAHEMLA

In the latter half of 63 BC, the king-men rebelled once again and took control of the city of Zarahemla. Chief Judge Pahoran was forced to flee for his life. At that time, though there were indications of problems in the center of the land, Moroni was completely unaware of the subversive actions, which was a powerful indication of the complete isolation of the perimeter armies from the capital city. The effects of the rebellion were unknowingly documented by Helaman in his previously noted correspondence to Moroni. The time frame of the takeover can therefore be temporally placed with a high degree of certainty.

According to Helaman, early in 63 BC, 6,000 men and supplies were sent from Zarahemla to Helaman's army,[1188] which enabled them to retake the city of Cumeni.[1189] Later in the same year,[1190] however, while Helaman's army contemplated how to recapture the city of Manti, their support was cut off over a period of "many months," in spite of an urgent request from Helaman conveyed by "an embassy"[1191] to the city of Zarahemla. Finally, they received 2,000 soldiers and food, without which they would have perished "for the want of food."[1192]

This critical lack of support was a basic indicator to troops all along the perimeter that all was not well in the center of the land. However, because of the isolation and general lack of communication during the war, the precise reason for the lack of support to the armies was not known.

62 BC

EASTERN SEABOARD

ONE LAST SETBACK FOR THE CAUSE OF FREEDOM

In 62 BC, repercussions from the latest resurgence of the king-men rebellion reverberated loudly along the eastern seaboard and in the nearby city of Nephihah. Beginning with Helaman's letter to Moroni, the defenders in Moroni's region experienced a roller coaster series of emotions. Initially in Alma 59, Chief Captain Moroni was delighted because of Helaman's epistle, which recounted the miraculous events along the southern border. He made it "known unto all his people, in all the land round about" (in the east region) and immediately sent a request to Pahoran for reinforcements and food to be sent to Helaman's army, which was distributed across the cities of Manti, Zeezrom, Cumeni, and Antiparah along the southwestern front, as well as the city of Judea. At last, it appeared the Nephites were on the verge of victory.[1193]

However, within Helaman's correspondence was implanted a subtle caveat concerning a potential Lamanite assault in the eastern region.[1194] The warning was simply the statement that a numerous army of the Lamanites had fled into the wilderness. Moroni may have expected a consequential increase in the Lamanite forces in the east, but he also expected reinforcements and supplies to be sent to Nephihah from the land of Zarahemla.[1195]

When the Lamanites had fled from the city of Manti, they likely moved eastward through the wilderness, following essentially the same course as that taken by the Zoramite and Lamanite army during the Zoramite War, but in reverse.[1196] Perhaps initially they were returning to Lamanite base cities located to the south of Jershon first established around 76 BC, from which Amalickiah had likely launched his attack against the city of Moroni at the beginning of the war. Ultimately, they joined with Ammoron's army in the east region.

The combined army was then sent by Ammoron to attack the city of Nephihah, which had been spared defeat in 67 BC, when Amalickiah opted to move along the coast in the direction of the narrow neck of land.[1197] Many of the Nephites defending Nephihah may have been there since being driven out of Moroni. In 62 BC, it was no longer a place of safety.

The Lamanites overwhelmed Nephihah and took possession of the city, slaying many Nephites. The Nephite survivors fled from Nephihah to the city of Morianton, where Moroni's army was stationed at that time. Morianton had likely been recaptured by the Nephites near the end of 63 BC,[1198] just before Moroni received Helaman's epistle at the beginning of 62 BC.[1199]

Moroni's elation over the marvelous results outlined by Helaman immediately turned to distress. His polite request that troops and aid be sent to the southern forces was soon replaced by a scathing denunciation of the leadership in Zarahemla and an ultimatum to Pahoran to come to their aid or face the bitter consequences. Moroni would come against them and take control of the government by force if they would not support the cause of freedom.[1200]

Communication was clearly a serious problem during the war because of the great distances between the various campaigns of the war and the limitations of communication in a pre-technological age.[1201] This made it difficult to coordinate the efforts in two or more regions. Until he received Pahoran's epistle, Moroni had no idea that Pahoran had been overthrown and driven from the city of Zarahemla, because what little communication there was had broken down. However, though Helaman's army on the south and Moroni's army on the east had no specific knowledge of the conditions in the city of Zarahemla, they knew a critical problem had caused support to be withheld from the perimeter battlefronts.

MORONI GOES TO PAHORAN'S AID

The courier who delivered Moroni's letter to Pahoran had to search for the deposed chief judge. Delivering such a communication could be a dangerous task if the messenger should be apprehended by enemy forces, in this case the king-men. Somehow, the courier successfully made his way to Gideon and delivered the critical message. Pahoran found great relief and hope in the strength of Moroni's letter. He had been faltering, in his desire not to offend God, in reacting with physical force against the king-men, but Moroni had informed him that he had been commanded by the Lord to defend the land against the rebellious dissenters. The courier waited while Pahoran penned his reply, and then he was on his way to deliver the message to Moroni that would provide the blueprint for ultimate victory.

In his response, Pahoran informed Moroni that it was the king-men who, after taking control of the government in the city of Zarahemla, "withheld our provisions and daunted our freemen that they have not come unto you."[1202] He outlined the series of events through which dissenters had taken control of the city of Zarahemla. At that time, they outnumbered the freemen in the city of Zarahemla, many of whom were likely absent, having joined the Nephite defensive effort at the borders of the land. While the Nephite armies were busy defending against the Lamanite assault, the king-men had begun anew, maligning the Nephite government, openly advocating its overthrow, and stirring up support for the Lamanite offensive. Ultimately, they had mounted a coup led by a man named Pachus, who had entered into correspondence with Ammoron.[1203] Pachus promised to support Ammoron in return for being made king over the land of Zarahemla. Pahoran was driven from the capital city and fled eastward to the land of Gideon, where he began rallying the people in the predominantly Christian region to come to his assistance.

After reading Pahoran's epistle, Moroni left Lehi and Teancum on the east coast, gathered a small force of men as instructed by Pahoran,[1204] and set off in the direction of Gideon.

CENTER OF THE LAND

MORONI ARRIVES WITH AN ARMY IN THE CENTER OF THE LAND

As he passed by towns and cities along the way, Moroni raised the rallying cry. People flocked to his army, and by the time he reached Gideon, he had gathered thousands of soldiers. After joining with the forces of Pahoran, they outnumbered the army of Pachus. The combined forces of Pahoran and Moroni went against the army of Pachus at the city of Zarahemla. In the ensuing battle, "Pachus was slain and his men were taken prisoners."[1205]

Pahoran and Moroni took control of the capital city, and Pahoran was restored to the judgment seat. The leaders of the insurrection (Pachus's men) were quickly tried and executed for the crimes of treason. Time was also taken at this point to conduct the trials of the king-men imprisoned at the beginning of the war.[1206] Though it is not mentioned in the text, there is little doubt they had been freed from prison by Pachus at the time he deposed Pahoran, because they were comrades with him in the war against the Christian Nephites. In all likelihood, they had joined the ranks of his army, which made them guilty of a second offense of treason, equally as grievous as the first one. Therefore, when apprehended the second time, they had no chance of being acquitted, unless they would "take up arms in the defence of their country," [1207]and were speedily put to death.

A DEATH BLOW FOR THE KING-MEN

As a political viewpoint or perspective, the treasonous creed of the king-men would no longer be tolerated as an expression of free speech among the Nephites. No faction advocating a return to monarchy would ever again be allowed to operate openly in Zarahemla. Following the conclusion to the Amalickiah and Ammoron Wars, there is no further reference to king-men throughout Nephite history. However, the new intolerance would not prevent dissenters from seeking to destroy the free government and install a dictatorial government.

Previously, the Amlicites, Amalickiah, and the king-men had been inflexible in their quest for a restoration of monarchy. In the future, dissenters would of necessity acquire the appearance of civility. In a subsequent publication, a new era of dissent will be identified, in which diplomacy and deception would become the signature characteristics of the dissent movement. The events, which both inspired and required this transformation, took place during the Amalickiah and Ammoron Wars.

61 BC
CENTER OF THE LAND
CRITICAL SUPPORT FROM ZARAHEMLA

As the thirty-first year of the judges commenced, with the free government back in control, resources in the interior of the land were freed to immediately provide reinforcements and food for the Nephite troops on the southern and eastern borders of the land. Six thousand soldiers and supplies were sent to Helaman's army on the south. An equal number were also sent to Lehi and Teancum's forces on the east coast.

EASTERN SEABOARD
THE CITY OF NEPHIHAH IS TAKEN BY STRATAGEM

When they had regained firm control in the center of the land, Pahoran and Moroni departed from Zarahemla in the direction of Nephihah, leaving a large army to protect the city from insurgents. Along the way, they encountered a Lamanite army, which they engaged, killing a large number of Lamanites. The Lamanites surrendered and swore the required oath never to return against the Nephites. They were allowed to depart in peace and join the people of Ammon.

Pahoran and Moroni then continued on to the city of Nephihah, intent on driving the Lamanites from the city. The Lamanite army in the city refused to come out for battle with such a numerous and determined Nephite army. Therefore, Moroni devised a plan to take the city by stratagem. Under cover of darkness, he climbed upon the wall of Nephihah and peered into the city to see where the Lamanite army was located. He found them encamped on the east side around the entrance.

Moroni had the Nephite army quickly prepare strong cords and ladders to let themselves down over the wall into the city on the west side. During the night, the entire army was lowered into the city without the Lamanites being aware. Obviously, the Lamanites did not post guards around the perimeter. When the morning came, they discovered the Nephite army within the walls of the city. In terror, they rushed frantically through the pass and fled toward the city of Moroni on the coast, where Ammoron was currently located.

The Nephite army followed after them in hot pursuit. They overtook many of them, taking prisoners of those who would surrender, and then returned to the city of Nephihah. By this time, the Lamanites were convinced that the Nephites would prevail, and they pleaded with Moroni to allow them to join the people of Ammon.[1208] Again, Moroni exhibited his unwavering compassion and mercy—even after such a long and tragic war in which thousands of Nephites had been slaughtered—and gave them their wish.

The people of Ammon welcomed the Lamanite war prisoners. They allowed them to spread out in the land and give up their weapons of war for pruning shears. From that time forth, these new converts became a great support to the Nephites. For the moment, the Nephites were relieved of a great burden of providing for thousands of prisoners of war.

THE NEPHITES DRIVE THE LAMANITES FROM THE CITIES OF LEHI AND MORONI

After the city of Nephihah was recaptured, Moroni left Pahoran in Nephihah and led the Nephite army eastward in pursuit of the fleeing Lamanites, not toward the city of Moroni, but rather the city of Lehi.[1209] This is another indication that Omner and Morianton were already in Nephite hands at that time,[1210] but not the city of Lehi. Moroni thus approached the city of Lehi from Nephihah on the west, while Lehi and Teancum[1211] approached from the city of Morianton on the north.

Without even trying to defend Lehi, the Lamanites fled from Moroni's army. Having nowhere else to go, they moved southward along the coast away from Lehi and Teancum's forces and toward the city of Moroni, where Ammoron was entrenched. Moroni had been the first city to fall when Amalickiah invaded the land. At this point, it was the only Nephite city still in Lamanite hands.

The Lamanites fled into the city of Moroni at nightfall, and the Nephites moved their armies into position to surround them on all sides, including on the south near the Nephite and Lamanite border. Due to the long march, both Nephite and Lamanite armies were weary. The Nephites did not attempt any further action that day, with the exception of Teancum.

Teancum was angry with Ammoron, who he felt was responsible—along with his brother, Amalickiah—for the widespread death, famine, and sorrow of the war. He went forth in his anger to the city of Moroni, scaling the wall and letting himself down into the city with the use of a cord.[1212] In utter silence, he crept forth from place to place until he found the sleeping Ammoron. As with Amalickiah, he slipped into Ammoron's tent and thrust a javelin into his heart, but unlike previously with Amalickiah, it was not an instantaneous kill. Ammoron was able to call to his servants before he died, who sounded the alarm across the Lamanite camp. The Lamanites awakened and pursued Teancum. They were able to slay him before he could go over the wall.

When Moroni and Lehi learned that Teancum had been killed, they mourned his loss. He had been a great and noble warrior, who had been unfailing in his devotion to the cause of peace and the defense of his country. Now he was dead, but his memory would live on. Single-handedly, he had killed both Amalickiah and Ammoron. If he had not sacrificed his life to seek out and kill Ammoron inside the walls of Moroni, the murderous dissenter might have escaped with his army into the land of Nephi to return later, given the time to recover and plan another attack.

The following day, the Nephites went against the Lamanites with great force,[1213] knowing it would be the last confrontation of the war. The Lamanites fled the city of Moroni and were driven and smitten. They fled across the border of Jershon into the land of Nephi and did not return at that time.

The Zoramite War in 74 BC had lasted only a period of months, perhaps no more than a few weeks. The destruction caused by Amalickiah and his brother, Ammoron, however, was a terrible scourge against the Nephites with episodes of war lasting for a period of seven years, during a total period of twelve years, beginning in late 73 BC and continuing until the end of 61 BC. It was a war that was largely carried out along the southern and eastern borders of Nephite lands, but it also affected the other areas of the land as well.

When Helaman returned to the city of Zarahemla and his duties in the Church, he found the same problems of corruption and apostasy that had plagued the Church following the Amlicite[1214] and Zoramite[1215] Wars, and that, in essence, had caused the most recent war.[1216] Again, he found it necessary to reestablish the Church across the land of Zarahemla and implement regulations that had been lost during the war. This difficult task was conducted between 61 and 57 BC, and Helaman died after its completion.

In 73 BC, Alma had referred to Helaman as being in his youth.[1217] His death came only sixteen years later[1218] in 57 BC, one year prior to Moroni's death. Like Moroni, he had answered the call to defend his country against the Lamanite invasion. The intense suffering and physical deprivation, not to mention the numerous wounds they had been subjected to over a period of four or five years, likely shortened his life, as it did Moroni's. Truly, these men were heroes, not only within their own cultures, but to members of the Church today who read the account of their ultimate sacrifice for the cause of freedom and of Christ.

LOOKING BACK

AMALICKIAH'S MANEUVERS AT THE BEGINNING OF THE WAR

From the order in which the cities along the southern border were recaptured by Helaman's forces, it can be concluded that they had fallen in exactly the reverse order. Furthermore, the order in which the cities were initially captured (first Manti, then Zeezrom, Cumeni, and Antiparah) is a strong indication, when considered in conjunction with the offensive along the eastern seaboard, that Amalickiah's campaign was initiated from the eastern lands of habitation, and not from the city of Nephi (see Map 5.0). On the basis of these simple observations, Amalickiah's initial plans and maneuvers are projected as follows.

At the end of 68 BC, Amalickiah departed out of the city of Nephi with a large Lamanite army. They proceeded along the narrow strip of wilderness to the eastern region on the south of Jershon. Gathering additional forces from that region, Amalickiah and

Ammoron (the second in command) planned a two-pronged attack, one along the eastern seaboard and one along the southern Nephite border.

Both Amalickiah and Ammoron accompanied the strike force along the eastern seaboard, which attacked the city of Moroni. Under the command of an unidentified Lamanite leader, the southern border attack was initiated at Manti. Instead of immediately moving northward after the fall of Manti toward the city of Zarahemla, where Moroni was putting down the king-men rebellion, this second army moved westward. Obviously, they were showing a great deal of patience in stripping away the entire outer layer of defensive cities before moving toward the center of the land, for the city of Zarahemla was no more than a day's travel to the north. This same level of paitence can be seen in the eastern seaboard attack following the capture of the city of Moroni when Amalickiah moved northward along the coast toward the city of Lehi, instead of moving westward in the direction of the Nephite capital city and attacking the city of Nephihah, as the Nephites expected.

AMMORON'S ACTIVITIES AND PURPOSES IN THE WAR, FOLLOWING AMALICKIAH'S DEMISE

Utilizing the geography of the land of Zarahemla, as it has been revealed through the account of the Amalickiah and Ammoron Wars, and previous accounts in the books of Mosiah and Alma, we now look at Ammoron's travels after he took the reins of the Lamanite forces. His direct involvement is recorded in the Book of Mormon at every point along the way. Whenever he was present in a region, he was always identified by name, through his communications with the Nephite military commanders. Therefore, his movements and frequently brief stops in his journey from the east sea to the west sea and back to the east sea during the period from 66 through 62 BC can be traced.

In 66 BC, after he was made king of the Lamanites, Ammoron left orders at the city of Mulek on the east coast before departing for the city of Nephi.[1219] He journeyed by each captured east coast city. After a stop in the city of Moroni, he apparently moved southward into the narrow strip of wilderness and made a wide swing around the perimeter cities of Nephihah and Aaron, which were still in

Nephite hands. Perhaps he stopped in the east wilderness, where the war had been initiated. Then, moving westward through the wilderness, he made stops at Manti, Zeezrom, Cumeni, and Antiparah, all of which were under Lamanite control. In Antiparah, he gave directions concerning the city of Judea.[1220] Judea was the location of the southern battlefront at that time.

Helaman's letter to Moroni describes his first arrival in company with the 2,000 stripling warriors in 66 BC at Judea. It is apparent that Ammoron had reached Antiparah, for he gave the order "to not come against the city of Judea, or against us, to battle."[1221] His order appears to have been a direct response to the arrival of the 2,000 stripling warriors, which strengthened Antipus' army.

Ammoron then journeyed south out of Antiparah to the city of Nephi.[1222] In Nephi, he informed the queen of Amalickiah's death and immediately began gathering additional troops across the land of Nephi.[1223] Near the end of the year he attacked the Nephites on the west coast.[1224]

AMMORON'S PERSPECTIVE IN THE WAR

Considering the order of development of the three separate battlefronts along the perimeter of Nephite lands under Ammoron's direction, a definite picture emerges of Ammoron's perspective and new battle plan as he made his way back to Nephi after the death of Amalickiah. No doubt he was plagued by a panorama of contrasting thoughts, some negative and some positive. First of all, he must have been demoralized, with intense feelings of vulnerability as a result of his brother's death, especially in the manner in which he died. Added to that was the thorough defeat of the Lamanite army at the borders of Bountiful at the hands of Teancum's elite force. They had been overwhelmed, driven back, and, following Amalickiah's death, had fled in terror[1225] into the safety of Mulek's fortifications.

On the positive side, however, he had been catapulted from a subordinate position into one of absolute power over the Lamanites upon the death of Amalickiah. Furthermore, he could now add vengeance to his list of justifications for his war of aggression against the Nephites.[1226] It was just another motivational tool he would use to spur the Lamanite warriors to action.

It is reasonable to assume that there was only one route available to Ammoron for his return to the land of Nephi, for he was in a hostile land. He had no choice but to retrace his steps down the east coast—the only route in the possession of the Lamanites. As he traveled from city to city along the eastern seaboard, he may have gained confidence because of the accomplishments of the previous year, for all six cities on the eastern border of Jershon were in Lamanite hands. In each of those cities, he established and confirmed his new authority and gave orders and instructions as in Mulek.[1227]

After he passed by the city of Moroni, he moved into the south wilderness beyond the borders of the Nephite lands to avoid the perimeter cities of Nephihah[1228] and Aaron,[1229] which were still under Nephite control. Emerging from the wilderness near Manti,[1230] he then continued westward along the line of four Lamanite-controlled cities[1231] on the southern border, before turning south toward the city of Nephi from Antiparah. The long journey gave him time to reflect on the present situation, in which the forward progress of the Lamanite forces had been stalled.

The planning stage of the war had been much simpler than what he was faced with now, and the supply of Lamanite warriors had seemed endless. During the five-year period between the attack at Noah and the subsequent attack at Moroni, there had been ample time for his brother and him to fully plan the assault of Zarahemla. The first projected phase had been to advance northward on the east all the way to Desolation, thus taking control of the eastern and northern borders in a single sweep. The narrow pass would be cut off, and in effect the Nephites would be surrounded. The second phase—a major offensive on the south—was to simultaneously strike the southern perimeter cities and take control of the southern border from Manti to Antiparah. At their leisure, they could then advance toward the Nephite heartland.

Without an avenue of escape into the land northward, the Nephites would be compelled to surrender themselves and their lands to Amalickiah. A third phase was to take advantage of internal strife, in coordination with the external invasion, which would reduce the number of soldiers available to strengthen the eastern and southern regions. The beginning of the war had been carefully timed to take advantage of the king-men unrest. In effect, the internal struggle became a genuine battlefront, fully coordinated with the east and south battlefronts.

Throughout the twenty-fifth year of the judges, their armies had continued to advance in both the eastern and southern regions, while Zarahemla crumbled from within. It appeared that the Nephite takeover would be achieved without a hitch. However, everything had changed suddenly when the eastern phase was halted suddenly by Teancum's army without reaching the narrow pass into the land northward and Amalickiah was slain in his sleep.

Attacking Nephite cities all around the perimeter had proven to be a very difficult proposition. With every Nephite city that fell, there was a great thinning of Lamanite forces and, effectively, an increase in the Nephite forces aligned against them. Thousands of Lamanite warriors were lost in each siege,[1232] and a large number of additional warriors had been required to secure each city and defend against Nephite retaliation. On the other hand, the Nephites from each city retreated to strengthen other cities not yet taken.[1233] There came a point where the Lamanite forces became spread too thin, as many warriors were employed simply to defend fortified cities in peripheral areas further and further removed from the battlefront, which removed them from effective participation in the war.

Such thoughts no doubt plagued Ammoron as he slipped quietly through the wilderness past Nephihah and Aaron. Arriving at Manti, he observed enough troops to hold the city, but not enough to advance toward Zarahemla. As he moved along the southern border, the same was true in the cities of Zeezrom and Cumeni. He concluded that the only answer to the current stalemate was more Lamanite warriors—as many as he could gather. He must also create another diversionary battlefront to replace the king-men revolt, which at that time had been put down.

Antiparah, located nearest the city of Nephi, was the Lamanite center of operations for the southern battlefront at that time and the location of the highest concentration of their forces. As Ammoron moved toward Antiparah, word apparently came to him that his field leaders were planning a new assault against the city of Judea, where the Nephite army was entrenched. His arrival at Antiparah coincided roughly with the arrival of Helaman at Judea with the 2,000 stripling warriors. Their arrival may have created a new illusion that thousands of Nephites were rallying to defend Zarahemla. Making one of his greatest mistakes of the war, Ammoron decided against attacking Judea in its vulnerable condition before fortifications were in place.[1234]

Alternatively, his decision may have reflected his overall perception of the war and the battle plan he had apparently conceived even before he left Mulek, which had become set in stone long before he reached Antiparah. His orders to "not come against the city of Judea"[1235] and "to maintain those cities which they had taken,"[1236] were essentially the same as those given at Mulek,[1237] though overall, they were less aggressive,[1238] and not necessarily because his plan had changed during the journey. Rather, it may have reflected a definite planned order in the siege of Zarahemla.

This planned order of attack is projected as follows: Phase 1 must be completed on the east to seal off the Nephite escape route into the land northward before Phase 2—the advancement toward the city of Zarahemla—could be continued on the south. Hence, it was imperative that the campaign on the east coast (which had faltered at Mulek) must continue to move forward toward Desolation, whereas the campaign on the south (focused presently at the city of Judea) must mark time until the east coast objectives were obtained.

Furthermore, the orders at Judea reflected the ramifications of that moment when he was a relatively short distance from the city of Nephi. He had already placed everything on hold until he could gather more warriors. Thus, his leaders at Antiparah would have to wait for an imminent attack on the west coast, which could be accomplished quickly, since the distances between Antiparah, Nephi and the west coast were relatively small. Success on the west coast would become a catalyst for victory on the east coast and its ultimate objective: control of Desolation. Only then could Judea and other second-tier cities to the south of the city of Zarahemla become the focal point of the war.

What Ammoron apparently did not know was that an attack on Judea at that moment would have brought the Nephite defensive operation to the point of defeat in that region. Failure to attack would give them time to recover, prepare internal cities for defense, and complete the training of the Nephite secret weapon—the stripling warriors. Therefore, the proper order of events would have been to crush Judea, and only then to mark time while waiting for the west coast offensive to commence and the east coast offensive to accomplish its objective.

Helaman's arrival with the stripling warriors at exactly the right moment was crucial to Ammoron's decision, for it is apparent that he did not realize the new troops were young and untrained. It gave an impression of strength where none yet existed,[1239] thereby supporting his belief that more Lamanite warriors and a new battlefront were needed to further spread and weaken the Nephite defenses. Had Helaman not arrived, Ammoron might have correctly understood the desperate condition of Antipus's army and their extreme vulnerability due to the terrible death toll they had suffered and the lack of fortifications at Judea.

The above projections of Ammoron's mental processes are not set forth as a definite and conclusive interpretation of his perspective, intents, and battle-plans following his brother's death. They are presented for the singular purpose of considering all factors surrounding the dilemma faced by Ammoron as he departed from Jershon and returned to the land of Nephi, as related to his course of action throughout the remainder of the war. It is hoped that they will stimulate further study and reflection by the reader.

LESSONS FROM THE AMALICKIAH AND AMMORON WARS

This war teaches many lessons; principal among them is the lesson that righteous, obedient children of God can find refuge in the Lord, regardless of what worldly powers might align against them. The many miracles performed by God on behalf of the Nephites during the war stand as an eternal symbol of His protective arm. It gives us the faith to find comfort and solace today, even as the world dips into the abyss of moral depravity and the wicked become more and more aggressive in their quest for power and more openly resolute in their hatred of others.

When righteous followers of Christ are faced with the aggression and violence of the sons of men, accounts such as the Amalickiah and Ammoron Wars, and other accounts in the Book of

Mormon and the Bible, should strengthen our faith and cause us to look upward for deliverance, even if all the forces of evil should combine against us. God has not changed. He is still a God of miracles!

TABLE 3.0
BATTLEFRONTS OF THE AMALICKIAH AND AMMORON WARS

Year of the Judges	Year BC	Eastern Seaboard Offensive	Southern Border Offensive	Center of Land (King-Men)	Western Seaboard Offensive
25	67	X	X	X	
26	66	X	X		X
27	65	X	X		X
28	64	X	X		
29	63	X	X	X	
30	62	X		X	
31	61	X			

EXPLANATION OF TABLE 3.0

At the beginning of 66 BC, the number of battlefronts fluttered briefly from three to two and then back to three as the first king-men rebellion was put down by the Nephites and the west coast offensive was immediately initiated by Ammoron.

At an unknown point during 65 BC, the number of battlefronts was reduced from three to two when Ammoron was repelled along the west coast, never to return. (See Alma 52:12–18.)

During 63 BC, the number of battlefronts returned briefly to three when the second king-men uprising took place, indicated by Helaman's epistle (Alma 58:34), but in the latter part of the same year (Alma 58:38) the Lamanites fled from the southern border (from Manti), and the number of battlefronts was again reduced from three to two.

At the end of 62 BC, the king-men were defeated once more (Alma 62:8–11), and the number of battlefronts was reduced from two to one. All that then remained to be done was to drive the Lamanites out of the land of Jershon.

BIBLIOGRAPHY

1. Doctrine and Covenants, published by The Church of Jesus Christ of Latter-day Saints.

2. Ginzberg, L., 1909, *The Legends of the Jews*, Vol. 1, trans. H. Szold (Philadelphia, Society of America).

3. Gosch, Stephen S. and Stearns, Peter N., *Premodern Travel in World History* (Routledge, NY, 2008).

4. Holy Bible, King James Version, (1979) published by The Church of Jesus Christ of Latter-day Saints, Salt Lake City, Utah.

5. Josephus, "The Antiquities of the Jews," trans. by William Whiston.

6. *Noah Webster's Dictionary*, copyright 1828.

7. Pearl of Great Price, the book of Moses, (1979) Published by The Church of Jesus Christ of Latter-day Saints, Salt Lake City, Utah.

8. Smith, Joseph, *History of the Church of Jesus Christ of Latter-day Saints*, Volume 4.

9. The Book of Mormon, translated by Joseph Smith, published by The Church of Jesus Christ of Latter-day Saints, Salt Lake City, Utah.

10. *Webster's Deluxe Unabridged Dictionary*, Copyright 1979 by Simon and Schuster.

ENDNOTES

1 Joseph Smith's History of the Church of Jesus Christ of Latter-day Saints, Volume 4, page 461.

2 Words of Mormon 1:7

3 The plates were buried in AD 421 and were received by Joseph Smith in 1827, which marks the passage of 1,406 years from the time when Moroni hid up the Plates of Mormon for the last time.

4 Mosiah 28:11-19—The Urim and Thummim are instruments used by prophets to translate ancient records written in unknown languages, and also to receive revelation from God. In the Book of Mormon they are called interpreters. Joseph Smith translated the Book of Mormon by means of the Urim and Thummim, which Moroni had sealed up with the records in the Hill Cumorah.

5 Unfortunately, the first 116 pages of the Book of Mormon, which were completed while Martin Harris served as Joseph Smith's scribe, never made it into the Book of Mormon as constituted today. Perhaps one day, if we as a church truly desire such of our Heavenly Father, we will be blessed with the discovery of the missing manuscript, or with its coming forth from the original plates, which Joseph returned to the Angel Moroni.

6 Enos 1:13-14

7 Prior to the discovery of the Americas by Christopher Columbus in 1492 AD

8 A codex (plural: codices) is a manuscript book written in ancient times, which (in reference to the Western Hemisphere) was painted by American Indian cultures prior to European contact, or written in the native manner during the early Spanish period. Only four Pre-Columbian codices are known to exist. Many were destroyed by the Spaniards.

9 Documents written by colonists and natives during the Spanish Colonial period of North and South America (after 1492 AD)

10 See Part 1, Chapter 1.2, "Nephite History in the Land of Nephi" and Part 2, Introduction

11 The pre-Christ period in Zarahemla lasted from *ca.* 200 BC until the Great Storm on the 4th day of AD 34.

12 Ginzberg, L., 1909, "The Legends of the Jews," Vol. 1, Chapter 4, Nimrod

13 Josephus, "The Antiquities of the Jews", Transl. by William Whiston, Chapter 4:2

14 Zedekiah was the last king of Judah prior to the Babylonian Captivity (2 Kings 24:17–20; Chapter 25).

ENDNOTES

15 See Helaman 6:10, 8:21. Also see Omni 1:14–18, in combination with Mosiah 25:2
16 2 Kings 24:18; 2 Chronicles 36:11
17 1 Nephi 1:4
18 1 Nephi 1:5
19 1 Nephi 1:13
20 1 Nephi 1:18
21 1 Nephi 2:1
22 1 Nephi 2:3,4
23 1 Nephi Chapter 4
24 1 Nephi Chapter 7
25 1 Nephi 2:5–9; 1 Nephi 16:12–14
26 1 Nephi 16:10
27 1 Nephi 18:12
28 1 Nephi 16:16
29 1 Nephi 16:34
30 1 Nephi 17:1
31 1 Nephi 17:5
32 1 Nephi 10:2-3
33 1 Nephi 11:1
34 1 Nephi 17:9
35 1 Nephi 18:12, 21
36 1 Nephi 18:23
37 2 Nephi 1:4
38 2 Nephi 25:6,10,11
39 2 Nephi 6:8
40 Omni 1:12
41 Omni 1:15
42 Omni 1:14
43 Helaman 8:21
44 The term "Samite" is not found in the Book of Mormon, and perhaps 2 Nephi 4:11 explains why.
45 A characteristic of a patrilineal society
46 2 Nephi Chapter 5
47 Omni 1:19
48 Alma 2:11
49 For example—Amalickiah (Alma 45:23–24; 46:1–7, 29)
50 Mosiah 25:19–24. Until Joseph Smith, there was no knowledge of Churches of Christ before the advent of Christ. See also 1 Nephi 4:26 and D&C 107:4.
51 Alma Chapter 27
52 Helaman Chapter 5
53 Moroni 1:2-3, Moroni 9:24
54 Helaman 6:34-41
55 4 Nephi 1:1–2, 20

56 4 Nephi 1:17

57 Alma 21:2-3

58 Alma 24:29–30; Alma 43:6–8; Alma 47:1; Alma 48:24; Alma 51:15-17; Helaman 1:15-17; Helaman 4:1–8

59 The abbreviated nature of the record of Ether is accentuated by the fact that the first five chapters take place in the Old World during a very short period of time. Chapters 12–15 contain Moroni's commentary, the prophecies of Ether, and an account of the final genocidal war. The balance of six chapters (6–11) covers a period of 2000 years with amazing detail.

60 This projection is based upon the arrival of the Nephites in the land of Zarahemla in about 200 BC, in combination with the recent arrival of the Mulekites, following their burial of Coriantumr, the last survivor of the Jaredites. See Part 3, Chapter 3.1: The Land of Zarahemla—Recently Settled.

61 2 Nephi 10:20; this interpretation depends upon the Nephite definition of "an isle of the sea" (as contained in this verse), and if they could be aware of the land northward (or its vastness) without venturing northward into the Mulekite land of Desolation, let alone the Jaredite capitol city of Moron, which bordered Desolation on the north (Ether 7:6).

62 Omni 1:22

63 Alma 22:30; See Part 3, Chapter 3.1.

64 Mosiah 8:7-8; Mosiah 21:25; Alma 22:31. This wilderness ultimately would become the lands of Zarahemla. In a sense, the wilderness was to both Nephites and Lamanites during the first Nephite period in the land of Nephi as fortified Nephite cities of Zarahemla were to the Lamanites during the second Nephite period—an obstacle to northern migration. This wilderness will be considered below in Part 3, Chapters 3.1 and 3.3, and in Book 2, Part 2, Chapter 2.1.

65 Alma 22:32. The narrow neck of land was a land bridge connecting the land southward to the land northward, that is, "...a small neck of land between the land northward and the land southward." Without the narrow neck of land, "...the land of Nephi and the land of Zarahemla..." (the land southward) would have been completely surrounded by water. See also Alma 50:33-34.

66 Mosiah 8:8

67 Ether 10:21

68 Alma 22:31. The northern portion of the south wilderness was later known to the Nephites as the land of Bountiful.

69 Omni 1:20–22

70 Alma 22:31. "And [the people of Zarahemla] came from [the land of Desolation] up into the south wilderness..." Mosiah 25:2. This verse speaks of Zarahemla (a descendant of Mulek) and those who came with him into the south wilderness.

71 Ramah was the site of the last Jaredite battle. It was the same hill known to the Nephites as Cumorah. See Ether 15:11

72 Moron: See Ether 14:6.

73 The city of Moron where Coriantumr ruled over the Jaredites was near the land of Desolation (Ether 7:6) where the Mulekites (people of Zarahemla) lived before their migration to the "south wilderness" (Alma 22:31), as the land southward was called by the Jaredites and the Mulekites in the previous cultural period in the land northward (Ether 10:21). It is reasonable that the location where the people of Zarahemla discovered Coriantumr was in the land of Moron, because it bordered upon their land (Desolation). Thus, Coriantumr returned home after the culmination of the war and was discovered by Mulekites who came into Moron from the neighboring land of Desolation, perhaps to view the great destruction, perhaps to search for the living among the dead, or perhaps to harvest (loot) the treasures left behind. The possibilities are many.

74 Omni 1:21

75 Omni 1:20-22

76 Mosiah 8:7–11

77 Mosiah 8:8

78 Ether 14:21–23

79 Mosiah 8:10–11

80 Mosiah 8:9; Ether 15:33

81 Mosiah 28:11–19

82 Omni 1:20–22

83 1 Nephi 18:23

84 Nephi did not provide detail in the small Plates of Nephi concerning the day of their landing. The small plates were not made until approximately 20 years after the arrival in the New World (See 2 Nephi 5:28–31). It is likely that more information concerning their arrival in the "promised land" is contained in the first 116 pages of Mormon's text, which were lost after being translated.

85 I Kings 2:2; Joshua 23:14; 2 Nephi 1:14

86 As implied in the Book of Mormon, the relationship of Nephi and Zarahemla was always given as "up to Nephi," and "down to Zarahemla." (See Mosiah 7:1; 9:3; 28:1, 5, 9; Omni 1:13)

87 2 Nephi 5:28, 34

88 1Nephi 1:24; 2 Nephi 5:25; Jacob 3:3

89 Jacob 3:4

90 Jarom 1:9

91 Jarom 1:7

92 Jarom 1:7, 9

93 Omni 1:3

94 Omni 1:5

95 Omni 1:6. Alma referred to the same principle of prosperity for obedience and righteousness, and destruction for disobedience and wickedness,

when he warned the Ammonihahites of coming destruction if they did not repent—See Alma 9:12–18. A similar idea is presented in Alma 50:19–22.

96 Omni 1:10

97 Jacob 3:4

98 2 Nephi 5:5 records the first time the Nephites fled from Lamanite violence.

99 Omni 1:13

100 1 Nephi 16:10; the Liahona had guided the Lehites following their departure from Jerusalem (See 1 Ne. 16:16).

101 Omni 1:12–13

102 Mosiah 7:1–5; Mosiah 21:25; Mosiah 22:15–16; Mosiah 23:30–35

103 Omni 1:13

104 Chapter 1.1 (above)

105 Omni 1:17–18

106 Omni 1:18

107 Omni 1:19

108 Omni 1:17. Compare with Mosiah 3:8. Christ is the Creator. Therefore, the phrase "denied the being of their Creator" is essentially the same as "denied the being of Christ."

109 1 Nephi 4:38

110 1 Nephi 1:17; 1 Nephi 9:2,4

111 1 Nephi 5:11–12

112 1 Nephi 5:16

113 Jacob 7:24

114 Omni 1:17

115 See the Books of Mosiah and Alma. Also see Words of Mormon 1:17.

116 Mosiah 8:2–3

117 Mosiah 8:13–18

118 Mosiah 1:3–4

119 Omni 1:18

120 Omni 1:14

121 Genesis 32:28

122 Genesis 49:8–12

123 Genesis 48; 49:22–26; Lehi was a descendant of Manasseh – See Alma 10:3.

124 Omni 1:14

125 Helaman 6:10

126 Omni 1:14

127 Omni 1:15

128 Alma 63:4

129 Alma 22:30–31

130 Omni 1:17

131 *Ibid.*

132 Mosiah 25:3. Note the comparison of the number of Lamanites to the number of Nephites and Mulekites. The number of Lamanites was only significant when they attacked the Nephites.

133 The first 116 pages of Mormon's abridgment, which unfortunately were lost after being translated by Joseph Smith, were abridged from the large Plates of Nephi and spanned Nephite history from the beginning in Jerusalem "down to the reign of this king Benjamin, of whom Amaleki spake" (Words of Mormon 1:3). Amaleki's reference to King Benjamin is found Omni 1:23–25.

134 The small Plates of Nephi were a spiritual record, not a secular or historical record.

135 Aminadi "interpreted the writing which was upon the wall of the temple, which was written by the finger of God" (Alma 10:2–3).

136 3 Nephi 5:12. This verse implies there was a church before the "transgression."

137 Omni 1:12

138 Though the 116 pages were lost, they were only copies, which Martin Harris, acting as Joseph's scribe, had penned on foolscap paper. The original record, inscribed on gold plates, was returned to the Angel Moroni. The lost record will come forth at the Lord's appointed time.

139 Omni 1:12–23

140 Mosiah 2:32

141 Omni 1:18

142 Omni 1:20–22. Mosiah utilized the Urim and Thummim (interpreters) to translate the writings on the large stone (See Mosiah 8:13).

143 Omni 1:27 (27–30)

144 Mosiah 2:11

145 Mosiah Chapters 1–6; 6:3

146 Omni 1:3-9

147 When Joseph Smith received the Plates of Mormon from the angel Moroni, the small plate of Nephi were sandwiched in between the two portions of the Plates of Mormon. The Plates of Mormon contain Mormon's abridgment of the large plate of Nephi. Joseph returned the Plates of Mormon to Moroni after the translation was completed, where they remain in reserve for the time when the sealed portion (containing the revelations given to the brother of Jared) will be revealed to the Saints, upon conditions of righteousness and faith. See Words of Mormon 1: 3-9.

148 Words of Mormon 1:17

149 Benjamin emphasized the point that the angel awoke him from sleep, apparently to establish to the people that it was not a dream, but a revelation from God. See Mosiah 3:2–3.

150 Mosiah 3:5

151 Mosiah 3:7

152 Mosiah 3:8. See also 1 Nephi 11:13-21; Alma 7:10

153 Mosiah 2:21
154 D&C 4:2
155 Romans 3:23
156 D&C 1:31
157 Mosiah 3:17–21
158 Mosiah 2:41
159 Mosiah 5:2–7
160 Mosiah 1:11 (10–11); See also Mosiah 2:1
161 Mosiah 5:5
162 Mosiah 5:7 (6–7)
163 See Alma 46:13–15; 48:10
164 Mosiah 25:18–23
165 Mosiah 1:2
166 Mosiah 1:10
167 Mosiah 6:5
168 Mosiah's grandfather, Mosiah I, fled with his people from the land of Nephi to escape escalating war and contention with the Lamanites (Omni 1:12–23). His father, Benjamin, experienced internal contention and war with the Lamanites during his reign (Omni 1:24; Words of Mormon 1:12–18).
169 Mosiah Chapters 26 and 27
170 Omni 1:27–30
171 Mosiah 7:1
172 Mosiah 7:2
173 Mosiah 7:4–5
174 Two towers were constructed by King Noah: one next to the temple in the city of Nephi and one on the hill bordering on the north of the land of Shilom (Mosiah 11:12–13).
175 The other city was Nephi, or Nephi-Lehi, as it was sometimes called (Mosiah 9:8).
176 Alma 46:40; 51:33
177 Mosiah 9:2
178 Mosiah 9:1
179 Omni 1:28
180 In Mosiah 7:1 and 9:8, the city of Nephi is called the city of Lehi-Nephi. Throughout the remainder of the Book of Mormon, as well as later in chapter 9 (verse 15), it is referred to exclusively as the city of Nephi.
181 Mosiah Chapters 9–22
182 2 Nephi 5:16
183 Mosiah 11:10-11
184 See 1 and 2 Kings in the Bible.
185 Mosiah 11:20
186 Mosiah 16:15
187 Mosiah 17:2
188 Mosiah 19:3

189 Mosiah 19:4
190 Mosiah 19:15, 25–26
191 Mosiah 7:22
192 Mosiah 21:3
193 Mosiah 21:6–12
194 Mosiah 21:16
195 *op. cit.* Mosiah 21:15
196 Mosiah chapters 7 and 21
197 See previous chapter.
198 Mosiah 7:5–6
199 Mosiah 7:7; 21:23–24
200 Mosiah 22:10
201 Mosiah 22:11
202 Mosiah 22:14; 28:11
203 3 Nephi 5:12
204 Mosiah 17:4
205 Mosiah 18:5
206 Mosiah 18:1; 23:9–10
207 Alma 5:3
208 Mosiah 18:4
209 Mosiah 18:5
210 Mosiah 18:8
211 According to the Noah Webster's dictionary in print at the time of the translation of the Book of Mormon (see the 1828 edition), the word "fountain" meant "1) A spring, or source of water; properly, a spring or issuing of water from the earth. This word accords in sense with well, in our mother tongue; but we now distinguish the [two words], applying fountain to a natural spring of water, and well to an artificial pit of water, issuing from the interior of the earth."
The fourth meaning of fountain in the same dictionary is: "the head or source of a river."
212 As will be seen, the pool was deep enough to serve as a baptismal font.
213 Mosiah 18:30
214 Omni 1:27–30. See also Mosiah 22:8–11. It is apparent from verse 11 of Mosiah chapter 22 that the wilderness between Zarahemla and Nephi bordered directly upon the cities of Nephi and Shilom. When the people of Limhi departed out of the city of Nephi, they entered the wilderness before circling around the land of Shilom.
215 Mosiah 17:4; 23:10
216 Mosiah 18:1–2
217 Mosiah 18:13
218 Joseph Smith, History 1:70
219 D&C 84:28
220 Mosiah Chapter 5; Mosiah 6:1–3
221 Mosiah 18:25

222 Mosiah 18:30. These words were written by Mormon during the twilight of Nephite civilization. Mormon cherished his membership in the Church of Jesus Christ and looked back fondly to its restoration by the prophet Alma.
223 Mosiah 18:25
224 Mosiah 18:32
225 Mosiah 18:33
226 Mosiah 23:1
227 Mosiah 23:2–3
228 Mosiah 23:4
229 Mosiah 23:5
230 Mosiah 23:7
231 Mosiah 23:27
232 Mosiah 23:28
233 Mosiah 23:29
234 Mosiah Chapter 20
235 Mosiah 23:33–34
236 Mosiah 23:35
237 Mosiah 23:36
238 Mosiah 23:37
239 Mosiah 24:1–2
240 Mosiah 20:12
241 Mosiah 24:1
242 Mosiah 24:4
243 *Ibid.*
244 Mosiah 24:6–7
245 Mosiah 24:5
246 Mosiah 24:6–7
247 Mosiah 24:7
248 Enos 1:20.
249 Mosiah 17:14–19
250 Alma 25:4–12
251 Mosiah 23:39
252 Alma Chapter 45.
253 Mosiah 24:8
254 Mosiah 24:10–12
255 Alma 24:13–14
256 Mosiah 24:15
257 Mosiah 24:17
258 Mosiah 24:19
259 Mosiah 24:21
260 Mosiah 24:23
261 Mosiah had already received the people of Limhi. See Mosiah 22:13–14.
262 Mosiah 24:25

263 The gospel is defined as literally "good news." It is the message of Jesus Christ, the kingdom of God, and the salvation of mankind.

264 The first 116 pages of the Joseph Smith translation of The Book of Mormon were lost shortly after being translated. The lost pages contained Mormon's abridgment of the large plate of Nephi through the reign of King Benjamin. See Joseph Smith History of the Church, Vol. 1, pp. 21–22.

265 See pages 1–143 of the Book of Mormon.

266 Jacob Chapter 7

267 Enos 1:20

268 Alma 1:32; 14:5; 31:1

269 Alma 21:2–5

270 See "The order of Nehor in the Land of Nephi" in Part 2, Chapter 2.3, The Order of the Nehors.

271 Moses 7:13–17

272 Omni 1:17; see Mosiah 3:8.

273 The term "indigenous" is frequently used as a characteristic of paganism, meaning developing naturally within a culture, without interference from Christianity through proselytizing. It fits well with the ideas expressed herein, in the vein of being from the earth—earthly, as opposed to being from God—godly.

274 Alma 43:6—These verses refer to the Amalekites and Zoramites.

275 Alma 47:36.

276 Alma 24:30 (28–30)

277 Alma 48:1–3

278 Alma 2:4; 44:2; 48:10; Helaman 4:1–2

279 3 Nephi Chapters 8–10.

280 Mosiah 25:15–19. Alma originally founded the Church at the Waters of Mormon in about 147 BC. See Mosiah 18:14–17.

281 Mosiah 25:19–24

282 Mosiah 26:37–38

283 Mosiah 27:1–2

284 Mosiah 27:10

285 Mosiah 25:23–24

286 Mosiah 26:10

287 Mosiah 26:6

288 Mosiah 26:1–4

289 Mosiah 26:7

290 Mosiah 26:9

291 Mosiah 26:10

292 Mosiah 26:11

293 Mosiah 26:13

294 Mosiah 26:36

295 Mosiah 27:1

296 Alma 1:24; 31:8–11; 46:1–7; Helaman 4:1–4

297 Mosiah 27:1–2
298 Mosiah 27:8–10
299 Mosiah chapter 27
300 Mosiah 27:32
301 Words of Mormon 1:16
302 Words of Mormon 1:12–18
303 Words of Mormon 1:15–16
304 Words of Mormon 1:16
305 Words of Mormon 1:17. Compare with Alma 23:1–7; Ether 7:23–27
306 Mosiah 26:5
307 Mosiah 27:1–3
308 Mosiah 27:10
309 Mosiah 10:11–17
310 4 Nephi 1:38–39
311 Ephesians 6:12
312 2 Nephi 5:18; Jacob 1:11
313 Nephi became the 1ˢᵗ king of the Nephites, as recorded in 2 Nephi 5:18. His reign began in *ca.* 588 BC, shortly after the flight from Laman, Lemuel, and Ishmael's sons. The total number of kings in the Land of Nephi is unknown.
314 Mosiah 29:30
315 Mosiah 29:39–42
316 Helaman 3:37. "Nephi began to reign in his stead." Alma 51:5. There were "those who were desirous that Pahoran should be dethroned."
317 Alma 2:1–7
318 Mosiah 29:42
319 Alma 4:20
320 Alma 4:16–17
321 Alma 4:16
322 Mosiah 25:19–24
323 Mosiah 29:26
324 Alma 1:2–6
325 The order established by Nehor is the first reference to pagan religion as an organization (church). However, the Amalekites had already practiced a religion that built synagogues according to the manner of the order of Nehor for the worship of God, though not His Son, Jesus Christ. See Alma 21:4; Alma 22:7.
326 Mosiah 26:1, 4–5
327 Alma 2:2
328 Helaman 6:31
329 Mosiah 29:30
330 Alma 10:19
331 Mosiah 29:31
332 D&C 101:78
333 Alma 2:24–27; 43:5–8; 46:4, 33; 48:1–4; Helaman 4:1–5

ENDNOTES

334 Mosiah 27:3; Alma 1:1, 19–21
335 Alma 1:6
336 Alma 1:3
337 Alma 1:12
338 Alma 1:4
339 Alma 1:5
340 Mosiah Chapter 19; 22:3–9
341 Alma 1:9
342 Alma 1:16
343 Alma 2:20
344 Alma 3:15. See verses 4–19.
345 Alma 3:20–24
346 Alma 4:4–5
347 Alma 4:11
348 Alma 5:2
349 Alma 6:3
350 Alma 7:6
351 Alma 4:4-12
352 Mosiah 27:8
353 Alma 8:4–5
354 Alma 8:6
355 Mosiah 27:1–6
356 Alma 14:16; 15:15; 16:11
357 Alma 8:11–12
358 Alma 8:10
359 Alma 8:13
360 Mosiah 27:11–17; Alma 8:15
361 Alma 8:17
362 Alma 8:18
363 Alma 8:27
364 Alma 8:29
365 Alma 9:12, 24–25
366 Alma 9:15–16
367 Alma 9:21
368 Alma 9:31–32
369 Alma 9:32–33. See also John 7:30; 8:20; 10:39
370 Alma 10:12
371 Alma 14:8–9
372 Alma 14:21–23
373 Alma 14:26
374 Alma 14:26–27
375 Alma 14:29
376 Alma 15:5–11
377 Alma 15:12; 31:32
378 Alma 15:15

266

379 Alma 15:16

380 Alma 1:7–9

381 Alma 1:5–6 (3–6)

382 Alma 21:4

383 Alma 21:4

384 Alma 17:20

385 Ether 7:4

386 Ether 7:6

387 Ether 7:9

388 Ether 7:8-10

389 Ether 6:23

390 Compare this with Alma 23:1–5, in which the Lamanite king gave power and authority to the sons of Mosiah to teach the gospel to his people.

391 Ether chapter 8

392 Ether 9:25–27

393 Alma 22:30

394 Alma 22:32. Until Zarahemla led them into the land southward in *ca.* 200 BC, the Mulekites occupied the land of Desolation.

395 Ether 7:6: "Now the land of Moron, where the king dwelt, was near [not in] the land which is called Desolation by the Nephites." Desolation remained the home of the Mulekites for almost 400 years. They remained in Desolation until Zarahemla led them into the south wilderness (Mosiah 25:2, Alma 22:31).

396 Omni 1:17

397 Alma 22:30–31

398 Consider the dissenter Coriantumr (a descendant of Zarahemla), Morianton who fled from the land of Lehi toward the land of Mulek, (Helaman 6:10), Alma's sons Corianton and Shiblom, and others.

399 The Mulekite scenario of interaction with the Jaredites is directly revealed in only a single verse in the Book of Mormon. (Omni 1:21) All other related information comes to us indirectly through the presence of Jaredite names, Jaredite religion (the order of the Nehor), etc.

400 Alma 1:6

401 Mosiah 28:8–9; 29:3

402 Mosiah 28:11–16

403 Mosiah 28:17–18

404 The time required for the people of Alma the Elder to travel from the borders of Nephi to the land of Zarahemla was 20 days. See "The Distance from Nephi to Zarahemla" in Part 3, Chapter 3.2. See also Mosiah chapters 23 and 24.

405 Alma 17:13, 17

406 Alma 21:4

407 Allowing time for fasting and prayer in preparation for a mission in a hostile land and a month-long journey from Zarahemla to Nephi, the maximum time between their departure from Zarahemla and arrival in

the land of Nephi would be no more than a couple of months. Most of their preparations had likely been made before they petitioned their father.

408 Alma 16:21

409 Alma 17:4

410 Alma 21:2 contains the first reference to the Amalekites in the Book of Mormon. Additional information concerning the Amalekites will likely one day be found in the 116 lost pages of Mormon's abridgment.

411 Alma 21:2—The Amulonites were not dissenters from the Nephites in Zarahemla, but they were dissenters from the gospel. At one time, they believed in their own version of the scriptures, but at some point after they joined with the Lamanites, they embraced the religion of the Amalekites, that is, the Order of the Nehors. See Mosiah chapters 23–24.

412 Alma 21:2, 4.

413 Words of Mormon 1:16 (12–18)

414 Following the Mulekite merger with the Nephites, the Book of Mormon became riddled with Jaredite names, whereas before there is no known instance of such.

415 The point being made is that the Amalekites did not dissent away from the Nephites while the Nephites remained in the land of Nephi, that is, before the people of Mosiah migrated to the land of Zarahemla. The Amalekite religion (The order of Nehor) came from the land of Zarahemla, after being brought by the people of Zarahemla from the land northward—the land of the Jaredites.

416 Alma 14:16

417 Alma 16:11

418 Alma 21:4

419 Alma 14:15–18; 16:11. The term "profession of Nehor," as expressed in these verses, is an apparent reference to the professional clergy first established by Nehor. The term alludes to the direct relationship between Nehor religion and the city of Ammonihah, which should be expected since Ammonihah was in the land of Zarahemla and its inhabitants were familiar with Alma who lived in the city of Zarahemla, where Nehor originally established his church.

420 Alma 21:3

421 Alma 21:4-10

422 Alma 21:6

423 Moses 8:21

424 Alma 20:30

425 Alma Chapters 18 and 19

426 Alma 22:1–26

427 Alma 23:1–13

428 The Lord blessed these honorable Lamanites through the mission of the sons of Mosiah.

429 Alma 23:6

430 The editorial nature of the Book of Mormon (from the standpoint of combining several accounts into one record) can be seen in the description of the Lamanite kingdom given in Alma chapter 22. Mormon had placed the account of Mosiah's sons' mission to the Lamanites inside Alma's account. In Alma's account, Mormon had already covered the period from 91 through 81 BC, which ended with the destruction of Ammonihah, at which time the Lamanites were first driven into the wilderness.

Alma chapter 22 is part of a flashback to the beginning of the Lamanite mission around 91 BC, yet the geographical description of Lamanite lands was accurate only after 81 BC, when the Lamanites first occupied the east wilderness bordering on the east sea. Until then, the region in Nephi lying eastward of the wilderness cities of Helam and Amulon (Chapter 1.6 above) was uninhabited wilderness. Therefore, it might be stated that until 81 BC, the full extent of the Lamanite kingdom (from ocean to ocean) was conceptual only, for no Lamanite subjects inhabited the eastern region prior to that time.

431 Alma 16:8; 28:2–3

432 Alma 23:5–13

433 Alma 23:4–5

434 Alma 23:14

435 Alma 16:1. The insertion of this precise date is made possible only by the merger of the account of the mission of the Sons of Mosiah with the account of Alma the Younger's mission to the city of Ammonihah. It was at this time that the Amalekites and Amulonites led the Lamanite army to inflict vengeance against the sons of Mosiah by attacking the city of Ammonihah in the land of Zarahemla, an attack that brought down the judgments of God upon Ammonihah for their persecution and murder of the innocent within their city.

436 Alma 24:1–2

437 Alma 24:3–4

438 Alma 24:5

439 Alma 23:17

440 Alma 24:16–17

441 Alma 24:23

442 Alma 25:1–2

443 D&C 63:33

444 Alma 8:17

445 It was the fifth day of the second month of the eleventh year of the reign of the judges (Alma 16:1). Assuming a twelve-month year, this day occurred seven days less than four months after the day Alma and Amulek were delivered from the prison in Ammonihah (Alma 14:23).

446 Alma 16:1. Ammonihah lay along the western perimeter of Nephite settled lands (Alma 8:3-6).

447 Alma Chapter 24

448 Alma 24:28

449 Alma 14:16

450 Alma 8:17

451 Alma 9:18–19

452 Alma 16:9

453 Alma 16:5. An important point is that the Nephites did not wish to pursue and destroy the Lamanite army, but to rescue the captives taken from the land of Noah. This point of war for defense only was always extremely important to the prophet Mormon, who abridged the record (See also Mormon 3:11–16). It was one of the things that endeared Chief Captain Moroni to him (See Alma 44:1–2; 48:11–16).

454 Alma 16:6

455 Alma 16:7–8

456 Alma 25:5 (3–5)

457 Alma 16:12

458 See Alma 16:1; 28:7

459 Alma 27:1

460 Alma 16:12; 25:5-9

461 Alma 24:1–2

462 Alma 24:6-26. The initial attack on the people of Anti-Nephi-Lehi occurred in 81 BC, shortly before the attack on Ammonihah (Alma 16:1).

463 Alma 27:3

464 Alma 27:4

465 Alma 27:6

466 Alma 27:7

467 Alma 27:12

468 Alma 22:27

469 Alma 27:14; Alma 22:27

470 Alma 16:21–17:1

471 Alma 27:25

472 It was at this time that Alma met the sons of Mosiah as he traveled from the land of Gideon to the land of Manti. See Alma 17:1.

473 Alma 27:23

474 Alma 27:22

475 The following information places the people of Ammon near the southern borders of the land of Jershon. 1) The city of Antionum was established by the Zoramites shortly after the people of Ammon settled in Jershon. Antionum was located immediately south of Jershon and lay at the boundary of the south wilderness (Alma 31:3). 2) The city of Antionum was also located near the land where the people of Ammon lived (Alma 35:6–9). The unnamed Ammonite city in Jershon (Alma 43:25) was situated close enough to Antionum to provide a convenient resting place for Alma and his brethren after completing their missionary labors in the Zoramite city (Alma 35:1–2).

476 Alma 1:12

477 Mormon 1:5

478 Mosiah 18:30

479 Mosiah 12:20-24; Alma 21:6

480 Alma 27:4–17

481 Alma 27:1–2

482 Alma 22:27

483 See Part 3, Chapter 3.3, "The Wilderness Regions of the land southward."

484 Alma 25:13

485 Alma 28:2 (1–2)

486 Alma 28:3–7

487 Alma 28:9–10

488 See Alma chapter 3.

489 Alma 28:1–7

490 Alma 30:59

491 By 75 BC, the city of Antionum must have been established only within the previous two years, for prior to 77 BC, the land of Jershon was uninhabited wilderness (except for Lamanites driven there by the Nephite armies), and was part of the undifferentiated east wilderness.

492 Alma 31:1

493 Alma 30:6

494 Alma 30:16

495 Alma 30:12

496 Alma 30:18

497 2 Nephi 28:7

498 Alma 30:23

499 Alma 30:28

500 Nephihah was chief judge from 83–68 BC, a period of 16 years. See Alma 4:17 and 50:37. Korihor came into the land during Nephihah's reign (74 BC).

501 Alma 30:44

502 Alma 30:45, 48

503 Alma 30:52

504 Alma 30:53

505 Alma 30:55

506 Alma 31:3. Antionum was therefore located against the northern border of the "wilderness south." Likely, it was very near the location of the future city of Moroni.

507 Alma 30:59

508 Alma 30:31

509 Alma 35:3

510 See John 8:44

511 Alma 30:53

512 Alma 31:3

513 *Ibid.*

514 Alma 16:8; 25:3–5

515 Alma 28:1–3 (See Maps A-4 & A-5 in Appendix A)

516 Alma 31:4

517 Alma 31:6–7

518 Alma 31:1

519 Alma 31:21

520 Alma 31:14

521 Alma 31:35

522 Alma 31:36

523 Alma 31:38

524 Alma 32:1

525 Alma 32:1–4

526 Alma 32:4

527 Alma 32:5

528 Alma 32:9–11

529 Alma 33:2-11

530 Alma 32:28–37

531 Alma 32:38–39

532 Alma 33:23

533 Alma 21:7–8

534 Alma 31:16–17. In contrast to the Nephite religious environment of AD 210 (4 Nephi 1:27), no reference is made to multiple Christian sects during the pre-Christ period of the Book of Mormon. The denial of Christ was the defining characteristic of pagan worship in ancient times. Between 121 BC and AD 34, all individuals were either believers in Christ or unbelievers.

535 Alma 31:1

536 Alma 32:28

537 Alma 33:1

538 Alma 33:3–8

539 Alma 33:12–13

540 Alma 33:14–22; Zenos and Zenock are prophets of Israel in Old Testament times whose prophecies of Christ's mission are found only in the Book of Mormon. The time will come when they will be further revealed to mankind.

541 Alma 34:1

542 Alma 34:8–16

543 Alma 34:3

544 Alma 34: 8

545 Alma 34:17–29

546 Alma 34:30–37

547 Alma 34:38

548 Alma 34:38–39

549 Alma 34:40–41

550 Alma 7:5–6

551 Alma 35:1–3
552 Alma 39:3–5
553 Alma 35:2
554 Alma 35:3
555 Alma 35:6
556 Alma 35:8. Obviously, the Zoramite leader wanted them to suffer for their decision to apostatize from the Zoramite faith.
557 Alma 35:9
558 Alma 35:12
559 Alma 35:10
560 Alma 35:11
561 Alma 8:3
562 Alma 43:4
563 Alma 43:19
564 The ditch-parapet system was a ditch excavated around the entire perimeter of a city, with the excavated soil piled on the inner lip of the ditch to form a barrier twice the vertical height of the ditch's depth. A parapet was a structure made of timbers constructed along the top of the inner mound of soil.
565 Alma chapter 49
566 Alma 50:1
567 Alma 50:7–15
568 Northern border: Alma 52:5–7; Western border: Alma 52:11–15.
569 Alma 43:4
570 Alma 43:5
571 Alma 43:6
572 Alma 43:7–8
573 Alma 43:19–21
574 Alma 43:22
575 Alma 43:23
576 Alma 43:24
577 Alma 43:25. This is the first and only direct reference to a city of the Ammonites in the land of Jershon, though the name of the city is not provided.
578 Alma 43:24
579 Alma 43:26
580 Alma 43:27, 32
581 Alma 43:28
582 Alma 43:31
583 Alma 43:32
584 Alma 43:34
585 Alma 43:35
586 Alma 43:36
587 Alma 43:37–40
588 Alma 43:41–42

589 Alma 43:43–44
590 Alma 43:45–48
591 Alma 43:49–50
592 Alma 43:51–53
593 Alma 43:54
594 Alma 44:1–2
595 *Ibid.*, 2
596 Alma 44:4 (3–4)
597 Alma 44:9
598 Alma 44:5–6
599 Alma 44:8
600 Alma 44:11 (10–11)
601 Alma 44:12
602 Alma 50:35; 51:33–34; 62:35–36
603 Alma 44:14 (13–14)
604 Alma 44:15
605 Alma 44:16
606 Alma 44:17–19
607 Alma 44:19–20
608 Alma 43:51
609 Alma 43:6
610 See Matthew 18:20.
611 Words of Mormon 1:16 (12, 15–18)
612 Words of Mormon 1:13–14
613 Words of Mormon 1:12
614 Words of Mormon 1:15–16
615 Words of Mormon 1:13–14
616 The period of peace may have been largely influenced by two factors: 1) absolute power in the hands of righteous Christian kings, who did not tolerate religious persecution, and 2) the slow development of organization within the pagan cults and associated pagan aggression against the Church of Christ.
617 As previously observed, the pagan groundswell actually began during Mosiah II's reign, but Mosiah was able to take measures to counteract the pagan-generated contentions.
618 The Amlicite War was the first encounter of the Nehor Wars and consisted of three battles. The first two battles are recorded in detail in Alma chapter 2. The third battle is referenced in Alma 3:20–24.
619 Alma 8:6 through15:19.
620 Alma 16:1–11
621 Alma chapters 36-42; 45:1–19
622 Alma 37:3
623 Alma 37:2
624 The small plate of Nephi are unmentioned even at this time only two generations from the time that Amaleki delivered them up to King

Benjamin. They are unmentioned likely for the same reason that Mormon found them only after he searched among the plates in his possession (Words of Mormon 1:3).

625 Alma 37:21

626 Alma 37:21, 24; see "Urim and Thummim" in the Bible Dictionary, 786–87.

627 Alma 37:38

628 Alma 50:38 (37–38)

629 Alma 37:14

630 Alma 45:18 (15–18)

631 Alma 45:19.

632 Alma 4:9–19; 6:3–7. The regulations had been first established by his father Alma, the first high priest of the Church through direct revelation from the Lord (See Mosiah 26:13–37).

633 Alma 45:21–22

634 According to Helaman, the hardening and softening effect of war was magnified in wars of greater duration. See Alma 62:41.

635 Alma chapter 2

636 Alma 45:23

637 Alma 46:4

638 Alma 45:24

639 Alma 46:10

640 Alma 46:1–2

641 Alma 46:10

642 Alma 46:10. "to seek to destroy the Church of God, and to destroy the foundation of liberty which God had granted unto them." The "foundation of liberty" may have been a free and protective government.

643 Mosiah 27:1–4; Alma 1:17; Alma 30:7–9

644 Luke 2:14

645 Alma 1:32

646 Alma 54:8–9. Moroni referred to Ammoron having once rejected gospel truths.

647 Alma 54:21 (italics added)

648 Alma 46:4

649 Mosiah chapters 26 and 27

650 Alma 45:21–24. "[They] would not give heed to their words, to walk uprightly before God (45:24)." These scriptures seem to indicate that the newly appointed church leaders (v. 22) walked uprightly before God (v. 24), whereas the angry ones did not meet the standard (Alma 46:1–2).

651 Alma 46:7

652 Mosiah 26:1–4

653 Alma 46:11

654 Alma 46:12–13

655 Alma 46:13. Through revelation, the title "Christian" or "children of Christ" was given to the Nephites by King Benjamin in 124 BC, only

three years before Alma established the Church of Christ in the land of Zarahemla (Mosiah 5).

656 Alma 46:19–20

657 Alma 46:23–24

658 Alma 46:28

659 Alma 46:34–35

660 Alma 46:33 (31–33)

661 Alma 47:1

662 Alma had departed the land of Zarahemla, leaving the large plate of Nephi in Helaman's possession (Alma 37:1–2).

663 Amalickiah's obsession for attaining power (and his complete lack of patience) is exemplified by his apostasy from the Church of Christ, his attempted takeover of Zarahemla, his takeover of Nephi, his inciting the Lamanites to rage, and his Lamanite invasion of Nephite lands that all occurred within the bounds of a single year (73 BC).

664 Alma 48:5

665 Alma chapter 16

666 Alma chapter 25

667 The war of King Benjamin's day, the Nehor Wars, which lasted from 87–77 BC (beginning with the Amlicite War), and the Zoramite War of 74 BC had all resulted in Lamanite defeats.

668 Alma 16:11

669 Alma 16:7

670 See Alma 16:11: "the people did not go in to possess the land of Ammonihah for many years."

671 Alma 48:7

672 Alma 43:19–21

673 Alma 49:6

674 Alma 44:18

675 The Lamanite attack occurred on the tenth day of the 11th month of the 19th year of the judges (See Alma 49:1)

676 Alma 49:1

677 Jarom 1:7

678 Alma 49:4

679 Alma 48:5, 11

680 Alma 49:13

681 Alma 43:17–22

682 Alma 43:19, 22

683 Alma 49:8–12

684 Alma 49:17

685 Alma 16:5

686 Alma 16:4–8

687 Alma 25:3

688 Alma 43:35–54

689 Alma 49:27

690 Alma 50:30–31

691 Alma 50:32

692 Alma 50:34. Note: Alma 22:32 states that the narrow pass was "a small neck of land" connecting the land northward to the land southward, without which the land Nephi and the land of Zarahemla (the land southward) would have been completely surrounded by water.

693 Alma 50:35–36

694 Nephihah began his reign in the beginning of the ninth year of the judges (Alma 4:20) and died near the end of the twenty-fourth year (Alma 50:37).

695 Alma 50:37

696 Alma 50:39

697 Alma 2

698 Alma 51:5

699 Alma 51:2

700 Alma 2:1-3

701 Alma 51:5

702 Alma 51:3: "Those who had sent in their voices with their petitions concerning the altering of the law." See Alma 51:15, in which Moroni abided by the same rule of law before taking his army against the king-men after their subsequent revolt. He "sent a petition, with the voice of the people, unto the governor of the land" to obtain the authority "to compel those dissenters [king-men] to defend their country or to put them to death."

703 Alma 51:3: "Pahoran would not alter nor suffer the law to be altered."

704 Alma 51:5–7

705 Mosiah 29:29

706 Alma 51:21

707 The Mulekites consisted of descendants of Mulek and those who came with him into the wilderness.

708 Alma 51:6; 60:25

709 Alma 51:7, 13

710 Alma 51:7

711 See "Amlici Seeks to be King" in Chapter 2.3, "The Order of the Nehors."

712 See "The Reign of the Judges" in Chapter 2.2, "The Evolving State of Nephite Government."

713 Alma 50:36

714 Alma 51:13

715 Alma 46:34–35. Covenants meant nothing to dissenters.

716 Alma 51:28; 27:22

717 Helaman 4:6–7

718 Alma 51:29

719 Alma 51:31

720 Alma 51:32

721 Alma 51:33–34

722 Alma 50:11

723 Alma 56:14–15
724 Alma 56:30–32
725 Alma 56:9
726 Alma 56:10
727 Alma 52:1
728 Alma 52:2
729 Alma 47:13, 17, 19, 31, 33
730 Amalickiah's ascent to the Lamanite throne required 1) that Lehonti, the chief military commander make him "second in command" (Alma 47:13), so that 2) upon Lehonti's death, Amalickiah was automatically appointed to his position, and then 3) Amalickiah, as head of the Lamanite army, was then entitled to ascend to the throne upon the death of the Lamanite king by merit of his own military power.
731 Alma 52:12
732 Alma 52:13
733 Alma 56:13–18
734 Mosiah 26:1–3; 27:2, 8, 32; Alma 4:11; 7:6
735 Mosiah 27:8
736 Alma 54:21
737 Alma 52:33
738 Alma 62:42
739 Alma 62:43
740 Alma 63:3
741 See Alma 48:11–18
742 Words of Mormon 1:12–18
743 Helaman 1:15
744 Helaman 1:2–7
745 Helaman 1:8–9
746 The people acted through elected public servants.
747 Helaman 1:12
748 Helaman 1:13
749 Moronihah was the son of Chief Captain Moroni. Leadership of the Nephite military forces was placed in his hands when his father retired around 59 or 58 BC. See Alma 62:43.
750 Apparently there was only one entrance into the city of Zarahemla.
751 Helaman 1:22
752 Alma 61:8
753 Helaman 1:23
754 Helaman 1:27–29
755 Alma 2
756 Alma 16:1
757 Alma 63:14–15
758 Mosiah 27:2
759 Mosiah 27:3
760 Mosiah 26:38; 27:1; Alma 1:3

761 Mosiah 27:10

762 Alma 21:4

763 Alma 1:6

764 Mosiah 25:19

765 Words of Mormon 1:12–18

766 The war against the Nephite free government was an adjunct to the war against the Church of God, for the two were inseparably connected.

767 Alma 30:7

768 Alma 51:21

769 See Alma 22:30–31; Mosiah 25:2

770 Ether 10:21

771 See Alma 2. Also see Part 2 above, Chapter 2.3, "The Order of the Nehors."

772 Alma 6:7

773 Alma 50:10; 56:14, 22

774 Alma 2:21

775 Upstream on the Sidon River

776 Alma 2:24

777 Alma 16:6–7

778 Alma 56:14

779 Alma 2:25

780 Alma 2:26

781 Alma 2:36–38

782 Mosiah 8:7–11; Mosiah 21:25–27

783 Alma 22:29, 33

784 Alma 50:9–11

785 Alma 50:25–36

786 Helaman 4:5–8

787 Helaman 4:5

788 Alma 2:36–38

789 3 Nephi 3:23

790 Alma 8; 16:1–3, 49

791 Alma 6:7

792 Alma 27:22–26

793 Omni 1:18

794 *Ibid.*

795 Omni 1:17.

796 Denying the Creator is synonymous with denying the existence of Christ. See Mosiah 3:8; 3 Nephi 9:15

797 Omni 1:19

798 Omni 1:12, 19

799 Mosiah 25:13

800 Mosiah 1:10

801 Mosiah 25:1–4

802 This group was comprised of all Nephites that had departed out of the land of Nephi with Mosiah I, plus the people of Limhi and the people of Alma, who were derivatives of the people of Zeniff.

803 Mosiah 25:4

804 Mosiah 29:42

805 Mosiah 3:5; Alma 7:7–13; Helaman 8:20–22; Helaman 14:2; 3 Nephi 1:9–14; 11:7–10

806 It is quite apparent that Mosiah carried the Liahona with him during the journey from Nephi to Zarahemla, and he transferred it to Benjamin at or near the time of his death. In about 124 BC, Benjamin transferred the Liahona, the written records, and other items to Mosiah II (Mosiah 1:16).

807 Mosiah 23:36–37

808 Mosiah 23:37

809 Helam was eight days from the city of Nephi along the relatively straight line of Alma's route of travel. It may have taken the Lamanites much longer to reach Helam due to the fact that they were lost and disoriented.

810 Stephen S. Gosch and Peter N. Stearns, *Premodern Travel in World History* (Routledge, New York, 2008), 37–59.

811 Mosiah 23:3

812 Mosiah 24:25

813 Mosiah 23:1–2

814 Mosiah 7:4

815 Mosiah 23:2.

816 Mosiah 24:23

817 Gosch, *op. cit.*

818 Omni 1:13

819 Alma 2:37–38

820 Alma 8:3–6

821 The Nehor Wars began with the Amlicite War of 87 BC and ended in 77 BC, when Lamanites pursued the people of Anti-Nephi-Lehi from Nephi to Zarahemla, only to be slain and driven by the Nephite armies into the wilderness.

822 Alma 25:3–5, 8

823 Alma 43:22–24

824 See Alma 22:32: "the land of Nephi and the land of Zarahemla were nearly surrounded by water, there being a small neck of land between the land northward and the land southward."

825 Alma 22:33–34

826 Omni 1:13

827 Omni 1:27–30. See also the record of Zeniff in Mosiah 9–22.

828 See the first section in the previous chapter (Chapter 3.2)

829 Omni 1:13

830 Mosiah 9:2

831 Zeniff's first journey through the wilderness was in company with King Mosiah (Omni 1:12).
832 Mosiah 9:4 (3–4)
833 Mosiah 9:5–7
834 Mosiah 9:7–8
835 Mosiah 7:2–3
836 Mosiah 7:1–2
837 Mosiah 7:4
838 Mosiah 8:7–8; 21:25
839 Mosiah 22:11; 24:23–25; 28:1–9
840 Limhi was the grandson of Zeniff—see Mosiah 7:9.
841 Mosiah 22:13
842 Alma 24:25
843 See Chapter 3.2 above.
844 Mosiah 23:36–38
845 Mosiah 23:30–36
846 In 87 BC, the Lamanite army journeyed to Zarahemla and fought with the Amlicites in the Amlicite War. See Alma chapter 2.
847 Omni 1:24, Words of Mormon 1:13–14
848 Helam was located eight days from the city of Nephi and twelve days from the city of Manti (which marked the southern border of Zarahemla prior to the sea to sea expansion of the land of Zarahemla beginning in 72 BC—See Alma 50:8).
849 Alma 17:1
850 Alma 17–26 contain the account of the fourteen-year mission of Mosiah's sons in the land of Nephi. See the commentary immediately preceding Alma 17.
851 Alma 20:8; 22:1
852 Alma 22:27
853 *Ibid.*
854 Alma 27:14. This verse must be combined with other verses to see that the sons of Mosiah traveled through the narrow strip of wilderness from a point near the city of Nephi to the borders of Manti.
855 The material enclosed in brackets is taken from Alma 22:27.
856 Alma 2:24; 3:20; 43:22; Mormon 1:10
857 Alma 16:2
858 Alma 25:1–2
859 Alma 16:1–6
860 Alma 16:7–8
861 Mosiah 18
862 Mosiah 22
863 Alma 22:27; 23:2–4
864 See Alma 50:9
865 Alma 52:9; 22:33–34.
866 See Alma 2.

867 Alma 2:24–25. The land of Minon at the southern border of Zarahemla was in the same approximate location as the land of Manti, which first referenced in 81 BC, six years after the Amlicite War. See Alma 16:6–7.

868 Mosiah 27:6

869 Alma 50:9–10

870 Alma 22:27; 43:22. The head (or headwaters) of a river is "the upper part of a river, near its source" (*Webster's Deluxe Unabridged Dictionary*, copyright 1979 by Simon and Schuster).

871 Alma 22:27

872 Alma 22:33: "The Nephites . . . with their guards and their armies, had hemmed in the Lamanites on the south, that thereby they should have no more possession on the north, that they might not overrun the land northward."

873 Mosiah 23:4

874 Mosiah 18:35

875 Mosiah 24:18

876 Alma 2:20–37

877 Alma 2:24

878 It is likely that King Mosiah simply followed the pointer of the Liahona without understanding the geography of the land through which they traveled. Therefore, the geography was first understood by Alma the Elder by revelation from God.

879 Five major confrontations occurred during a 26-year period: 1) 87 BC—Amlicite War, 2) 81 BC—destruction of Ammonihah and related battles, 3) 77 BC—Defense of people of Ammon, 4) 74 BC—Zoramite War, and 5) 73–60 BC—Amalickiah and Ammoron War. In each war, a Lamanite army invaded the land of Zarahemla.

880 Alma 22:29: "And also there were many Lamanites on the east by the seashore, whither the Nephites had driven them."

881 Alma 25:5, 8

882 Alma 25:6–7

883 Alma 27:1

884 Alma 28:1–2 identifies the beginning of permanent Lamanite occupation of the east wilderness. The year was 77 BC.

885 Alma 50:7

886 Alma 28:2–3

887 Alma 50:13–14 (See Map A-5 in Appendix A)

888 See Alma 43:25.

889 Alma 31:3

890 Alma 31:4; 35:10

891 Alma 50:7

892 Alma 50:9

893 Alma 49

894 Alma 50:12

895 Mosiah 27:6. This verse represents the first recorded founding of cities in Zarahemla other than the city of Zarahemla.

896 Alma 2:37

897 Alma 16:2

898 Alma 16:3

899 Alma 8:3. Melek lay three days to the south of Ammonihah (Alma 8:6).

900 Alma 8:13. Alma turned from Ammonihah toward Aaron during his 82 BC missionary travels to the west of the city of Zarahemla.

901 Alma 15:1. Sidom was also established to the west of the city of Zarahemla at the time. Like the city of Aaron, it was relatively near Ammonihah, but the specific direction is not given.

902 Alma 49

903 Alma 50:7–11

904 Alma 52:12–15

905 Mosiah 23:3–4

906 Mosiah 24:24–25

907 Mosiah 18:4

908 Alma 21:1–2

909 The first reference to Manti was given in 81 BC. See Alma 16:6–7.

910 Alma 50:10–11; 56:13–14

911 Alma 56:30–32

912 Alma 56:14–17

913 Alma 22:28: "Now, the more idle part of the Lamanites . . . were spread through the wilderness . . . on the west of the land of Zarahemla, in the borders by the seashore, and on the west in the land of Nephi, in the place of their fathers' first inheritance."

914 3 Nephi 3:23

915 3 Nephi 3:13–14

916 Alma 22:28

917 Alma 28:2–3; 31:3; 50:7

918 Alma 22:29

919 Alma 22:33

920 2 Nephi 5:28, 34

921 Alma 52:15

922 Alma 52:1–14

923 Alma 50:11: "fortifying the line between the Nephites and the Lamanites . . . from the west sea, running by the head of the river Sidon."

924 Alma 52:11–15; verse 15: "Moroni—who had established armies to protect the south and the *west borders of the land*" (emphasis added).

925 Alma 56:31

926 Ether 9:33

927 Ether 10:20

928 Mormon 3:5. The city of Lib lay at the northern border of the south wilderness, "at the place where the sea divides the land," except for the narrow neck of land that connects the two continents together. Likely, it

was located at or near the Nephite "line Bountiful and the land Desolation" (Alma 22:32), that is the northern border of the land of Bountiful.

929 Ether 10:21–22

930 Alma 22:30: Desolation "was discovered by the people of Zarahemla [Mulekites], it being the place of their first landing."

931 Alma 22:30–32: The land of Bountiful "bordered upon the land which they called Desolation, it [extending] so far northward that it came into the land which had been peopled and destroyed."

932 Ether 7:6. This scripture places Moron at the southern edge of Jaredite lands.

933 Alma 22:31: "And [The people of Zarahemla] came from [Desolation] up into the south wilderness."

934 Omni 1:21; Ether 13:21

935 This wilderness later became the land of Zarahemla.

936 Ether 10:19, 21: "For the land [southward] was covered with animals of the forest. . . . And they did preserve the land southward for a wilderness, to get game. And the whole face of the land northward was covered with inhabitants."

937 The city of Bountiful was located at the eastern border of the land of Bountiful (Alma 51:26–28). See Appendix A, Map A-6.

938 Helaman 1:27–29

939 Ether 11:6–7; 14:1

940 Ether 10:21

941 Mosiah 8:7–8; 21:25–27

942 Alma 50:11

943 Alma 50:7–12

944 See Map A-6 in Appendix A.

945 Alma 50:25–35

946 Alma 52:9; see also Alma 50:32.

947 Alma 50:34 (34–36)

948 Alma 16:1–8

949 Alma 24:3–4; 25:1–5

950 Alma 50

951 Alma 16:1–9; see also 25:1–5.

952 Alma 24:4

953 Alma 22:27

954 Alma 50

955 Alma 51:26–27

956 Alma 52:9

957 Alma 62:14

958 Alma 52:15

959 No information is provided of the land southward after the appearance of the Savior other than in the brief account of the first stages of the Final Nephite Civil War. See Mormon 1–2.

960 Alma 22:32: The "line Bountiful and the land Desolation"

961 The clash between Teancum's army and the people of Morianton in 68 BC was the first military encounter on the narrow neck of land. Moronihah's defense of the same location was the second.

962 Helaman 4:6–7

963 3 Nephi 7:12–13

964 Alma 52:9

965 *Ibid.*

966 The first and second descriptions of the narrow neck of land are found in Alma 22:29–34 and 50:34.

967 Helaman 4:7

968 Alma 22:32

969 *Ibid.*; emphasis added.

970 Alma 50:34

971 Mosiah 8:7–8

972 Mosiah 8:8

973 1 Nephi 13:10, 12–13, 17, 29

974 1 Nephi 17:5

975 Ether 2:6

976 Ether 2:13

977 Mormon 6:4: "we did pitch our tents round about the hill Cumorah; and it was in a land of many waters."

978 Ether 15:11

979 Ether 15:8; Coriantumr "came to the waters of Ripliancum, which, by interpretation, is large, or to exceed all."

980 Dennis, Jerry, *The Living Great Lakes, Searching for the Heart of the Inland Seas,* (New York. NY: St Martin's Press, 2003), 4.

981 "Running from the east towards the west."

982 See Alma 25:1–8.

983 Alma 27:20–30

984 Other factors included 1) the geographic knowledge obtained by the sons of Mosiah, 2) the recent Zoramite War, and 3) the impending Amalickiah and Ammoron Wars.

985 Alma 16:7–8; 25:2–5

986 Alma 25:3

987 Alma 25:5–9

988 Alma 27:1–2

989 Alma 27:10–14

990 Alma 28:1–2

991 Alma 50:1

992 Alma 50:7

993 Alma 25:3–9

994 Alma 25:13; 27:1

995 Alma 27–28

996 After their arrival in the land of Zarahemla, the people of Anti-Nephi-Lehi became known among the Nephites as the people of Ammon, or Ammonites (Alma 27:26).

997 Alma 31:8

998 Alma 50:7

999 Alma 50:13–15

1000 Alma 50:14

1001 Alma 25:5, 8

1002 Alma 43:25

1003 Alma 31:3

1004 Alma 50:11

1005 Alma 28:2

1006 Alma 43.

1007 Alma 50:11; emphasis added. The city of Manti was located by the head of the river Sidon (Alma 22:27).

1008 Alma 51:26. Jershon's eastern seaboard cities included Moroni, Lehi, Morianton, Omner, Gid, and Mulek. As previously explained, though included in this verse, Nephihah was not a coastal city. The city of Moroni, located at the southeastern corner of Nephite lands, was a common element of both the southern border configuration of fortified cities and the eastern seaboard configuration.

1009 Alma 51:28–30.

1010 This boundary marked the beginning of the narrow neck of land

1011 Alma 22:28

1012 *Ibid.*

1013 Alma 52:15: Moroni "established armies to protect . . . the west borders of the land."

1014 Unnamed city at the southwest corner of Nephite lands (Alma 56:31) and "the line Bountiful and the land Desolation" (Alma 22:32; see also Helaman 4:7)

1015 Alma 52:11–12: "And [Moroni] also said unto [Teancum], I would come unto you, but behold, the Lamanites are upon us in the borders of the land by the west sea. . . . Ammoron . . . had gathered together a large number of men, and had marched forth against the Nephites on the borders by the west sea."

1016 Alma 50:12

1017 Alma 22:32

1018 Ether 7:6

1019 Ether 10:20–22

1020 Alma 22:32

1021 The city of Desolation is not referenced in the Book of Mormon until Mormon 3:7. No indication is given that a city was established there in the pre-Christ period. However, just as Moroni established fortifications at cities around the southern, eastern, and western borders of Nephite lands, it is assumed that "the line Bountiful and the land Desolation"

(Alma 22:32) was the location of fortifications placed at the northern border of the land Bountiful.

1022 Alma 22:32–34; 50:29–35; 51:30; 52:9; Helaman 4:6–7

1023 Alma 50:33–34

1024 Alma 52:5–9

1025 Helaman 4:5–7

1026 See Alma 43:53; 56:24. Coriantumr ignored this principle and soon found his army trapped in the land of Zarahemla (Helaman 1:14–34). It cost him his life.

1027 Alma 50:2: "Works of timber built up to the height of a man."

1028 See Alma 62:36 for an account of Teancum's entry over the wall into the fortified city of Moroni

1029 Alma 2:36–38

1030 3 Nephi 3:23; see also Helaman 4:5

1031 This record is not lost. Joseph simply lost the opportunity to translate it following the Martin Harris incident. The record remains in the angel Moroni's care, custody, and control.

1032 Alma 22:28

1033 1 Nephi 6:3; Jacob 1:2–4

1034 Alma 22:28. This reference was not placed in the Nephite record until 91 BC when the sons of Mosiah returned from their mission to the Lamanites. However, verse 28 refers to lands occupied by the Lamanites even from the time of Lehi's landing, and therefore during the period of Nephites living within the land of Nephi.

1035 Helaman 1:18

1036 Alma 2:26

1037 Alma 2:20

1038 Alma 6:7

1039 Alma 16:6–7

1040 Helaman 1:23–24, 27

1041 See Alma 27:26; 43:25; 50:14

1042 Alma 50:34

1043 Alma 22:32; see also 3 Nephi 3:23

1044 Helaman 1:23

1045 Alma 50:13

1046 Omni 1:5

1047 Jarom 1:10

1048 1 Nephi 12:14–19; Alma 9:18

1049 Omni 1:6–7

1050 Omni 1:10

1051 Omni 1:12

1052 See Mosiah 2–5, 12–16.

1053 See Mosiah 5–6

1054 Ether chapter 7

1055 Ether 14:6

1056 Omni 1:17

1057 Alma 22:31 (30–31): "And [the people of Zarahemla] came from [the land of Desolation] up into the south wilderness." Their journey to the land southward took place after they laid Coriantumr to rest.

1058 Alma 31:7; Ether 1:12, 14

1059 Helaman 56; if Mormon had included the southern border attack, in his account of the war (Alma Chapters 51–55), it would be identified above as the second battlefront, with the King-Men Rebellion being moved to the third position.

1060 Alma 51:13

1061 Alma 54:23

1062 Alma 46:1–6

1063 Alma 51:14

1064 Alma 51:16–17

1065 Alma 51:18–19. See Alma 62:9 for the conclusion of the king-men affair.

1066 Alma 51:21

1067 Alma 51:12–13, 22–23

1068 Alma 51:22–23

1069 Alma 52:4

1070 Alma 49:10

1071 Alma 51:24

1072 It was Moroni's understanding that Amalickiah sought to gain control of the narrow neck of land whereby he would "have power to harass them on every side" (Alma 52:9; see also Alma 51:30).

1073 A mistake appears in Alma 51:26. In verse 25, it is stated that Amalickiah did not go against Nephihah, preferring to remain on the coast where the city of Moroni was located. Verse 26 states he went on, capturing many cities (including Nephihah), "all of which were on the borders by the seashore" (which Nephihah was not). Later, in 62 BC ("the thirtieth year"), it is reiterated (as in verse 25) that Nephihah had not fallen at that time, having been the place of refuge for many of the people who had fled from Moroni, Lehi, and Morianton (Alma 59:5–11). The mistake therefore is likely a simple one—that of incorrectly including Nephihah in the list of captured cities (Alma 51:26). Concerning mistakes in the Book of Mormon, see the comments on Moroni's title page at the front of the Book of Mormon.

1074 Alma 51:26

1075 Alma 27:22

1076 Alma 51:25

1077 Alma 51:28; 27:22. The eastern border of Bountiful touched the northern border of Jershon.

1078 Alma 51:31

1079 Alma 51:32

1080 Alma 51:37

1081 Alma 50:11. The five-year period from 72 through 68 BC provided ample time to fully complete the fortifications along the southern border from the west coast to the east coast.

1082 Alma 56:9

1083 Alma 53:8 is a preface for a brief account of the stripling warriors, who joined the war in 66 BC.

1084 Described in Alma 53:8 as the "west sea, south"

1085 Alma 56:13–15

1086 Alma 52:1

1087 Alma 52:2

1088 Alma 52:4

1089 Alma 52:13

1090 Alma 52:8

1091 Alma 52:5

1092 Alma 52:6

1093 Alma 52:7

1094 Alma 56:57; see Alma 27:26 for "people of Ammon."

1095 Alma 56:1-9

1096 Alma 53:8

1097 Alma 53:22

1098 They were called people of Ammon, or Ammonites after Ammon, the son of Mosiah.

1099 See "The People of Anti-Nephi-Lehi Suffer More Persecution" in Chapter 2.3, "The order of Nehor."

1100 Alma 53:14–15

1101 Alma 53:17

1102 Alma 53:19

1103 Alma 56:1

1104 Alma 56:13–15

1105 Alma 56:31

1106 Alma 56:34

1107 Alma 56:9, 33

1108 Alma 56:31–33

1109 Alma 56:22–23

1110 Alma 50:11. Moroni fortified only the line separating Zarahemla from Nephi. Cities were placed along the border at intervals from Manti to the west sea. Interior cities were not fortified at that time.

1111 Alma 56:15, 18, 20

1112 Alma 56:24–26

1113 Alma 56:15

1114 Alma 52:12

1115 Alma 56:18

1116 Alma 56:19

1117 Alma 56:20

1118 Alma 56:20: "And in the commencement of the twenty and seventh year we had prepared our city *and ourselves* for defence" (emphasis added); also see Ether 13:16.

1119 Alma 52:12

1120 Alma 52:13

1121 Alma 56:13–18

1122 Alma 51:14–22

1123 Alma 52:11–12, 18

1124 Alma 52:8–13

1125 Alma 52:11, 14

1126 Alma 56:31

1127 Alma 52:15: "Moroni established armies to protect the south and the west borders of the land."

1128 Alma 56:31

1129 Alma 56:42

1130 Moroni lay at the east end of the southern border by the east sea, whereas the unnamed city lay at the west end of the southern border by the west sea.

1131 Alma 52:18

1132 Alma 52:14

1133 Alma 56–58

1134 Alma 52:15–18

1135 Alma 56:20–28

1136 Alma 56:18

1137 Alma 56:10

1138 Alma 56:31

1139 Alma 56:30–42. Verse 42 establishes the calendar date on the third day of the Nephite and Lamanite encounter.

1140 Alma 56:50–51

1141 Alma 56:57

1142 Alma 56:34

1143 Alma 56:30–31

1144 Alma 52:18

1145 The fact that Helaman led his army in the direction of the coastal city may imply that they were aware that the city was in Nephite hands. It may be an indication that communication was maintained between the two battlefronts, which would have been integral to successful coordination of the overall defense operation. On the other hand, the later communication between Moroni and chief judge Pahoran reveals that communication between regions was not always in place, even when it was sorely needed. It therefore is also possible that Antipus and Helaman were making an assumption that the city on the coast was in Nephite hands, and that the Lamanites would have no way of knowing the current status of the west coast war.

1146 Alma 52:15, 18

1147 Alma 52:19

1148 Alma 52:20

1149 Alma 52:19–40

1150 See "Moroni Plans a Pincer Movement to Trap the Lamanites" in Chapter 2.4, "The Zoramites."

1151 Alma 52:27–28

1152 Alma 53:5

1153 Alma 57:1–3

1154 Alma 57:4

1155 Alma 57:1–4

1156 Alma 55:1

1157 Alma 55:2

1158 Alma 55:4–5; see also Alma 47:20–30

1159 Alma 55:6

1160 Alma 55:8

1161 Alma 55:13

1162 Alma 55:16

1163 Alma 55:17

1164 Alma 55:33

1165 Alma 55:33–35

1166 Alma 56:1

1167 Alma 59

1168 Alma 62:30. As explained above, the Nephites likely would not have gone against Lehi without having first taken Morianton? See also "The Nephites Drive the Lamanites from the City of Lehi" below in this chapter.

1169 Alma 57:11

1170 Alma 57:12

1171 Alma 57:14

1172 Alma 57:17

1173 Alma 57:29–33

1174 Alma 57:34

1175 Alma 57:36

1176 Alma 57:26

1177 Alma 56–58

1178 The city of Zeezrom is not mentioned at this time, though apparently it was no longer in the hands of the Lamanites in 63 BC (Alma 58), when the entire focus of the southern campaign was on the city of Manti.

1179 Alma 58:5

1180 Alma 58:7

1181 Alma 58:8

1182 Alma 58:10–11

1183 Alma 58:13

1184 Alma 22:27–29

1185 Alma 58:15

1186 Alma 58:16–17

1187 Alma 58:39

1188 Alma 57:6

1189 Alma 57:12

1190 Alma 58

1191 Alma 58:4, 7

1192 Alma 58:7

1193 Alma 59:2–3

1194 Alma 58:29–30

1195 Alma 59:9

1196 Whereas the Zoramite and Lamanite army had traveled from the vicinity of the Ammonite city of Aaron to the city of Manti, the Lamanite army that fled from Helaman's army traveled from Manti to Moroni on the east coast. See "The Zoramite War" in Part 2, Chapter 2.4, "The Zoramites." See Map A-6 in Appendix A.

1197 Alma 51:24–25

1198 Alma 55:33–35

1199 Alma 56:1

1200 Alma 60

1201 Messages before the modern age must have been borne of necessity by messenger on foot or on horseback, or at best in some cultures by carrier pigeon.

1202 Alma 61:4

1203 Alma 61:8; 62:6

1204 Alma 61:15

1205 Alma 62:8–9

1206 See Alma 51:19.

1207 Alma 62:9

1208 Alma 62:27

1209 Alma 62:30

1210 See "Cities of Omner and Morianton" mentioned previously during 63 BC.

1211 Alma 62:32

1212 Alma 62:36

1213 Alma 62:38

1214 Alma 4:15–20

1215 Alma 45:21–22

1216 Alma 62:44–45

1217 Alma 36:3

1218 Alma 62:52

1219 Alma 52:4. Mulek represented the leading edge of the eastern assault at the time. It was the location where Amalickiah was killed.

1220 Alma 56:18

1221 Alma 56:18; it is noted that this verse if considered alone might seem to indicate Ammoron was not present but sent orders. His direct presence is noted, however, in the first verse of chapter 57, when he sent an epistle to Helaman, who was in the city of Judea, as noted in the previous verse (Alma 56:57).

1222 The city of Nephi was likely south of Antiparah due to the fact that the next city along the line of southern perimeter cities was the unnamed city lying on the west coast. Since Nephi was inland from the west coast, it is assumed that Antiparah was closest to Nephi, lying northward of the city on the Nephite side of the narrow strip of wilderness.

1223 Alma 52:12

1224 *op. cit*

1225 Alma 52:1–2

1226 Alma 54:16; Ether 14:24

1227 Alma 52:4

1228 Alma 51:24, 25

1229 Alma 50:14. Though Aaron is not mentioned during the course of the war, its existence is noted in this verse.

1230 Ammoron likely took the same general path from Moroni to Manti that the Lamanite and Zoramite army had taken in 74 BC. See Alma 43:22.

1231 Manti, Zeezrom, Cumeni, and Antiparah—Alma 56: 13–15

1232 Alma 52:4

1233 Alma 51:24

1234 Alma 56:18

1235 Alma 56:18

1236 Alma 56:20

1237 Alma 52:12

1238 At Mulek, Ammoron left instructions to maintain the Nephite cities under their control and additionally to "harass the Nephites on the east sea" and "take possession of their lands as much as it was in their power " (see Alma 52: 13). At Antiparah, he told the Lamanite army to maintain the cities they had already taken (Alma 56:20), but to hold back and not take the opportunity available to them at Judea (Alma 56:18). Thus, in the east: "Maintain and try to take more cities." Whereas in the south: "Maintain, but do not try to take more cities"—a distinct variation.

1239 When the time to fight arrived, the stripling warriors went forth in the strength of the Lord. They were more powerful and invincible than seasoned warriors.

ABOUT THE AUTHOR

Troy J. Smith is an LDS author and researcher. He grew up in Arkansas as a Baptist but joined The Church of Jesus Christ of Latter-day Saints at the age of twenty-eight. Ever since then, he has had a profound interest in the Book of Mormon.

To better understand the physical world of the Book of Mormon, Troy obtained a BA degree in Latin American studies at Tulane University in 1984. In 1987 and 1988, he became involved in the publication of the *Zarahemla Quarterly*, for which he authored and coauthored articles pertaining to Book of Mormon archaeology. In the subsequent years, Troy has continued to research and study Mesoamerican culture, pre-Columbian cultures, and New World archeology. *The War against Christianity* is the result of years of Book of Mormon study and archeological research.

Troy lives with his wife, Debbie, in Utah. They have eight children and nineteen grandchildren.